D0792881

Qualitative Inquiry and the Politics of Evidence

Dedication
For Katherine E. Ryan
and Kathryn M. Giardina

Qualitative Inquiry and the Politics of Evidence

Norman K. Denzin
Michael D. Giardina
Editors

Left Coast
Press Inc.

Walnut Creek, California

Left Coast
Press Inc.

Walnut Creek, CA 94596
http://www.LCoastPress.com

ISBN 978-1-59874-321-0 hardcover
ISBN 978-1-59874-322-7 paperback

Library of Congress Cataloging-in-Publication Data

Qualitative inquiry and the politics of evidence / Norman K. Denzin, Michael
D. Giardina, editors.
p. cm.
Includes bibliographical references.
ISBN 978-1-59874-321-0 (hardback : alk. paper) -- ISBN 978-1-59874-322-7
(pbk. : alk. paper)
1. Qualitative research. 2. Evidence. I. Denzin, Norman K. II. Giardina,
Michael D., 1976-
H62.Q347 2008
001.4'3--dc22
2008013787

Printed in the United States of America

∞™ The paper used in this publication meets the minimum requirements of
American National Standard for Information Sciences—Permanence of Paper
for Printed Library Materials, ANSI/NISO Z39.48–1992.

08 09 10 11   5 4 3 2 1

CONTENTS

Acknowledgments

We thank Mitch Allen at Left Coast Press for his continued enthusiastic support of our endeavors. We also thank Carole Bernard for her editorial expertise and patience with us throughout the production process and Hannah Jennings for her production design of the volume.

Many of the chapters contained in this book were presented as plenary or keynote addresses at the Third International Congress of Qualitative Inquiry, held at the University of Illinois, Urbana-Champaign, in May 2007. We thank the Department of Advertising, the Institute of Communications Research, the College of Communications, and the Center for Qualitative Inquiry for institutional support of the congress, as well as those campus units that contributed time, funds, and/or volunteers to the effort.

The congress, and by extension this book, would not have materialized without the tireless efforts of Himika Bhattacharya (diplomatic liaison), Christina Ceisel (logistics and planning), Li Xiong (communications guru), Yiye Liu (webmistress), Kevin Dolan (program designer), Grant Kien (organizational sage), and James Salvo (the glue who continues to hold the whole thing together). For information on future congresses, please visit http://www.icqi.org.

Norman K. Denzin
and Michael D. Giardina
Champaign, Illinois
December 2007

Available from the Same Editors

Qualitative Inquiry and the Conservative Challenge:
  Confronting Methodological Fundamentalism (2006)

Ethical Futures in Qualitative Research:
  Decolonizing the Politics of Knowledge (2007)

These volumes emanate from the International Congress on Qualitative Inquiry held annually in May on the campus of University of Illinois, Urbana-Champaign and sponsored by the International Center for Qualitative Inquiry. More information on the congress can be found at www.icqi.org. To order these volumes, go to www.LCoastPress.com.

Introduction

The Elephant in the Living Room, OR Advancing the Conversation about the Politics of Evidence[1]

Norman K. Denzin and
Michael D. Giardina
University of Illinois, Urbana-Champaign

There is a current dispute between qualitative and quantitative research. It is international, acrimonious, and there are elements of state-sponsored support "in the West" for a return to a kind of neopositivist quantitative inquiry.

—Stronach, 2006, p. 758

To serve evidence-based policymaking we probably need to invent a ... myth for qualitative work, that is we too have clear-cut guidelines and criteria, maybe not randomized control trials, but we have our criteria.

—Hammersley, 2005a, p. 4

Proem

What is evidence to the Bush administration other than something that gets in its way? On December 3, 2007, a National Intelligence Estimate (NIE) report was released by the United States and its sixteen interagency intelligence community. The eight-page summation of its findings[2] stated with "high confidence" that Iran had suspended its effort to procure or produce nuclear weapons in 2003. This revelation came as news to many in the West, for as late as October 2007, U.S. President George W. Bush had made numerous statements to the contrary.

What followed in the wake of the NIE's release was the stuff of fairy tales, similar to the rhetoric surrounding the rationale for the unilateral invasion and illegal occupation of Iraq: Despite the findings, Bush nevertheless stated in a press conference that Iran was still dangerous and that nothing had changed concerning how Iran should be viewed on the world stage. More specifically, Mr. Bush stated:

> Look, Iran was dangerous, Iran is dangerous, and Iran will be dangerous if they have the knowledge necessary to make a nuclear weapon. ...The NIE says that Iran had a hidden—a covert nuclear weapons program. That's what it said. What's to say they couldn't start another covert nuclear weapons program?[3] (Baker & Wright, 2007, p. A23)

More shocking, however, was that the NIE in question had, as Kevin Drum (2007) reported, been

> finished a year ago [2006], and its basic parameters were almost certainly common knowledge in the White House well before that. This means that all the leaks, all the World War III[4] stuff, all the blustering about the IAEA [International Atomic Energy Association]—all of it was approved for public consumption after Bush/Cheney/Rice/etc. knew perfectly well most of it was baseless. (Drum 2007, n.p.)

Yet, despite this knowledge, the administration—clearly cognizant of the status of Iran's nuclear program—bombarded us with doomsday scenarios and "evidence" allegedly proving otherwise.[5] Such posturing was furthered by a public relations effort within the United States to ramp up support for action toward Iran (e.g., Fox News perpetuated the White House lies about Iran; Republican presidential hopefuls like John McCain and Mitt Romney took an ultra-hard line in debates over how to deal with Iran; there were repeated media profiles of Iranian President Mahmoud Ahmedinejad as the second-coming of Hitler, etc.).

These coarticulated efforts culminated in the public sphere in September 2007, when the Kyl-Lieberman amendment (H.R. 1585; Amendment No. 3017)—which "ratchet[ed] up the confrontation with Iran by calling for the designation of its Revolutionary Guard as a terrorist organization responsible for killing U.S. troops" (Sargent, 2007)—passed in the Senate by a vote of 76 to 22. Note that this vote came roughly one month *after* Adm. Mike McConnell informed the president of the impending NIE findings.[6]

The larger meaning here is clear: The president of the United States participated in misleading the American people as to the state of Iran's nuclear program and potential capabilities—primarily for partisan political gains and a right-wing, religious-inflected neoconservative agenda—even while evidence existed to the contrary.[7]

But this blatant rejection of evidence is nothing new; we've seen it all before. Consider Iraq. Or global warming. Or No Child Left Behind. Or abstinence-only education. The state of the economy. Even evolution. For the last seven years, on every aforementioned topic, the Bush administration has pushed forward policies that fly in the face of the evidence on hand or has shaped evidence to fit its own ring-wing fundamentalist agenda: Iraq? No weapons of mass destruction, which means that it had weapons of mass destruction. Global warming? A real phenomena agreed on by the vast majority of the world's scientific community, so obviously it is a left-wing conspiracy that needs more study to be rejected. No Child Left Behind? Doesn't work, which means that it does. Abstinence-only education? A tragic farce, which means it should be promoted instead of safe sex in public schools. And the list goes on and on. Indeed, as Keith Olbermann (2007) remarked on his MSNBC news program, *Countdown with Keith Olbermann*, the current regime has led us down a path "in which the facts have become optional" and where "intel is valued less than the hunch." Under Bush, the "politics of evidence" has truly taken on new meanings.[8]

This is the sociopolitical context within which qualitative researchers currently reside, all the while being caught in the middle of a global conversation concerning the *evidence-based research movement*, and emerging standards and guidelines for conducting and evaluating qualitative inquiry (St. Pierre, 2006). This conversation turns on issues surrounding the politics and ethics of evidence and the value of qualitative work in addressing matters of equity and social justice (Lather, 2006, p. 789). In some ways, this is like old wine in old bottles: 1980s battles in a new century.

Like an elephant in the living room, the evidence-based model is an intruder whose presence can no longer be ignored. Within the global audit culture,[9] proposals concerning the use of

Cochrane and Campbell criteria,[10] experimental methodologies, randomized control trials, quantitative metrics, citation analyses, shared databases, journal impact factors, rigid notions of accountability, data transparency, warrantablity, rigorous peer-review evaluation scales, and fixed formats for scientific articles now compete, fighting to gain ascendancy in the evidence-quality-standards discourse (Feuer, Towne, & Shavelson, 2002; Lather, 2004b, p. 21; NRC, 2002, p. 47; Thomas, 2004). The interpretive community must mount an articulate critique of these external threats to our "collective research endeavor" (Atkinson & Delamont, 2006, p. 751). We must create our own standards of quality, our own criteria (see Lather, 2006; St. Pierre & Rouleston, 2006). *This volume is one step in that direction.*

• • •

The term "politics of evidence" is, as Morse observes, an oxymoron, and in more than one way. Evidence "is something that is concrete and indisputable, whereas politics refers to 'activities concerned with the … exercise of authority [and power]'" (2006b, p. 395). Evidence in a countable or measurable sense is not something to which all qualitative researchers attend. Few critical ethnographers think in a language of evidence; they think instead about experience, emotions, events, processes, performances, narratives, poetics, the politics of possibility (see Madison, 2005).

Moreover, evidence is never morally or ethically *neutral*. But Morse, quoting Larner (2004, p. 20), argues that the politics and political economy of evidence is *not* a question of evidence or no evidence. Rather, it is a question of who has the power to control the *definition* of evidence, of who defines the kinds of materials that *count* as evidence, of who determines what methods best produce the best forms of evidence, and of whose criteria and standards are ultimately used to evaluate quality evidence. On this, Morse is quite clear (2006a, pp. 415–16): "Our evidence is considered soft … it is considered not valid, not replicable, not acceptable! We have failed to communicate the nature of qualitative evidence to the larger scientific community … we have failed to truly understand it ourselves." In short, the *politics* of evidence cannot be separated from the *ethics* of evidence (see Denzin & Giardina, 2007).

Additionally, there are tensions over the politics of evidence within the interpretive community itself: (1) Interpretivists dismiss postpositivists; (2) poststructuralists dismiss interpretivists; and now (3) the postinterpretivists dismiss the interpretivists (Preissle, 2006, p. 692; see also Hammersley, 2005b; Hodkinson, 2004; MacLure, 2006). For example, some postpositivists are drawn to the scientifically based research (SBR) standards movement, seeking to develop mixed- or multiple-methodological strategies that will conform to the new demands for improving research quality. Others reject the gold standard movement and argue for a set of understandings unique to the interpretive, or postinterpretive, tradition (St. Pierre & Rouleston, 2006). Atkinson and Delamont (2006), meanwhile, call for a return to the classics in the Chicago School tradition. And the American Education Research Association (AERA) (2006) aims to strike a middle ground, neither too postpositivist nor too interpretivist (see also the chapters by Howe, Stronach, and Torrance, this volume).

The immediate effects of this conversation start at home, in departments and in graduate education programs where Ph.D.s are produced and tenure for qualitative research scholars is granted. Many fear that the call for SBR will drown out instruction, scholarship, and the granting of tenure in the qualitative tradition or confine it to a narrow brand of interpretive work (Eisenhart, 2006, p. 697). Worse yet, it could lead to a narrow concept of orthodoxy.[11]

In this Introduction, we read the controversies surrounding these evidence-based discourses within a critical pedagogical framework, showing their contradictions, their overlaps, and the gaps and fissures that stand between them (Denzin, 2003). Standards for assessing quality research are pedagogies of practice: moral, ethical, and political institutional apparatuses that regulate and produce a particular form of science, a form that may be no longer workable in a transdisciplinary, globalizing, and postcolonial world (Denzin & Giardina, 2006; see also McCarthy et al., 2007). Within the evidence-based community, many believe that qualitative research does not count as research *unless* it is embedded in a randomized clinical trial (RCT). Further, within this community, there are no agreed-on procedures, methods, or criteria for extracting information from qualitative studies. These narrow interpretations must be resisted.

In reviewing these multiple discourses, this chapter—and those that follow—endeavor to chart a path of resistance. Because the qualitative research community is not a single entity, guidelines and criteria of quality need to be fitted to specific paradigmatic and genre-driven concerns (e.g., grounded theory studies versus performance ethnographies). We favor flexible guidelines that are not driven by quantitative criteria. We seek a performative model of qualitative inquiry, one that enacts a performance ethic based on feminist, communitarian assumptions. We further align these assumptions with the call by First and Fourth World scholars for an indigenous research ethic (Bishop, 1998; Rains, Archibald, & Deyhle, 2000; Smith, 1999). This call opens the space for a discussion of ethics, science, causality, trust, and a reiteration of moral and ethical criteria for judging qualitative research (Denzin, 2003, In press; Denzin & Giardina, 2006, 2007; Denzin, Lincoln, & Giardina, 2006).

The Elephant in the Living Room

We agree with Atkinson and Delamont (2006) when they state, "We are appalled by the absurd proposal that interpretive research should be made to conform to inappropriate definitions of scientific research. ... Equally disturbing is the argument that qualitative research should not be funded if it fails to conform to these criteria" (p. 751; see also Erickson & Gutierrez, 2002, p. 221). Hammersley (2005a, p. 3), in turn, observes that, "Qualitative research tends to suffer by comparison with quantitative work because there is a myth that quantitative researchers have clearcut guidelines which are available for use by policymakers (Was it a randomized controlled trial? Was there a control group?)."

Morse (2006a) extends the argument: "Indeed, qualitative inquiry falls off the positivist grid. Why it barely earns a Grade of C– on the Cochrane scale! It gets worse! It receives the 'does not meet evidence standard' on the 'What Works Clearinghouse' (WWC) Scale" (Morse, 2006a, p. 396; see also Cheek, 2005, 2006).

Feuer, Towne, and Shavelson (2002) offer the counterargument:

Although we strongly oppose blunt federal mandates that reduce scientific inquiry to one method ... we also believe that the field should use this tool in studies in education more often then is current practice. ... Now is the time for the field to move beyond particularized views and focus on building a shared core of norms and practices that emphasize *scientific* principles. (p. 8, emphasis added)

Furthermore, a report by the National Center for the Dissemination of Disability Research Standards states: "We need criteria for comparing research methods and research evidence, we need terms like *credibility* (internal validity), *transferability* (external validity), *dependability* (reliability), *confirmability* (objectivity)"[12] (see http://www.ncddr.org).

A good skeptic, though, must ask, "Whose science?" "Whose scientific principles?"

• • •

Evaluative criteria, as pedagogical practices, are shaped by what is regarded as the proper relationship between qualitative inquiry and social policy. Within the critical qualitative inquiry community, at least four pedagogical stances or identities can be distinguished. Each has its own history (Hammersley, 2005a): (1) discipline-based qualitative research focused on accumulating fundamental knowledge about social processes and institutions; (2) qualitative policy research aimed at having an impact on current programs and practices; (3) critical qualitative approaches that disrupt and destabilize current public policy or social discourse; and (4) public intellectuals, public social scientists, and cultural critics who use qualitative inquiry and interpretive work to address current issues and crises in the public arena (Hammersley, 2005a, p. 3).

Hammersley (2005a, p. 5) cautions, though, that "we should not allow the close encounters promised by the notion of evidence-based policymaking, or even 'public social science,' to seduce us into illusions about ourselves and our work." On this point, Torrance (2006, p. 127) is quite assertive: "This new orthodoxy seems perversely and willfully ignorant of many decades of debate over whether—and if so, in what ways—we can conduct enquiry and build knowledge in the social sciences, pausing only to castigate educational research for not being more like … medical research."

This ethical, epistemological, and political discourse is historically and politically situated. It plays out differently in each national context (see Atkinson & Delamont, 2006; Cheek, 2006; Gilgun, 2006; Lather, 2004a, 2004b; Morse, 2006a, 2006b; Preissle, 2006; Stronach, this volume; Torrance, 2006, this volume). In the United States, the United Kingdom, the European Union, New Zealand, and Australia, the conversation criss-crosses audit cultures, indigenous cultures, disciplines, paradigms, and epistemologies as well as decolonizing initiatives. Depending on the nation-state, the discourse goes by various acronyms. In the United States, it is called scientifically based research (SBR) or scientific inquiry in education (SIE). In the United Kingdom, the model goes by letters RAE (research assessment exercise). And, in Australia, scholars must deal with the research quality framework (RQF). Each of these models is based, more or less, on the assumption that because medical research is successful and because randomized experimental designs are used and appreciated in medical science, this should be the blueprint for *all* good research (but see Timmermans & Berg, 2003).

Within the postpositivist, foundational, and quasi-foundational U.S. research communities,[13] there are multiple institutions (and conversations) competing for attention, including: (1) the Institute of Education Science (IES) within the U.S. Department of Education; (2) the What Works Clearinghouse (WWC), funded by IES; (3) the Cochrane-Campbell Collaboration (CCC), which contracts with WWC; (4) the National Research Council-SBR framework (2002, 2006), which implements version of CCC and WWC; (5) the recently IES-funded ($850,000) Society for Research on Educational Effectiveness (SREE); and (6) the 2006 standards for reporting adopted by the American Education Research Association (AERA), which explicitly addresses standards for qualitative research, some of which are contained in documents prepared by members of the Cochrane Qualitative Methods Group (Briggs, 2006).[14] The following section examines several of these institutional formations in greater detail.

"Institutionally" Speaking ...

The National Research Council and Scientifically Based Research

The federally funded National Research Council's (NRC) SBR, or evidence-based movement, argues that educational, health care, and other social problems can be better addressed if we borrow from medical science, upgrade our methods, and create new gold standards for evaluating evidence (NRC, 2002, 2005). For this group, quality research is scientific, empirical, linked to theory, uses methods for direct investigation, and produces coherent chains of causal reasoning based on experimental or quasi-experimental findings, offering generalizations that can be replicated, and used to test, and refine theory. According to the NRC, if research has these features, it has high quality and is thus scientific (NRC, 2005, p. 20).

In the United States, such research must also conform to the Office of Human Subject Research definition of scientific inquiry. That is, scientific research is

> any activity designed to test an hypothesis, permit conclusions to be drawn, and thereby to develop or contribute to generalizable knowledge expressed in theories, principles, and statements of relationships. Research is described in a formal protocol that sets forth an objective and a set of procedures designed to reach that objective. (Title 45, Part 46, U. S. Code of Federal Regulations; AAUP, 2001, p. 55; also, AAUP, 1981, 2002, 2006)

Hand in hand, ethics and models of science now flow into one another. Institutional review board (IRB) panels rule on research that is simultaneously ethically sound and of high quality. *If these assumptions are allowed, we have lost the argument even before it starts.* Cannella and Lincoln (2004) are clear on this point:

> The NRC report is a U.S. government-requested project designed to clearly define the nature or research that is to be labeled as representing quality. ... Accurately referred to as methodological fundamentalism ... contemporary conservative research discourses ... have ignored critical theory, race/ethic studies, and feminist theories and silenced the voices and life conditions of the traditionally marginalized (p. 165, paraphrase; see also Feuer,

2006; Hammersley, 2005a; St. Pierre, 2006; St. Pierre & Roulston, 2006).

Thirteen recommendations for implementing the NRC model are directed to federal funding agencies, professional associations and journals, and schools of education. These recommendations state that:

Research agencies should:

- define and enforce better quality criteria for peer reviewers;
- ensure peer reviewer expertise and diversity; and
- create infrastructures for data sharing.

Publishers and professional associations should:

- develop explicit standards for data sharing;
- require authors to make data available to other researchers;
- create infrastructures for data sharing;
- develop standards for structured abstracts; and
- develop manuscript review systems that support professional development.

Schools of education and universities should:

- enable research competencies;
- ensure students develop deep methodological knowledge; and
- provide students with meaningful research experiences.

There are several problems with these NRC formulations and recommendations. We start with Maxwell (2004a, 2004b). He unravels and criticizes the centrally linked assumptions in the model with six points of contention that constitute powerful criticisms of SBR. He argues that the model assumes a narrow, regularized view of causation; privileges a variable-oriented (as opposed to a process-oriented) view of research; denies the possibility of observing causality in a single case; neglects the importance of context, meaning, and process as essential components of causal and interpretive analysis; erroneously asserts that qualitative and quantitative research share the same logic of inference;

and presents a hierarchical ordering of methods for investigating causality, giving priority to experimental and other quantitative methods (Maxwell, 2004b, p. 3).

Feuer, Towne, and Shavelson (2002, p. 8) attempt to finesse this criticism, creating a "special" place for qualitative research and suggesting that it can be used to capture the complexities involved in teaching, learning, and schooling:

> [W]hen a problem is poorly understood, and plausible hypotheses are scant—qualitative methods such as ethnographies … are necessary to describe complex phenomena, generate theoretical models and reframe questions. … We want to be explicit … we do not view our strong support for randomized field trials and our equally strong argument for close attention to context … as incompatible. Quite the contrary: When properly applied, quantitative and qualitative research tools can both be employed rigorously and together.

Finessing aside, the NRC is clear on this point: "a randomized experiment is the best method for estimating [causal] effects" (Feuer, Towne, & Shavelson, 2002, p. 8).

But as Yogi Berra would say, it's like déjà vu all over again. Flashback to 1926, and Lundberg, sociology's archpositivist, is arguing against the use of the case method:

> The case method is not in itself a scientific method at all, but merely the first step in the scientific method … the statistical method is the best, if not the only scientific method … the only possible question … is whether classification of, and generalizations from the data, should be carried out by random, qualitative, and subjective method … or through the systematic, quantitative, and objective procedures of the statistical method. (Lundberg, 1926, p. 61)

Now fast forward to 1966, to Howard S. Becker:

> The life history method has not been much used by contemporary sociologists, a neglect which reflects a shift in the methodological stance of the researcher. Rigorous, quantitative, and (frequently) experimental designs have become the accepted modes of investigation. This situation is unfortunate because the life history, when properly conceived and employed can become one of the sociologist's most powerful observational and analytic tools. (Becker, 1966, p. xviii)

The presumption that only quantitative data can be used to identify causal relationships is problematic. Maxwell (2004a) shows how the SBR model neglects meaning, context, and process. He demonstrates that causality can be identified (after Hume) in the single case; that is, multi-case, variable-based causal arguments are just one form of causal interpretation. Other causal or quasi-causal models, of course, are based on multi-variant, process-, contextual-, and interactionist-based assumptions. Further, causality as a type of narrative is only one form of interpretation. Autoethnographic, performative, arts-based, ethnodramatic, poetic, action-based, and other forms of narrative representation are equally powerful methods and strategies of analysis and interpretation.

In additional to Maxwell's original six criticisms, we would add the following five.

First, amazingly, there is little attention given to the process by which evidence is turned into data. This is not a simple process, one certainly not accomplished by waving Harry Potter's magic wand over a body of observations.

Second, there is no detailed discussion of how data are to be used to produce generalizations, test and refine theory, and permit causal reasoning. It is clear, though, that data become commodities that do several things.

Third, in other words, evidence as data carries the weight of the scientific process. This process works through a self-fulfilling, self-validating prophecy: You know you have quality data that are scientific when you have tested and refined your theory. But how you have addressed problems in the real world remains a mystery left for a Dashiell Hammett character to unravel.

Fourth, the focus on data sharing is critical and of central concern. It is assumed that quality data can be easily shared. But complex interpretive processes shape how evidence is turned into data, and how data, in turn, are coded, categorized, labeled, and assembled into data banks (Charmaz, 2005). *Data are not silent!* Data are commodities, produced by researchers, perhaps owned by the government or by funding agencies. What would it mean to share my data with you? Why would I want to do this? If I own my data, I want to have ownership over how they are used, including what is published from them. The injunction to engage in data sharing requires amplification. Data sharing involves complex moral and ethical considerations that go beyond sending a body of coded data to another colleague or governmental agency.

Fifth, money, and concerns for auditing from the audit culture, seems to drive the process. This is evidenced in the emphasis placed on funding and quality peer reviews. If quality data can be produced and shared, then granting agencies get more science for less money. However, for greater data sharing to occur, more quality projects need to be funded. For this to happen, granting agencies need a better peer review system with better trained reviewers who are using more clearly defined rating scale levels. And so, the thinking goes, reviewers will be helped if researchers write proposals that use rigorous methodologies and the very best research designs. Such projects will surely have high standards of evidence. Thus does the self-fulfilling process reproduce itself. We know we are getting quality science of the highest order because we are using methods of the highest order. Reviewers can easily identify such work. The blind peer review, based on presumptions of objectivity, is the key to this system.[15]

We must also bear in mind that the peer review system is not immune to political influence. Kaplan (2004), especially, has demonstrated that the George W. Bush administration has systematically stacked federal advisory and peer review committees with researchers whose views match the president's fundamentalist neoconservative orientation on issues ranging from stem cell research to ergonomics, faith-based science, AIDS, sex education, reproductive health,[16] family values, global warming, and environmental issues in public parks (see also Denzin & Giardina, 2006, 2007; Goldberg, 2007; Kaplan, 2004; Klein, 2007; Maher, 2007; Monastersky, 2002; Phillips, 2006).

Society for Research on Educational Effectiveness (SREE)

The Society for Research on Educational Effectiveness (SREE) serves to extend the federally sponsored NRC agenda. It also appears to oppose recent efforts within the AERA to soften NRC guidelines (see below). The code words for SREE, which has its own journal (*Journal of Research on Educational Effectiveness*), handbook (*Handbook of Research on Educational Effectiveness*), and electronic journal (*Research Notes on Educational Effectiveness*), are rigorous research design and randomized control experiment: The mission of SREE is to:

> advance and disseminate research on the causal effects of education interventions, practices, programs, and policies. As support for researchers who are focused on questions related to educational effectiveness, the Society aims to: (1) increase the capacity to design and conduct investigations that have a strong base for causal inference; (2) bring together people investigating cause-and-effect relations in education; and (3) promote the understanding and use of scientific evidence to improve education decisions and outcomes.[17] (http://www.sree-net.org; see also Viadero, 2006).

By its own standards, there is no place in SREE for qualitative research. This is hardcore, fundamentalist SBR: evidence-based inquiry. Scientific research becomes a commodity to be sold in a new journal, a commodity that serves, embodies, and emboldens the interests of educational science as narrowly defined

The Cochrane-Campbell-What Works Clearinghouse Collaborations

The Cochrane, Campbell, and What Works Clearinghouse Collaborations are inserting themselves into the qualitative research conversation. All three represent state-sponsored projects dedicated to producing so-called scientific peer reviews of quality (that is, evidence-based) research that can be used by policymakers. The Cochrane Qualitative Methods Group focuses on methodological matters arising from the inclusion of findings from qualitative studies into systematic reviews of evidence-based inquires. The Campbell Methods Group focuses on methodological issues associated with process evaluations, which use mixed methods, while including evidence gathered via qualitative methods. It is understood that qualitative research can help in understanding how an intervention is experienced, while providing insight into factors that might hinder successful implementation. And, likewise, the What Works Clearinghouse, under the aegis of the Department of Education's Institute of Education Sciences, "aims to promote informed education decision making through a set of easily accessible databases and user-friendly reports that provide education consumers with high-quality reviews of the effectiveness of replicable educational interventions ... that intend to improve student outcomes" (see http://ies.ed.gov/ncee/wwc/overview/).

Randomized controlled trials are central to all three collaborations. Hence, qualitative evidence is of primary interest only when it is included as a data-gathering technique in an experimental or quasi-experimental study (Briggs, 2006). There is some debate on this point; that is, whether "only qualitative research embedded within relevant RCTs should be included" (Briggs, 2006). The Campbell Collaboration only includes qualitative materials if they are part of controlled observations (Davies, 2004, p. 30). However, there is no consensus on how to include qualitative *evidence* in such work—namely, how to identify, record, appraise, and extract data from qualitative studies.

Enter CASP—the Critical Appraisal Skills Program (Briggs, 2006), which was developed in conjunction with the Cochrane Qualitative Research Methods Group. The Cochrane Group (Briggs, 2006) has a broad but conventional definition of qualitative research, encompassing specific methods (interviews, participant and nonparticipant observation, focus groups, ethnographic fieldwork), data types (narrative), and forms of analysis (NUDIST, ethnography, grounded theory, thematic categories).

CASP, like any number of other checklists (Dixon-Woods, Shaw et al., 2004; Jackson & Waters, 2005; Popay, Williams, & Williams, 1998; Spencer et al., 2003) is an assessment tool developed for those unfamiliar with qualitative research. The tool presents a series of questions, focused around three broad issues: rigor, credibility, and relevance. Ten questions concerning aims, methodology, design, subject recruitment, data collection, researcher-participant relationship, ethics (IRBs), data analysis, statement of findings, and value of research are asked. The reviewer of a study writes comments on each of these issues.

CASP implements a narrow model of qualitative inquiry. Methods are not connected to interpretive paradigms (e.g., feminist, critical theory, etc.). Multiple strategies of inquiry and analysis (case or performance studies, narrative inquiry, critical ethnography, etc.) go unidentified. Nor is the complex literature from within the interpretive tradition on evaluating qualitative research addressed (see Christians, 2005). Thus, CASP offers the reviewer a small, ahistorical tool kit for reading and evaluating qualitative studies.

Here Hammersley is again relevant. This is the myth of the checklist, the myth of the guideline (Hammersley, 2005a). Consider the guidelines prepared for the British Cabinet Office (Spencer et al., 2003). This is another checklist with sixteen categories (scope, timetable, design, sample, data collection, analysis, ethics, confirmability generalizability, credibility, etc.), eighty specific criteria (clearly stated hypotheses, outcomes, justify analysis methods, triangulation, etc), and thirty-five broad criteria (explicit aims, appropriate use of methods, assessment of reliability and validity, etc). This is old-fashioned postpositivism—applying a soft quantitative grid (confirmability, hypotheses, credibility) to qualitative research.

But there is more going on. Like CASP, the Spencer et al. toolkit introduces the notion of credibility; that is, can the findings be trusted? If they can be trusted, they must be confirmable, valid, and reliable. Which means they can be generalized. If they are not credible, the whole house of cards falls down. Torrance (e-mail, 2007) exposes the underlying theory at work here, noting that "it is a traditional, positivist model, that is the truth is out there to be discovered." Yet, as he observes, "these scholars still cannot solve the problem of epistemological incommensuration [...] [T]his is little more than experts 'rating' qualitative evidence on an agreed scale so it can be included in meta-analyses of effect sizes" (2007).

American Education Research Association

The AERA (2006) has recently added its collective voice to the conversation, supplementing, and departing from the NRC recommendations. Its 2006 guidelines for reporting on empirical social science research are also intended to foster excellence in the production of high quality research. Two global standards are offered: *warrantability* and *transparency*[18] (AERA, 2006, p. 2). Reports of research should be warranted; in other words, adequate evidence, which would be credible (internal validity), should be provided to justify conclusions. Reports should be transparent, making explicit the logic of inquiry used in the project. This method should produce data that have external validity, reliability, and confirmability (objectivity). Like the NRC guidelines, these standards are to be used by peer reviewers, research scholars, journal publishers, and in graduate education programs where researchers are trained.

There is extensive discussion of quantitative procedures (AERA, 2006, pp. 6–10), but trust is not an issue; trust is left for *qualitative* researchers. The report is explicit, asserting that

> it is the researcher's responsibility is to show the reader that the report can be trusted. This begins with the description of the evidence, the data, and the analysis supporting each interpretive claim. The warrant for the claims can be established through a variety procedures including triangulation, asking participants to evaluate pattern descriptions, having different analysts examine the same data (independently and collaboratively), searches for disconfirming evidence and counter-interpretations. (AERA, 2006, p. 11)

This is all clear enough, but these validating procedures and standards are not held up for quantitative researchers. When qualitative evidence does not converge, the report recommends that

> critical examination of the preexisting perspective, point of view, or standpoint of the researcher(s), of how these might have influenced the collection and analysis of evidence, and of how they were challenged during the course of data collection and analysis, is an important element in enhancing the warrant of each claim. (AERA, 2006, p. 11)

Here is the heart of the matter: As the AERA sees it, the perspective of the qualitative researcher can influence the collection of evidence in such a way as to introduce a lack of trust into the research process. That presence potentially undermines the credibility and warrantabilty of the report. But why would the qualitative researcher's effects on the research process be greater than, or even less than, the effects of the quantitative researcher? Doesn't the quantitative researcher have an effect on the collection, analysis and interpretation of evidence, including deciding what is evidence?!?!?

The AERA recommendations call for the responsible use of quasi-foundational tools; in other words, it believes that threats to trust can be overcome. Transparency (née trust) is increased by clearly discussing the process of interpretation, highlighting the evidence and alternative interpretations that serve as a warrant for each claim, providing contextual commentary on each claim. When generalizations extend beyond a specific case, researchers must clearly indicate the sampling frame, population, individuals, contexts, activities, and domains to which the generalizations are intended to apply (external validity). The logic supporting such generalizations must be made clear.

A magician's sleight of hand is at work in the AERA recommendations. The intent of the report is now clear—two things are going on at once. A familiar pattern. Qualitative research is downgraded to the status of a marginal science, or second-class academic citizenship. Because it lacks trustworthiness, it can be used for discovery purposes, but not for the real work of science, which is verification. Only under the most rigorous of circumstances can qualitative research exhibit the qualities that would make it scientific, and even then trust will be an issue. Trust becomes a proxy for quality; transparency and warranted evidence function as proxies for objectivity.

But trust in this discourse resurfaces as a proxy for more than quality. It spills over to the researcher who does research that lacks trustworthiness. Untrustworthy people lie, misrepresent, cheat, engage in fraud, alter documents. They are not governed by measurement and statistical procedures that are "objective" and free of bias. They may not be shady characters—they may in fact be well-intended, gifted actors, poets, fiction writers, performers—but they are not scientists! Qualitative researchers are not to be trusted because their standpoints can influence what they study, and report. Yet, somehow, quantitative researchers are freed from these influences. *This is, of course, a complete and total sham!*[19]

• • •

Clearly, AERA wants a space for qualitative research that is not governed by the narrow NRC experimental and quasi-experimental guidelines. We all want this. To its credit, AERA wants a broad-based, multimethod concept of quality. But it falters in asserting that empirical research reports should be warranted and transparent. These are criteria for doing business as usual. No wonder SREE was created: AERA's educational science does not require randomized control experiments; SREE's does.[20]

Moreover, it is as if the NRC, SREE, and AERA guidelines were written in a time warp. Over the last three decades, the field of qualitative research has become an interdisciplinary field in its own right. The interpretive and critical paradigms, in their multiple forms, are central to this movement. Complex literatures are now attached to research methodologies, strategies of inquiry, interpretive paradigms, and criteria for reading and evaluating inquiry itself. Sadly, little of this literature is evident in any of the recent national documents. It seems that the qualitative community is hemmed in from all sides. But before this judgment is accepted, the "for whom" question must be asked; that is, "High quality science, or evidence, for whom?" (Cheek, 2006).

The NRC, AERA, and SREE's umbrellas are too small. Or, to put it more bluntly, we need a larger tent. We must resist the pressures for a single gold standard, even as we endorse conversations about evidence, inquiry, and empirically warranted conclusions (Lincoln & Cannella, 2004). We cannot let one group define the key terms in the conversation. To do otherwise is to allow the SBR group to define the moral and epistemological terrain that we stand on. Neither they, nor a government, own the word "science." Habermas (1972) anticipated this thirty-five years ago:

> The link between empiricism, positivism and the global audit culture is not accidental and it is more than just technical. Such technical approaches deflect attention away from the deeper issues of value and purpose. They make radical critiques much more difficult to mount ... and they render largely invisible partisan approaches to research under the politically useful pretense that judgments are about objective quality only. In the process human needs and human rights are trampled upon and democracy as we need it is destroyed. (Habermas, 1972, p. 122, 2006, p. 193; see also Smith & Hodkinson, 2005, p. 930)

Bourdieu (1998) elaborates further: "The dominants, technocrats, and empiricists of the right and the left are hand in glove with reason and the universal. ... More and more rational, scientific technical justifications, always in the name of objectivity, are relied upon. In this way the audit culture perpetuates itself" (p. 90).

There is more than one version of disciplined, rigorous inquiry—counter-science, little science, unruly science, practical science—and such inquiry need not go by the name of science. We must have a model of disciplined, rigorous, thoughtful, reflective inquiry, a "postinterpretivism that seeks meaning but less innocently, that seeks liberation but less naively, and that ... reaches toward understanding, transformation and justice" (Preissle, 2006, p. 692). It does not need to be called a science, contested or otherwise, as some have proposed (Eisenhart, 2006; Preissle, 2006; St. Pierre & Rouleston, 2006).

Lather (2006), paraphrasing slightly, extends the argument:

> The commitment to disciplined inquiry opens the space for the pursuit of "inexact knowledges" (p. 787), a disciplined inquiry that matters, applied qualitative research ... that can engage strategically with the limits and the possibilities of the uses of research for social policy (p. 789). The goal is a critical counter-"science" ... that troubles what we take for granted as the good in fostering understanding, reflection and action (p. 787). We need a broader framework where such key terms as science, data, evidence, field, method, analysis, knowledge, truth, are no longer defined from within a narrow policy-oriented, positivistic framework. (p. 788)

A New Terrain—Trouble with the Elephant

Let's return to the elephant in the living room. Consider the parable of the blind men and the elephant by Lillian Quigley (1996)[21]:

> In my children's book, *The Blind Men and the Elephant* (1959), I retell the ancient fable of six blind men who visit the palace of the Rajah and encounter an elephant for the first time. Each touches the elephant, and announces his discovery. The first blind person touches the side of the elephant and reports that it feels like a wall. The second touches the trunk and says an elephant is like a snake. The third man touches the tusk and says an elephant is like a spear. The fourth person touches a leg and says it feels like a tree. The fifth man touches an ear and says it must be a fan, while the sixth man touches the tail and says how thin, an elephant is like a rope.

There are multiple versions of the elephant in our parable. Multiple lessons. We can never know the true nature of things. We are each blinded by our own perspective. Truth is always partial, fractured, contested, performed.

To summarize:

Truth One: The elephant is not one thing. If we call SBR the elephant, then, according to the parable, we can each know only our version of SBR. For SBR advocates, the elephant is two things: an all-knowing being who speaks to us, and a way of knowing that produces truths about life. How can a thing be two things at the same time?

Truth Two: For skeptics, we are like the blind persons in the parable. We only see partial truths. There is no God's eye view of the totality, no uniform way of knowing.

Truth Three: Our methodological and moral biases have so seriously blinded us that we can never understand another blind person's position. Even if the elephant called SBR speaks, our biases may prohibit us for hearing what she or he says. In turn, her or his biases prevent her or him from hearing what we say.

Truth Four: If we are all blind, if there is no God, and if there are multiple versions of the elephant, then we are all fumbling around in the world just doing the best we can.

This is the blind person's version of the elephant. But there are at least two other versions: version 2.1 and version 2.2. Both versions follow from another fable: Now the elephant refers to a painfully problematic situation, thing, or person in one's life space. Rather than confront the thing and make changes, people find that is easier to engage in denial, to act like the elephant isn't in the room. This can be unhealthy, because the thing may be destructive. It can produce codependency. We need the negative presence of the elephant to feel good about ourselves.

This cuts two ways at once:

In Fable 2.1, SBR advocates treat qualitative research as if it were an elephant in *their* living room. They have ignored our traditions, our values, our methodologies; they have not read our journals, or our handbooks, or our monographs. They have not even engaged our discourses about SBR. Like the six blind men, they have acted as if they could create us in their own eye. They say we produce findings that can not be trusted, that we are radical relativists, that we think anything goes, that with our values we would not have stopped Hitler! They dismiss us when we tell them they only know one version of who we are, and when we tell them their biases prevent them from understanding what we do, they assert that we are wrong and they are right.

In Fable 2.2, the elephant is located in *our* living room. With notable exceptions, we have tried to ignore this presence. Denial has fed codependency. We need the negative presence of SBR to define who we are. For example, we have not taken up the challenge of better educating policymakers, showing them how qualitative research and our views of practical science, interpretation, and performance ethics can positively contribute to projects embodying restorative justice, equity, and better schooling (Preissle, 2006; Stanfield, 2006). We have not engaged policymakers in a dialog about alternative ways of judging and evaluating quality research. Nor have we engaged SBR advocates in a dialog about these same issues (but see St. Pierre, 2006). And they have often declined the invitation to join us in a conversation (but see Feuer, 2005). As a consequence, we have allowed the SBR elephant to set the terms of the conversation.

If we are to move forward in a positive fashion, we have to get beyond Fable 2.2, beyond elephants, blind persons, and structures of denial. We must create a new narrative, a narrative of passion, and commitment, a narrative that teaches others that ways of knowing are always already partial, moral, political, and contested. This narrative will allow us to put the elephant in proper perspective. Here are some of the certain things we can build our new fable around:

1. We have an ample supply of methodological rules and interpretive guidelines.
2. They are open to change and to differing interpretation, and this is how it should be.
3. There is no longer a single gold standard for qualitative work.
4. We value open peer reviews in our journals.
5. Our empirical materials are performative. They are not

commodities to be bought, sold, and consumed.
6. Our feminist, communitarian ethics are not governed by IRBs.
7. Our science is open-ended, unruly, disruptive (MacLure, 2006; Stronach et al. 2007, p. 197).
8. Inquiry is always political and moral.
9. Objectivity and evidence are political and ethical terms.

The Chapters

Qualitative Inquiry and the Politics of Evidence is comprised of three sections that actively seek to intervene into contemporary debates concerning the nature of evidence. Section I (Policy Intentions) focuses on policy-oriented concerns to qualitative researchers, such as those with the RAE in the United Kingdom and other bibliometric standards and frameworks taking hold throughout the world. Section II (Theoretical and Methodological Interruptions) offers several distinctive contributions regarding the production of knowledge and human understanding that work to unsettle any concept of a fixed or finite view of "evidence." Section III (Performative Interventions) moves from the policy-oriented and theoretical/methodological imperatives of the previous two sections to a performative set of chapters that deploy autoethnographic methods and narrative collages located at the intersection of various constructs of evidence.

Section I launches the volume with Harry Torrance's exposition on the articulation of evidence and politics in the contemporary moment. Reflecting on the current situation in both the United States and the United Kingdom, Torrance begins by reviewing arguments for and against random clinical trials within the broad spectrum of educational research, particularly how they are enmeshed within policy-oriented discursive spaces. From there, he discusses some initial responses of the "qualitative research community," taking care to point out that this is a diverse and disunified arena comprised of numerous scholarly disciplines (e.g., anthropology, psychology, social work, etc.) and differently arrayed national contexts, each with its own applied research and policy settings (education, social work, health studies, etc.). Torrance goes on to focus specifically on responses within the United Kingdom, particularly the government Cabinet Office's commissioned report by the National Center for Social Research (*Quality in Qualitative Evaluation: A Framework for Assessing Research Evidence* [Cabinet Office, 2003]), which, he argues, "comprise[s] a banal and inoperable set of standards which beg all the important questions of conducting and writing up qualitative fieldwork." He follows this examination of the UK context by next turning his attention to similar developments in the United States, such as those conducted under the auspices of the National Science Foundation or by scholarly associations such as AERA. He concludes by offering that we must be willing to engage with policymakers and draw them into the discussion in the pursuit of productive, organic relationships rather than retreating and becoming focused solely on "standards" and "frameworks."

Ian Stronach's chapter follows, presenting a closely nuanced interrogation of the RAE (an appraisal model within the United Kingdom that has spawned copies from Hong Kong to New Zealand). He begins by deconstructing the RAE Education sub-panel's rubrics, drawing also on the broader RAE regulations, procedures, and associated documentation and research. In so doing, he highlights the political, rather than purely academic, concerns that gave rise to the current iteration of the RAE in the face of criticisms to previous RAE metrics. He further takes on the RAE's appraisal terms of "originality, significance, and rigor" and how these terms are given seemingly ever-changing hierarchical purchase throughout various fields, especially with respect to rigor. He concludes with a scathing philosophical polemic against the larger academic community for its lack of "civil courage" in not challenging en masse "a process that is so clearly flawed, inexpertly researched, ill-thought out, and obviously manipulated by politicians and policymakers," but one that has nevertheless achieved acceptance "by a research community that should, by its very nature, be the first to criticize and dismiss it."

Kenneth R. Howe's chapter similarly engages with the prevailing methodological orthodoxy of our contemporary moment, especially as exemplified by documents such as the NRC's *Scientific Research in Education* and *Advancing Scientific Research in Education* and the AERA's *Standards for Reporting on Empirical Social Research*. In particular, Howe criticizes the new orthodoxy as being a throwback to positivist reductionism and the "two dogmas" of educational research: the quantitative/qualitative incompatibility thesis and fact/value dichotomy. He then finds fault with the new orthodoxy for fostering a "third dogma" of educational research cut from the same cloth as the first two: the empirical science/humanities dualism. Moreover, he advances the view that no fundamental epistemological dividing line can be drawn between the empirical sciences and the humanities and that, accordingly, empirical research should not be cordoned off from the humanities, particularly, the focus on values. The chapter concludes with several observations about the problems and prospects for interdisciplinary research in education across the empirical science/humanities divide.

The section concludes with Julianne Cheek's provocative chapter, which argues that proponents of qualitative inquiry are both positioned, and, in turn, position themselves, in the wake of the effects of the politics of evidence. Such positioning is thus a dynamic process. It is not simply imposed or determined by others. Qualitative researchers are both worked on by, and in turn work on, understandings of research and research evidence. One potentially hidden or unexplored outworking of such a dynamic is the possible rise within qualitative inquiry itself of new forms of research fundamentalism in response, but also as reaction, to attempts to normalize and define research related evidence. This paradigm, Cheek argues, creates a fine line for qualitative research to tread in terms of positioning and transforming practice(s) in the wake of the politics of evidence.

David Altheide's chapter opens Section II and presents an exploratory analysis of the evidentiary narrative, which symbolically joins an actor, an audience, a point of view, assumptions, and a claim about a relationship between two or more phenomena. In so doing, he focuses on evidence as *process*, to provide another way to understand how everyday life perspectives inform what we see as relevant, confirming or disconfirming various beliefs, assumptions, and theories. Altheide argues that knowledge and belief systems in everyday life are tied to epistemic communities that provide perspectives, scenarios, and scripts that reflect symbolic social and moral orders. Viewing evidence as part of a communication process suggests that evidence is not about facts per se, but is about an argument, a narrative that is appropriate for the purpose-at-hand. By way of example, documents about the Iraq War are used to illustrate the interpretive stances that follow from the evidentiary process.

Joseph Maxwell follows, presenting a cogent explication of how realism can do useful work for qualitative methodology and practice if it is taken seriously and its implications for qualitative research systematically developed. One of the most important contributions that realism can make, he argues, derives from a realist understanding of causality; in particular, "supporting the use of qualitative research for causal explanation and defending this against the criticisms of quantitative researchers," as well as "helping qualitative researchers to further develop their theoretical understanding of, and methods for developing, causal explanations." Such an approach, he explains, can be helpful in "developing and assessing evidence" for qualitatively informed research projects.

Patti Lather's chapter tackles "recent feminist reinscriptions of practices of critique and analysis in qualitative research in order to begin to grasp what is on the horizon in terms of new analytics and practices of inquiry." Specifically, she develops what she calls a "philosophical ethnography," one based in part on aspects of Eve Sedgwick's (1997) reparative reading, Gayatri Spivak's (1993) dislocating negotiation, and Elizabeth Wilson's (1998) analytics of breaching. Here, Lather is concerned with troubling the categories of knowing and understanding in the context of a feminist effort to unsettle scientism and scientificity, where "openness and unknowingness are part of the process, a self-reflexive, non-dogmatic feminism that relishes conflicting interpretations without domesticating them, a permanent unsettlement in what might be termed a postfoundational feminism." In turn, the spectre of "not knowing" becomes our greatest ally in our quest for, as Spivak would say, "learning from below."

Section II concludes with Janice Morse, Linda Niehaus,

Stanley Varnhagen, Wendy Austin, and Michele McIntosh's chapter, which reports on a web-based survey of 517 qualitative researchers' perceptions of the "risks" inherent in qualitative unstructured interviews. Although emotions manifest during these qualitative interviews may be viewed as "natural" in the context of the types of losses experienced by the interviewees, they argue that emotional responses cannot be identified in an IRB review of the proposal. As such, the mitigation of this emotional response becomes the responsibility of the researcher, and ethics education and short courses must include such instruction. Moreover, they report that psychological harm to the researcher, although rare, is a possibility for which researchers must be prepared. The authors conclude by suggesting six principles of ethical conduct for qualitative researchers.

Section III opens with D. Soyini Madison's striking essay, which examines the intersecting vectors of power, politics, and poetry within the oral narrative performances of local human rights activists in Ghana, West Africa, who are working for the rights of women and girls against traditional cultural practices that impede their freedom and well-being. Focusing on the voices of human rights activists as related to their work against the cultural practice known as Trokosi/Troxovi, these narratives serve as examples of poetic transcription as critical performance ethnography in which "each narrator poetically narrates their own indigenous and critical methodologies based on the politics of their performative interventions in defending the human rights of Others." The author concludes with a "wish list" for future research in this area.

From there, we find Christopher Darius Stonebanks's chapter, which examines to what extent political pressure through mediated circuits of production exerts control over educational policy and educators' curriculum and thus denies respected counternarratives in qualitative research to enter public schools. To do so, he presents us with various slices of life—ranging from the controversy over Ward Churchill's post-9/11 statements, to a family outing at a local Thanksgiving festival, to a popular Hollywood film (*Addams Family Values*)—that together and in isolation speak to the contested nature of knowledge in the contemporary moment. Stonebanks then ties these narratives (and counternarratives) together in a discussion of curricular knowledge and how the political considerations afforded the production of knowledge present us with an ongoing cultural pedagogy of contemporary social relations.

A co-constructed performance text on the affective power of autoethnography follows, authored by a hendecagon group of scholars organized by Mary E. Weems and Carolyne J. White. Using music, artifacts, and a spirit of community togetherness to forge a "sacred space" for their poetry to spring forth, each contributor pens (and in some cases, comments on) his or her own own group-inspired poetic verse. Topics such as love, sex, race, family, jazz, and chicken noodle soup spring forth from "being in the moment," revealing the deeper, creative, emotional ties that bind us to our research, our selves, and our communities.

Leah Vande Berg and Nick Trujillo's chapter closes out the section. Written from multiple perspectives, and with the addition of numerous friendly voices to the narrative, they present an intensely personal journey about Leah's battle with cancer. Narrating a heartfelt story shared by many, we're taken deep inside their dual struggles with hospitals, hopes for recovery, pains of surgery, values of friendship, and love for each other. The he said/she said/they said format of showing, not telling, further reveals the shifting and ever complex viewpoints on life and living in the moment.

The volume concludes with a performative chapter by Carolyn Ellis, Arthur Bochner, Norman Denzin, Bud Goodall, Ron Pelias, and Laurel Richardson on the state of autoethnography and the place of personal narratives within the larger qualitative research community. Focusing on issues ranging from personal history and presentation of self, to broader debates such as major challenges and goals of autoethnographers in an age of global uncertainty, the authors highlight and comment on the changing landscape confronting the next generation of qualitative researchers.

By Way of a Conclusion

Qualitative Inquiry and the Politics of Evidence marks the third entry in our series on qualitative research in the historical present. Each of these three volumes has found its genesis in and come out of our parallel involvement in organizing the annual International Congress of Qualitative Inquiry at the University of Illinois, Urbana-Champaign. The first, titled *Qualitative Inquiry and the Conservative Challenge: Confronting Methodological Fundamentalism* (2006), sought to actively contest the right-wing/neoconservative-dominated direction of regulatory policy governing scientific inquiry. Such regulatory efforts—primarily those obsessed with enforcing scientifically based, biomedical models of research—raise fundamental philosophical, epistemological, and ontological issues for scholarship and freedom of speech in the academy.

Our second volume, *Ethical Futures in Qualitative Research: Decolonizing the Politics of Knowledge* (2007), charted a radical path for a future in which ethical considerations transcend the Belmont Principles (which focus almost exclusively on the problems associated with betrayal, deception, and harm), calling for a collaborative, performative social science research model that makes the researcher responsible not to a removed discipline or institution, but to those he or she studies. In so doing, personal accountability, the value of expressiveness, the capacity for empathy, and the sharing of emotionality are stressed. As such, scholars were directed to take up moral projects that decolonize, honor, and reclaim (indigenous) cultural practices, where healing leads to multiple forms of transformation and the personal and social levels, and where these collective actions can help persons realize a radical politics of possibility, hope, love, care, and equality for all humanity.

And here, with our third volume, our collected authors challenge the very ground on which evidence has been given cultural and canonical purchase: What is truth? What is evidence? What counts as evidence? How is evidence evaluated? How can evidence—or facts—be "fixed" to fit policy? What kind of evidence-based research should inform this process? How is evidence to be represented? How is evidence to be discounted or judged to be unreliable, false, or incorrect?

Taken together, all three volumes work in tandem to address a fundamental question: How are we as qualitative researchers to move forward in this new paradigm? Let us address this question for a moment. We agree with Amos Hatch (2006) when he states:

> Let us engage in the paradigm wars. Let us defend ourselves
> against those who would impose their modern notions of science
> on us by exposing the flaws in what they call scientifically-based
> research. Let us mount a strong offense by generating qualitative
> studies that are so powerful they cannot be dismissed.[22] (p. 407)

Like us, Hatch (2006) wants research done within all the
qualitative paradigms to be considered legitimate. He does not
want knowledge "and how it is created to be in the hands of those
who happen to hold political power" (p. 406). He does not want to
take a giant step back to the pre-1980s paradigm wars. He wants
a strong line of defense in order to reestablish qualitative inquiry
as a valuable and "respected form of inquiry" (p. 406).

Hatch (2006) outlines several ways to fight back: (1) publishing well-designed qualitative research in high quality journals; (2)
increasing support for new scholars doing qualitative research; (3)
lobbying journals and editors to publish more qualitative work;
(4) defending our territory by "exposing the flaws, faulty logic,
shaking assumptions, and sheer banality that characterizes many
of the arguments in the SBR movement" (p. 406); (5) rejecting
SBR criteria for evaluating our work; (6) critiquing SBR studies
that are held up as models for the field; and (7) refusing to accept
SBR's concepts of science and knowledge and proper inquiry.

We endorse Hatch's conclusions. "If we do not fight back,
qualitative research ... could become self-absorbed, fragmented
and ineffectual. And the neo-conservative dream of a return to
modernity will have come true" (2006, p. 407). In short, we will
have lost.

• • •

We live in a depressing historical moment: violent spaces; unend-
ing wars against persons of color; oppression; the falsification of
evidence; the collapse of critical, democratic discourse; repres-
sive neo-liberalism disguised as dispassionate objectivity prevails.
Global efforts to impose a new orthodoxy on critical social science
inquiry must be resisted—a hegemonic politics of evidence cannot be allowed. Qualitative researchers belong to such a global

community. The SBR battles in the United States are also being fought in Europe, Australia, South America, Africa, and elsewhere. The interpretive community needs to draw together into one large community so we can share our problems and experiences with these new discourses. Scholars who share the values of excellence, leadership, and advocacy need venues to engage in debate, frame public policy discourse, and disseminate research findings. We need to a community that honors and celebrates methodological diversity and showcases scholarship from around the world. If we can do this the rewards will be "plentiful and the opportunity for professional [and societal] impact unsurpassed" (Guba, 1990, p. 378). Too much is at stake to do otherwise. We have a job to do; let's get to it!

Notes

1. This chapter reworks Denzin, Forthcoming a, "The Elephant in the Living Room, Part II," which is forthcoming in *Qualitative Research* 8(4). It also draws philosophically from Denzin and Giardina, 2006, 2007.

2. As of this writing, the NIE is available for download as a .pdf document on the *New York Times*'s website (http://graphics8.nytimes.com/packages/pdf/international/20071203_release.pdf).

3. This blatant insularity to and rejection of reality likewise stretched beyond Bush and his usual farrago of babysitters to such prominent neoconservative figures as Norman Podhoretz (one of the original signatories of the Project for the New American Century's "Statement of Principles," and a foreign policy advisory to former Republican presidential hopeful Rudolph Giuliani) and John Bolton (former U.S. ambassador to the United Nations [2005–2006], currently a Senior Fellow at the conservative American Enterprise Institute), both of whom not only rejected the NIE's finding, but also went so far as to suggest that the findings were part of a State Department conspiracy to undermine the president's credibility. Said Bolton during a live interview with CNN's Wolf Blitzer,

   > Well, I think [the NIE] is potentially wrong, but I would also say, many of the people who wrote this are former State Department employees who during their career at the State Department never gave much attention to the threat of the Iranian program. Now they are writing as [fingers quote] "members of the intelligence community" the same opinions that they've had four and five years ago. (CNN, Situation Room, December 4, 2007).

   And, similarly, as Podhoretz (2007) stated in Commentary Magazine:

> [T]he intelligence community, having been excoriated for supporting the then universal belief that Saddam had weapons of mass destruction, is now bending over backward to counter what has up to now been a similarly universal view ... that Iran is hell-bent on developing nuclear weapons. ...But I entertain an even darker suspicion. It is that the intelligence community, which has for some years now been leaking material calculated to undermine George W. Bush, is doing it again. (n.p.)

4. With respect to WWIII, Bush stated in an October 2007 speech:

> But this—we got a leader in Iran who has announced that he wants to destroy Israel. So I've told people that if you're interested in avoiding World War III, it seems like you ought to be interested in preventing them from have the knowledge necessary to make a nuclear weapon. I take the threat of Iran with a nuclear weapon very seriously. And we'll continue to work with all nations about the seriousness of this threat. Plus we'll continue working the financial measures that we're in the process of doing. In other words, I think—the whole strategy is, is that at some point in time, leaders or responsible folks inside of Iran may get tired of isolation and say, this isn't worth it. And to me, it's worth the effort to keep the pressure on this government.

5. In one rather bizarre development in mid-July 2007, as William Broad and David Sanger (2007) reveal, "American intelligence officials called the leaders of the international atomic inspection agency to the top of a skyscraper overlooking the Danube [River] in Vienna and unveiled the contents of what they said was a stolen Iranian laptop computer." Information was presented, they say, that contained "thousands of computer simulations" and "descriptions of experiments" that were alleged to show a long-standing and on-going effort on the part of Iran to construct a nuclear warhead. Presented as hard evidence of Iran's nuclear ambitions dating to at least 2004, the data were nonetheless considered suspicious by those privy to it; a senior European diplomat said of the documents: "I can fabricate that data. It looks beautiful, but it is open to doubt" (Broad & Sanger, 2007).

6. Moreover, a careful analysis of the president's public statements over the last year with respect to Iran indicates an ever-so-subtle shift in orientation, that, when viewed with the knowledge of the NIE, seems to suggest that the president *knew* he was lying to the public about Iran's nuclear ambitions since at least August 9, 2007. Writing in the *Washington Post*, Dan Froomkin presents a timeline of quotes from 2007—both before and after the president was made aware of the impending NIE and its findings—that seem to make clear what the president knew:

> | | |
> |---|---|
> | March 31: | "Iran is trying to develop a nuclear weapon ..." |
> | June 5: | Iran's "pursuit of nuclear weapons ..." |
> | June 19: | "consequences to the Iranian government if they continue to pursue a nuclear weapon ..." |

July 12: "the same regime in Iran that is pursuing nuclear weapons …"
August 6: "this is a government that has proclaimed its desire to build a nuclear weapon …"
August 9: "They have expressed their desire to be able to enrich uranium, which we believe is a step toward having a nuclear weapons program …"
August 28: "Iran's active pursuit of technology that could lead to nuclear weapons …"
October 4th: "You should not have the know-how on how to make a (nuclear) weapon …"
October 17: "Until they suspend and/or make it clear that they, that their statements aren't real, yeah, I believe they want to have the capacity, the knowledge, in order to make a nuclear weapon."

To wit, before August 9, it is: "Trying to develop, build or pursue a nuclear weapon." After August 9, it is: "Desire, pursuit, want … knowledge, technology, know-how to enrich uranium" (Olbermann, 2007).

7. This is perhaps the only logical conclusion. To believe, as Bush has suggested, that he was only informed of the findings in August 2007—and even then kept mainly in the dark about its specifics—one would also have to accept the following scenario laid out by Sen. Joe Biden:

Are you telling me a president that's briefed every single morning, who's fixated on Iran, is not told back in August that the tentative conclusion of 16 intelligence agencies in the U.S. government said [Iran] had abandoned their effort for a nuclear weapon in '03? … If that's true, he has the most incompetent staff in modern American history, and he's one of the most incompetent presidents in modern American history.

In response to Biden's charges, White House spokesperson Dana Perino went on the Fox News Channel's *O'Reilly Factor* to call Biden's comments inappropriate and to perpetuate the lies of the president. She stated to host Bill O'Reilly that "[The White House] just found out that Iran has a covert nuclear weapons program. It proves that we were right, and that international pressure is what caused them to halt it." Of course, the operative word here should be "had," not "has," as in, Iran *had* a nuclear weapons program, which the NIE confirmed was suspended in 2003. But why let that get in the way, right?

8. In January 2008, the Center for Public Integrity, a nonprofit, nonpartisan, nonadvocacy, independent journalism organization based in Washington, DC, published on its website a report titled "The war card: Orchestrated deception on the way to war," which documents 935 false statements made in the two years following 9/11 by George W. Bush and seven of his administration's top officials (including Vice President Richard Cheney, Secretary of State Condoleeza Rice, and Secretary of Defense Donald Rumsfeld) about the national security threat posed by Saddam Hussein's Iraq. Of these

935 false statements, the report catalogs "at least 532 separate occasions (in speeches, briefings, interviews, testimony, and the like)," in which "Bush and these three key officials, along with Secretary of State Colin Powell, Deputy Defense Secretary Paul Wolfowitz, and White House press secretaries Ari Fleischer and Scott McClellan, stated unequivocally that Iraq had weapons of mass destruction (or was trying to produce or obtain them), links to Al Qaeda, or both." (Of these, Bush himself accounts for 232 false statements about weapons of mass destruction). The report concludes with this devastating assessment:

> [The] Bush administration led the nation to war on the basis of erroneous information that it methodically propagated and that culminated in military action against Iraq on March 19, 2003. Not surprisingly, the officials with the most opportunities to make speeches, grant media interviews, and otherwise frame the public debate also made the most false statements, according to this first-ever analysis of the entire body of prewar rhetoric." The report can be found online at http://www.publicintegrity.org/WarCard/

9. Audit culture refers to a technology and a system of accounting that measures outcomes and assesses quality in terms of so-called objective criteria, such as test scores. Some argue that the global audit culture implements conservative, neoliberal conceptions of governmentality (Bourdieu, 1998, p. 90; Habermas, 1972, p. 122, 2006, p. 193).

10. Lather (2004a, 2004b) offers a history and critical reading of this alphabet soup of acronyms CC (Cochrane Collaboration), C2 (Campbell Collaboration), AIR (American Institutes for Research), WWC (What Works Clearinghouse), IES (Institute of Education Science) (see http://w-w-c.org/whoweare/overview.html). There has been a recent move within CC and C2 to create protocols for evaluating qualitative research studies (see Briggs, 2006; National CASP Collaboration, 2006).

11. In the last two decades, qualitative researchers have gone from having fewer than three journals dedicated to their work to having twenty or more (Chenail, 2007).

12. The elephant wears two other garments: the cloak of meta-analyses and the disguises of mix-methods research. The meta-analysis disguise invites the production of systematic reviews that incorporate qualitative research into meta-analyses (Dixon-Woods, Bonas et al., 2006). The mixed-method disguise revisits the concept of triangulation, asking how qualitative and quantitative methods can be made to work together (Moran-Ellis et al., 2006). There are problems with both disguises. Meta-analyses of published articles hardly count as qualitative research in any sense of the word. The return to mix-methods inquiry fails to address the incommensurability issue—the fact the two paradigms are in contradiction (Smith and Hodkinson, 2005, pp. 922–24). Any effort to circumvent this collision—

through complimentary strengths, single-paradigm, dialectical, or multiple paradigm, mixed methods approaches—seems doomed to failure (see Teddlie & Tashakkoroi, 2003, pp. 19–24). It should be further noted that over the past four decades, the discourse on triangulation, multiple operationalism, and mix-method models has become quite complex and nuanced (see Saukko, 2003, p. 32 and Teddlie & Tashakkori, 2003 for reviews). Each decade has taken up triangulation and redefined it to meet perceived needs.

13. Extending Smith and Deemer (2000), within the qualitative inquiry community there are three basic positions on the issue of evaluative criteria: foundational, quasi-foundational and non-foundational (see also Creswell, 2007, pp. 203–20; Guba & Lincoln, 1989, 2005; Lincon & Guba, 1985; Spencer et al., 2003, p. 39). **Foundationalists,** including those who apply the Cochrane and Campbell Collaborations are in this space, contending that *research is research*, quantitative or qualitative. That is to say, all research should conform to a set of shared criteria (e.g., internal, external validity, credibility, transferability, confirmability, transparency, warrantability [see Dixon-Woods, Bonas et al., 2006; Dixon-Woods, Shaw et al., 2004; Teddlie and Tashakkori, 2003, p. 13]). **Quasi-foundationalists** contend that a set of criteria, or guiding framework unique to qualitative research need to be developed. These criteria may include terms like reflexivity, theoretical grounding, iconic, paralogic, rhizomatic, and voluptuous validity (Eisner, 1993; Lather, 1993; Lincoln & Guba, 1985). In contrast, **nonfoundationalists** stress the importance of understanding, versus prediction (Denzin, 1997; Wolcott, 1999). They conceptualize inquiry within a moral frame, implementing an ethic rooted in the concepts of care, love, trust, respect, and kindness (see also Christians, 2005).

14. The common thread that exists between WWC and CCC is the No Child Left Behind (NCLB) Act, and the Reading First program mandated under NCLB, which requires a focus on identifying and using scientifically based research in designing and implementing educational programs (see http://www.ed.gov/programs/readingfirst/index.html).

15. Ironically, the blind peer review recommendation flies in the face of a recent CC study, which argues that there is little hard evidence to show that blind peer reviews improves the quality of research (Jefferson et al., 2003; see also White, 2003, p. 241 and Judson, 2004, pp. 244–86). Indeed, the Cochrane researchers found few studies examining this presumed effect.

16. In December 2002, for example, Bush appointed W. David Hagar, a physician and anti-abortion activist, to the Food and Drug Administration's Advisory Committee for Reproductive Health Drugs. Prior to his appointment, the vehemently pro-life Hagar had campaigned against FDA approval for RU-486 (an emergency contraceptive) and had authored numerous books advocating prayer and reading of scripture to cure medical ailments (see McGarvey, 2005).

17. Their first annual conference (March 2–4, 2008) is outcomes based, calling for rigorous studies of reading, writing, and language skills, mathematics, and science achievement, social and behavioral competencies, dropout prevention and school completion (see http://educationaleffectiveness.org).

18. Warrantability and transparency are key terms in the new managerialism, which is evidence based and audit driven; that is, policy decisions should be based on evidence that warrants policy recommendations, and research procedures should be transparently accountable (Hammersley, 2004, p. 141) Transparency is also a criterion advanced by the Cochrane Qualitative Methods Group (Briggs, 2006).

19. By implication, quantitative scientists are not being charged with fraud and misrepresenting their data. This may be because many qualitative researchers don't have data and findings, tables and charts, statistics and numbers. We have stories, narratives, excerpts from interviews. We perform our interpretations and invite audiences to experience these performances, to live their way into the scenes, moments and lives we are writing, and talking about. Our empirical materials can't be fudged, misrepresented, altered, or distorted because they are life experiences. They are ethno-dramas.

20. Like the NRC, AERA's ethical guidelines focus on issues relevant to reporting results. Authors have an obligation to address the ethical decisions that shaped their research, including how the inquiry was designed, executed, and organized. Incentives for participating, consent waivers and confidentiality agreements, and conflicts of interest should be presented and discussed. Reporting should be accurate, free of plagiarism, fully accessible to others, and without falsification or fabrication of data or results. Data should be presented in such a way that any qualified researcher with a copy of the relevant data could reproduce the results. Thus are interpretive materials turned into data. The interpretive process becomes an exercise in seeking patterns of evidence, presenting evidence in a way that will engender trust on the part of the reader while avoiding charges of misrepresentation or fabrication (more on ethics below). But this is not how qualitative researchers work.

21. The text that follows borrows from and paraphrases Koukl (2007, http/www.str.org/site/News2?page=NewsArticle&id=6191).

22. For more on the paradigm wars, see Denzin, Forthcoming b, "The New Paradigm Wars and Qualitative Inquiry."

References

American Association of University Professors (AAUP). 1981. Regulations governing research on human subjects: Academic freedom and the Institutional Review Board. *Academe* 67(6): 358–70.

American Association of University Professors (AAUP). 2001. Protecting human beings: Institutional Review Boards and social science research. *Academe* 87(3):55–67.

American Association of University Professors (AAUP). 2002. Should all disciplines be subject to the Common Rule? Human subjects of social science research. *Academe* 88(1):1–15.

American Association of University Professors (AAUP), Committee A. 2006. *Report on human subjects: Academic freedom and the institutional review boards.* http://www.aaup.org/AAUP/About/committees/committee+repts/CommA (accessed March 25, 2007).

American Education Research Association (AERA). 2006. *Standards for reporting on empirical social science research in AERA publications.* http://www.aera.net/opportunities/?id = 1480 (accessed February 6, 2007).

Atkinson, P., & S. Delamont. 2006. In the roiling smoke: Qualitative inquiry and contested fields. *International Journal of Qualitative Studies in Education* 19(6):747–55.

Baker, P., & R. Wright. 2007. U.S. renews efforts to keep coalition against Tehran: Bush says new NIE shows Iran is still a threat. *The Washington Post*, p. A23 (December 5).

Becker, H. S. 1966. Introduction. In C. R. Shaw, *The Jack-Roller: A delinquent boy's own story*, pp. v–xviii. Chicago: University of Chicago Press.

Bishop, R. 1998. Freeing ourselves from neo-colonial domination in research: A Maori approach to creating knowledge. *International Journal of Qualitative Studies in Education* 11(2): 199–219.

Bourdieu, P. 1998. *Practical reason*. Cambridge, UK: Polity.

Briggs, J. 2006. What is qualitative research? What is its role in evidence review? Cochrane Qualitative Research Methods Group. University of Adelaide and the Joanna Briggs Institute. http://www.joannabriggs.edu.au/cqrmg/about.html (accessed October 11, 2007).

Broad, W. J., & D. E. Sanger. 2005. How did a 2005 estimate go awry? *The New York Times* online. http://www.nytimes.com/2007/12/04/washington/04policy.html (accessed February 20, 2008).

Cabinet Office. 2003. Quality in qualitative evaluation. A framework for assessing research evidence. London: Government Chief Social Researcher's Office. [Report prepared on behalf of the Cabinet Office by L. Spencer, J. Ritchie, J. Lewis, & L. Dillon, National Centre for Social Research.]

Cable News Network (CNN). 2007. *Situation Room*. Interview with John Bolton. December 4.

Cannella, G. S., & Y. S. Lincoln. 2004. Dangerous discourses II: Comprehending and countering the redeployment of discourses (and resources) in the generation of liberatory inquiry. *Qualitative Inquiry* 10(2):165–74.

Charmaz, K. 2005. Grounded theory in the 21st century: Applications for advancing social justice studies. In N. K. Denzin and Y. S. Lincoln (eds.), *Handbook of qualitative research*, 3rd ed., pp. 537–46. Thousand Oaks, CA: Sage.

Cheek, J. 2005. The practice and politics of funded qualitative research. In N. K. Denzin & Y. S. Lincoln (Eds.), *Handbook of qualitative research*, 3rd ed., pp. 387–410. Thousand Oaks, CA: Sage.

Cheek, J. 2006. What's in a number? Issues in providing evidence of impact and quality of research(ers). *Qualitative Health Research* 16(3):423–35.

Chenail, R. J. 2007. Qualitative research sites. *The Qualitative Report: An Online Journal.* htpp://www.nova.edu/sss/QR/web.html (accessed December 14, 2007).

Creswell, J. W. 2007. *Qualitative inquiry & research design: Choosing among five approaches*, 2nd ed. Thousand Oaks, CA: Sage.

Christians, C. 2005. Ethics and politics in qualitative research. In N. K. Denzin and Y. S. Lincoln (Eds.), *Handbook of qualitative research*, 3rd ed., pp. 139–64. Thousand Oaks, CA: Sage.

Davies, P. 2004. Systematic reviews and the Campbell Collaboration. In G. Thomas & R. Pring (Eds.), *Evidence-based practice in education*, pp. 21–33. New York: Open University Press.

Denzin, N. K. 1997. *Interpretive ethnography.* Thousand Oaks, CA: Sage.

Denzin, N. K. 2003. *Performance ethnography: Critical pedagogy and the politics of culture.* Thousand Oaks, CA: Sage.

Denzin, N. K. 2007. The secret Downing Street memo and the politics of truth: A performance text. *Symbolic Interaction* 30(4):447–64

Denzin, N. K. Forthcoming a. The elephant in the living room, Part II. *Qualitative Research* 8(4).

Denzin, N. K. Forthcoming b. The new paradigm dialogs and qualitative inquiry. *International Journal of Qualitative Studies in Education* 21(6).

Denzin, N. K., & M. D. Giardina. 2006. Qualitative inquiry and the conservative challenge. In N. K. Denzin & M. D. Giardina (Eds.), *Qualitative inquiry and the conservative challenge*, pp. ix–xxxi. Walnut Creek, CA: Left Coast Press.

Denzin, N. K., & M. D. Giardina. 2007. *Ethical futures in qualitative research: Decolonizing the politics of evidence.* Walnut Creek, CA: Left Coast Press.

Denzin, N. K., Y. S. Lincoln, & M. D. Giardina. 2006. Disciplining qualitative research. *International Journal of Qualitative Studies in Education* 19(6):769–82.

Dixon-Woods, M., S. Bonas, A. Booth, D. R. Jones, T. Miller, A. J. Sutton, R. L. Shaw, J. A. Smith, & B.Young. 2006. How can systematic reviews incorporate qualitative research? A critical perspective. *Qualitative Research* 6(1):27–44.

Dixon-Woods, M., R. L. Shaw, S. Agarwal, & J. A. Smith. 2004. The problem of appraising qualitative research. *Qual Saf Health Care* 13:223–25.

Drum, K. 2007. Why was the NIE released? *Washington Monthly*. http://www.washingtonmonthly.com/archives/individual/2007_12/012623.php (accessed December 12, 2007).

Eisenhart, M. 2006. Qualitative science in experimental time. *International Journal of Qualitative Studies in Education* 19(6):697–708.

Eisner, E. W. 1991. *The enlightened eye*. New York: Macmillian.

Erickson, F., & K. Gutierrez. 2002. Culture, rigor, and science in educational research. *Educational Researcher* 31(8):21–24.

Feuer, M. J. 2006. Response to Bettie St. Pierre's "Scientifically based research in education: Epistemology and ethics." *Adult Education Quarterly* 56(3):267–72.

Feuer, M. J., L. Towne, & R. J. Shavelson. 2002. Science, culture, and educational research. *Educational Researcher* 31(8):4–14.

Gilgun, J. F. 2006. The four cornerstones of qualitative research. *Qualitative Health Research* 16(3):436–43.

Goldberg, M. 2007. *Kingdom coming: The rise of Christian nationalism*. New York: W. W. Norton & Co.

Guba, E. 1990. Carrying on the dialog. In E. G. Guba (Ed.), *The paradigm dialog*, pp. 368–78. Newbury Park, CA: Sage.

Guba, E., & Y. S. Lincoln. 1989. *Fourth generation evaluation*. Newbury Park, CA: Sage.

Guba, E., & Y. S. Lincoln. 2005. Paradigmatic controversies and emerging confluences. In N. K. Denzin & Y. S. Lincoln (Eds), *Handbook of qualitative research*, 3rd ed., pp. 191–216. Thousand Oaks, CA: Sage.

Habermas, J. 1972. *Knowledge and human interests*, 2nd ed. London: Heinemann.

Habermas, J. 2006. *The divided West*. Cambridge, UK: Polity.

Hammersley, M. 2004. Some questions about evidence-based practice in education. In G. Thomas & R. Pring (Eds.), *Evidence-based practice in education*, pp. 133–49. New York: Open University Press.

Hammersley, M. 2005a. Close encounters of a political kind: The threat from the evidence-based policy-making and practice movement. *Qualitative Researcher* 1(December):2–4.

Hammersley, M. 2005b. Countering the "New Orthodoxy" in educational research: A response to Phil Hodkinson. *British Educational Research Journal* 31(2):139–56.

Hatch, A. 2006. Qualitative studies in the era of scientifically-based research: Musings of a former QSE editor. *International Journal of Qualitative Studies in Education* 19(4):403–7.

Hodkinson, P. 2004. Research as a form of work: Expertise, community and methodological objectivity. *British Educational Research Journal* 30(1):9–26.

Jackson, N., & E. Waters. 2005. Criteria for the systematic review of health promotion and public health interventions. *Health Promotion International* 20(4):367–74.

Jefferson T, M. Rudin, F. S. Brodney, & F. Davidoff. 2006. Editorial peer review for improving the quality of reports of biomedical studies. *Cochrane Database of Methodology Reviews* 6(1)MR000016. DOI: 10.1002/14651858.MR000016.pub2. The Cochrane Colloboration: http:/www.cochrane.org/reviews/en/mr000016.html (date of last Substantial Update: October 3, 2005). The full text is available in *The Cochrane Library* (ISSN 1464-780X).

Judson, H. F. 2004. *The great betrayal: Fraud in science.* New York: Harcourt Brace.

Kaplan, E. 2004. *With God on their side: How the Christian fundamentalists trampled science, policy and democracy in George W. Bush's White House.* New York: New Press.

Klein, N. 2007. *The shock doctrine: The rise of disaster capitalism.* New York: Metropolitan Books.

Koukl, G. 2007. The trouble with the elephant. http/www.str.org/site/News2?page=NewsArticle&id=6191 (accessed December 14, 2007).

Larner, G. 2004. Family therapy and the politics of evidence. *Journal of Family Therapy* 26(1):17–39.

Lather, P. 1993. *Getting smart: Feminist research and pedagogy with/in the postmodern.* New York: Routledge.

Lather, P. 2004a. Scientific research in education: A critical perspective. *British Educational Research Journal* 30(6):759–72.

Lather, P. 2004b. This is your father's paradigm: Government intrusion and the case of qualitative research in education. *Qualitative Inquiry* 10(1):15–34.

Lather, P. 2006. Foucauldian scientificity: Rethinking the nexus of qualitative research and educational policy analysis. *International Journal of Qualitative Studies in Education* 19(6):783–92.

Lincoln, Y. S., & G. S. Cannella. 2004. Dangerous discourses: Methodological conservatism and governmental regimes of truth. *Qualitative Inquiry* 10(1):5–10.

Lincoln, Y. S., & E. Guba. 1985. *Naturalistic inquiry.* Beverly Hills, CA: Sage.

Lundberg, G. 1926. Quantitative methods in sociology. *Social Forces* 39(October):19–24.

MacLure, M. 2006. The bone in the throat: Some uncertain thoughts on baroque method. *International Journal of Qualitative Studies in Education* 19(6):7239–746.

Madison, D. S. 2005. *Critical ethnography: Methods, ethics and performance.* Thousand Oaks, CA: Sage.

Maher, B. 2007. *The decider* [DVD]. HBO Home Video.

McGarvey, A. 2005. Dr. Hagar's family values. The Nation. May 11. http://www.thenation.com/doc/20050530/mcgarvey (accessed December 4, 2007).

Monastersky, R. 2002. Research groups accuse Education Department of using ideology in decisions about data. *Chronicle of Higher Education* 25(November):2. http://chronical.com/dailyk/2002/22/200211250n.htm (accessed January 31, 2008).

Moran-Ellis, J., V. D. Alexander, A. Cronin, M. Dickenson, J. Fielding, J. Sleney, & H. Thomas. 2006. Triangulation and integration: Processes, claims and implications. *Qualitative Research* 6(1):45–60.

Maxwell, J. A. 2004a. Causal explanation, qualitative research, and scientific inquiry in education. *Educational Researcher* 23(2):3–11.

Maxwell, J. A. 2004b. Using qualitative methods for causal explanation. *Field Methods* 16(3):243–64.

McCarthy, C. R., A. Durham, L. Engel, A. A. Filmer, M. D. Giardina, & M. Malagreca (eds.) 2007. *Globalizing cultural studies: Ethnographic interventions in theory, method, and policy.* New York: Peter Lang.

Morse, J. M. 2006a. Reconceptualizing qualitative inquiry. *Qualitative Health Research* 16(3):415–22.

Morse, J. M. 2006b. The politics of evidence. *Qualitative Health Research* 16(3):395–404.

National CASP Collaboration. 2006. 10 questions to help you make sense of qualitative research, critical appraisal skills program (CASP). Milton Keyenes Primary Care Trust (*The Cochrane Collaboration.* http://www.joannabriggs.eduau/cqrmg/role.html (accessed June 17, 2007).

National Research Council (NRC). 2002. *Scientific research in education*, Committee on Scientific Principles for Education Research, R. J. Shavelson & L. Towne, Eds. Washington, DC: National Academy Press.

National Research Council (NRC). 2005. *Advancing scientific research in education*, Committee on Scientific Principles for Education Research, L. Towne, L. Wise, & T. M. Winters, Eds. Washington, DC: National Academy Press.

Olbermann, K. 2007. *Countdown with Keith Olbermann.* MSNBC, December 6, 2007.

Phillips, K. 2006. *American theocracy: The peril and politics of radical religion, oil, and borrowed money in the 21st century.* New York: Viking.

Podhoretz, N. 2007. Dark suspicions about the NIE. *Commentary Magazine.* December 12. http://www.commentarymagazine.com/blogs/index.php/podhoretz/1474 (accessed January 3, 2008).

Popay, J. R., A. Rogers, & G. Williams. 1998. Rationale and standards for the systematic review of qualitative literature in health services research. *Qualitative Health Research* 8(3):341–51.

Preissle, J. 2006. Envisioning qualitative inquiry: A view across four decades. *International Journal of Qualitative Studies in Education* 19(6):685–96.

Quigley, L. 1996. *The blind men and the elephant.* New York: Charles Scribner's Sons.

Rains, F. V., J. Archibald, & D. Deyhle. 2000. Introduction: Through our eyes and in our own words—the voices of indigenous scholars. *International Journal of Qualitative Studies in Education* 13(4):337–42.

Sargent, G. 2007 (September 26). Kyl-Lieberman Iran Amendment passes by huge margin. *Talking Points Memo.* http://tpmelectioncentral.talking-pointsmemo.com/2007/09/kyllieberman_iran_amendment_passes_by_huge_margin.php (accessed December 12, 2007).

Saukko, P. 2003. *Doing research in cultural studies: An introduction to classical and new methodological approaches.* London: Sage.

Schwandt, T. 2006. Opposition redefined. *International Journal of Qualitative Studies in Education* 19(6):803–10.

Sedgwick, E. 1997. Paranoid reading and reparative reading, or, you're so paranoid, you probably think this essay is about you. In E. Sedgwick (Ed.), *Novel gazing: Queer readings in fiction*, pp. 1–37. Durham NC: Duke University Press.

Smith, J. K., & D. K. Deemer. 2000. The problem of criteria in the age of relativism. In N. K. Denzin & Y. S. Lincoln (Eds), *Handbook of qualitative research*, 3rd ed, pp. 877–96. Thousand Oaks, CA: Sage.

Smith, J. K., & P. Hodkinson. 2005. Relativism, criteria and politics. In N. K. Denzin & Y. S. Lincoln (Eds.), *Handbook of qualitative research*, 3rd ed., pp. 915–32. Thousand Oaks, CA: Sage.

Smith, L. T. 1999. *Decolonizing methodologies: Research and indigenous peoples.* Dunedin, New Zealand: University of Otago Press.

Spencer, L., J. Ritchie, L. Lewis, & L. Dillion. 2003. *Quality in qualitative evaluation: A framework for assessing research evidence.* London: Government Chief Social Researcher's Office, Crown Copyright.

Spivak, G. 1993. *Outside in the teaching machine.* New York: Routledge.

Stanfield, J. H., II. 2006. The possible restorative justice functions of qualitative research. *International Journal of Qualitative Studies in Education* 19(6):723–28.

St. Pierre, E. A. 2006. Scientifically based research in education: Epistemology and ethics. *Adult Education Quarterly* 56(3):239–66.

St. Pierre, E. A., & K. Roulston. 2006. The state of qualitative inquiry: A contested science. *International Journal of Qualitative Studies in Education* 19(6:673–84.

Stronach, I. 2006. Enlightenment and the "heart of darkness": (Neo)imperialism in the Congo, and elsewhere. *International Journal of Qualitative Studies in Education* 19(6):757–68.

Stronach, I., D. Garratt, C. Pearce, & H. Piper. 2007. Reflexivity, the picturing of selves, the forging of method. *Qualitative Inquiry* 13(2):179–203.

Teddlie, C., & A. Tashakkori. 2003. Major issues and controversies in the use of mixed methods in the social and behavioral sciences. In A. Tashakkori & C. Teddlie (Eds.), *Handbook of mixed-methods in social and behavioral research*, pp. 3–50. Thousand Oaks, CA: Sage.

Thomas, G. 2004. Introduction: Evidence: Practice. In G. Thomas & R. Pring (Eds.), *Evidence-based practice in education*, pp. 1–20. New York: Open University Press.

Timmermans, S., & M. Berg. 2003. *The gold standard: The challenge of evidence-based medicine and standardization in health care*. Philadelphia: Temple University Press.

Torrance, H. 2006. Research quality and research governance in the United Kingdom. In N. K. Denzin & M. D. Giardina (Eds.), *Qualitative inquiry and the conservative challenge*, pp. 127–48. Walnut Creek, CA: Left Coast Press.

Viadero, D. 2006. New group of researchers focuses on scientific study. *Education Week* 25(21):1, 16.

White, C. 2003. Little evidence for effectiveness of scientific peer review. *British Medical Journal* 326(7383):241.

Wilson, E. 1998. *Neural geographies: Feminism and the microstructure of cognition*. New York: Routledge.

Wolcott, H. F. 1999. *Ethnography: A way of seeing*. Walnut Creek, CA: AltaMira Press.

Section 1

Policy Intentions

Building Confidence in Qualitative Research

Engaging the Demands of Policy

Harry Torrance
Manchester Metropolitan
University, UK[1]

Introduction

Recent U.S. legislation has privileged "scientifically based research" in decisions about funding educational programs and educational research; moreover "scientific" is defined largely in terms of experimental design and methods, especially randomized controlled trials (RCTs), also sometimes known as randomized field trials (Eisenhart, 2006; Eisenhart & Towne 2003). This seems to be related to prior criticism, and review of the quality of educational research (NRC, 2002) has been interpreted as an attack on more qualitative approaches to educational research (Denzin & Giardina, 2006) and one that warrants urgent response from what might loosely be called the "qualitative research community" (St. Pierre & Roulston, 2006).

Attacks on the quality of educational research, particularly qualitative educational research, have their parallels in the United Kingdom (Hargreaves, 1996; Hillage et al., 1998; Tooley & Darby, 1998), have similarly impacted on debate in Australia (Yates, 2004), and are beginning to emerge in the European Union (Bridges, 2005; Brown, 2003). The argument has been that educational research (and, in some respects, social science research more generally) is too often conceived and conducted as a "cottage industry": producing too many small-scale, disconnected, non-cumulative studies that do not provide convincing explanations of educational phenomena or how best to develop teaching and learning. There is not a cumulative or informative knowledge base in the field and what is there is characterized as being of both poor quality and limited utility.

Thus, it can be argued that those working in educational research, in general, and in qualitative traditions, in particular, are facing a global movement of neopositivist interest in so-called "evidence-based" policy and practice, where what counts as legitimate evidence is construed very narrowly indeed. This is manifest not only in country-specific initiatives and legislative action (e.g , No Child Left Behind [2001] in the United States and the English National Curriculum and Testing system [Torrance, 2003]), but also in international assessment and evaluation activities such as Trends in International Mathematics and Science Study and the Program for International Student Assessment (Torrance, 2006) and the Campbell Collaboration, which seeks to review and disseminate social science knowledge for policymakers (Davies & Boruch, 2001; Wade et al., 2006). Clearly, these various manifestations differ in their origins, orientations, and specific intentions; they are not a coherent and homogeneous movement. But equally, they do seem to represent a concerted attempt to impose (or perhaps reimpose) scientific certainty and system management on an increasingly complex and uncertain social world.

It is apparent, then, that what is happening in the United States is not unique: It is almost certainly connected to movements elsewhere, and it should probably be understood in these terms (indeed, an exploration of links and policy flows would be a very interesting study). However, the legislative obsession with RCTs does seem to be peculiar to the United States, and I begin by exploring this before moving on to reflect on the British experience of responding to calls for better quality educational research, in particular better quality qualitative research.

The Cases for and against RCTs

The case for RCTs seems to derive from a combination of the methods of natural science with the supposed needs of policy. It is argued that randomized experiments means that any systematic observed differences between the sample that has received the "treatment," and the "control" group that has not must be attributable to the treatment. The design reveals whether there is a "causal link"; the treatment can be said either to "work" or "not work"; and some calculations can be made about the size of the effect: "[T]he experiment is the design of choice for studies that seek to make causal conclusions, and particularly for evaluations of educational innovations" (Slavin, 2002, p. 18).

Of course, experimental design can also be more subtle and complicated than this, with different elements of such designs potentially revealing different aspects of program impact (on different subsamples of students, for example, if the overall sample is large enough), but it is the appeal to certainty about "what works" that is claimed to attract policymakers: "If we implement Program X instead of Program Y, or instead of our current program, what will be the likely outcomes for children?" (Slavin, 2002, p. 18). Such attraction is easy to appreciate. It sounds seductively simple. When charged with dispensing millions of tax dollars on implementing programs and supporting research, one can understand that policymakers would value this sort of help.

This is not the place to discuss all the criticisms (and rejoinders) about the nature of causality and the place of RCTs in understanding social interaction and evaluating human services. They have been well rehearsed in recent issues of *Educational Researcher* (e.g., Burkhardt & Schoenfeld, 2003; Erickson & Gutierrez, 2002; Feuer, Towne, & Shavelson, 2002; Maxwell, 2004; Riehl, 2006; Slavin, 2002). The relevant point about RCTs and policy, particularly when comparing the United States with England, is that so much prior qualitative work has to be accomplished before any RCT might be designed, and much policy is decided well before any RCT might be implemented, let alone the results made public. Thus, Slavin's deceptively simple question about Program X versus Program Y begs many more questions about where Program X and Y come from in the first place. Such decisions are already a long way down the road of policy development and implementation, and often too far down the road for it to be worthwhile doubling back. Prior questions would include how and why have Program X and Y been developed? What sort of perceived problem are they trying to fix? What is the research evidence that indicates the nature of the problem and the specific different approaches to fixing it? These are all questions that require prior investigation of both outcomes (perhaps secondary analysis of test result data) and processes (e.g., ethnographic studies of why the test data are as they are), not to mention value judgments about whether particular practices and/or inconsistencies in the data do indeed indicate the existence of a "problem" that needs to be "solved."

It might be argued that this view of how RCTs are developed renders such earlier investigative work as somehow less "scientific," or even "prescientific" (see Shavelson et al., 2003, p. 28). But we know that RCTs are difficult and expensive to organize (Slavin, 2002) and therefore that the evidence on which the design is based has to be pretty secure in the first place. If various forms of qualitative work can be trusted in this respect, why can't they be trusted in their own right? Certainly in England, although there are criticisms of the quality of educational research and regular calls for more and more rigorously trained quantitative researchers in the social sciences generally (Hillage et al., 1998; OECD, 2002), qualitative studies of the sort indicated above are still funded by government departments and the UK Economic and Social Research Council (ESRC). The value of qualitative studies in exploring the nature of a particular problem is well recognized by government and other research users/sponsors, though their link to policymaking is often indirect: Even when commissioned by government departments, research is not necessarily utilized in the policymaking process in any straightforward way (see below).

Furthermore, the thrust of the evidence-based policy movement in England at present tends to favor *reviews* of research—synthesizing findings from multiple studies—rather than relying on the results of a single study, no matter how well conducted. Arguments in favor of conducting such reviews, particularly those known as "systematic reviews," derive from the critiques of social and educational research outlined earlier: that the findings of empirical studies are often too small-scale, noncumulative, and/or contradictory to be useful (Gough & Elbourne, 2002; Oakley, 2000, 2003). Advocates are closely associated with the Cochrane

Collaboration in medical and health care research and the Campbell Collaboration in social science, both of which favor the accumulation and dissemination of research findings based on scientific methods, particularly randomized control trials. As such, systematic reviewing is often associated with criticisms of qualitative research and is very much located within the "evidence-based policy and practice" movement (Davies, 2004).

For these reasons and others, systematic reviewing has its critics in the United Kingdom (e.g., Hammersley, 2001; MacLure, 2005).[2] Nevertheless, for the purposes of the argument here, the development and use of systematic reviewing points to a policy caution about relying on single studies, experimental or otherwise, and further demonstrates the divergent manifestation of apparently similar policy concerns in the United Kingdom and the United States. Moreover, even one of the leading proponents of systematic reviewing and the use of RCTs in England concedes that "RCTs generally find smaller effects than other designs, and the effects of most interventions, whether medical or social, are modest" (Oakley, 2006, p. 76).

This, of course, links with another set of issues: that of the timeliness, cost, and utility of research. It is often incumbent on policymakers to be seen to be doing something about a perceived problem or be acting in response to what seems to be a good idea (be it research based or not) without waiting for the definitive results of science (supposing these can be produced). Even the results of systematic reviews can take months to appear, let alone the results of newly commissioned studies; policymakers in England are just as likely to ask for very rapid reviews of research or rapid evidence assessment (Boaz, Solesbury, & Sullivan, 2004, p. 12), to be conducted over a few days or weeks, and possibly assembled via an expert seminar, as to commission longer term systematic reviews. An investigation of research reviewing by the UK's ESRC-funded Centre for Evidence-based Policy and Practice noted that the shortest period devoted to producing a commissioned research review was fifteen days, whereas the longest period was thirty months (Boaz, Solesbury, & Sullivan, 2007, p. 8).

Similar issues pertain to commissioned studies and evaluations. Colleagues at Manchester Metropolitan University (MMU) are currently involved in several projects evaluating the impact of information and communications technology on schools and teaching in England, including the impact of placing tools such as interactive whiteboards in classrooms (Somekh et al., 2002, 2005). Introducing the latest computer technology into schools is a politically good thing: There is no way that the UK Department for Education and Skills is going to rip out all the whiteboards that have been put into schools if the evaluation is not particularly positive. At the same time, schools and local authorities (school districts) that have not yet had what they would consider to be their "fair share" of this investment are unlikely to be satisfied by a blunt report that simply says it "doesn't work." They want the hardware and the chance to try it out for themselves.[3] Thus, the MMU evaluations are expected to report, through survey, observation, interview, and action research activities with participating teachers, on what *seems* to work and what problems have been encountered; how, and why it works, or not; and what lessons can be learned for future "roll out" of the program to other local authorities, initial training, and continuing professional development activities.

Thus, policy builds, one initiative on another, incrementally over time, with many more issues other than the scientific evidence coming into play. It might be argued that policy shouldn't develop like this, but it does, and in a democracy (rather than a "scientocracy"), it is not clear how it could be otherwise. Scientific evidence is but one element in a democratic policymaking process. Public values and interests influence matters at the macro level of the decision-making process, and the professional judgment of innumerable local actors mediate policy at the micro level.[4]

Interestingly, much of this sort of incremental, practice-oriented research activity seems to be reflected in current debates about design experiments. And, just as criticism of qualitative research is not unique to the United States (although the focus of attention on RCTs seems much sharper there than elsewhere), so, too, the debate about design experiments seems to indicate that RCT advocacy in the United States is not uniquely an attack on the specific field of qualitative research. *All* approaches to research that do not employ RCTs seem to be subject to critical scrutiny.

Thus, a recent special issue of *Educational Researcher* (32[1], 2003) devoted to exploring design experiments included a response from Shavelson et al. (2003) that dismissed the approach by asserting that "an entirely different conceptualization of 'evidence-based' education has captured the imagination of federal policymakers" (p. 25). Shavelson and colleagues further asked: "Should we believe the results of design experiments?" (p. 25). In other words, they invoke political power as the determining factor in methodological debate while simultaneously undermining the claims of one particular methodological approach.

Design experiments involve testing hypotheses about learning, embedded in specific materials and pedagogic approaches, in small-scale "real-life" situations (classrooms, after school clubs, etc.); learning the lessons of how the materials and pedagogies work; and trying to "scale up" for more general testing and application. The approach now seems to be associated with psychologists who wanted to "get out of the lab" and conduct field-based experiments (Brown, 1992; The Design Collective, 2003). However, similar approaches have been associated with curriculum research and development and action research for many years (see Elliott, 1989; James, 2006; Stenhouse, 1975) and have parallels in related endeavors such as mixed methods and "deliberative" and "realist" approaches to evaluation (Chatterji, 2005; House & Howe, 1999; Pawson & Tilley, 1997).

A more practical and policy-friendly set of approaches to applied educational research and development is hard to imagine. Yet, such work is dismissed because it relies "on narrative accounts to communicate and justify [its] findings" (Shavelson et al., 2003, p. 25). Shavelson et al. invoke their membership of the NRC Committee (which, interestingly, they describe at one point as "Our committee" [p. 28]) to "scrutinize the knowledge claims from design studies through the lens of the [NRC Report] guiding principles" (p. 26). Shavelson and colleagues conclude that "experiments should [be used] for choices among important design alternatives" (p. 28); by "experiment." in this statement, they mean "randomized experiments" (p. 28). To be fair, design experiments are treated seriously by Shavelson et al.; they are not arbitrarily dismissed, but ultimately they are treated as just another "prescientific" preparatory stage (p. 28), before the "real science" of RCTs begins.

So what is going here? Many different research perspectives and approaches to applied research, curriculum development, and program evaluation cast doubt on RCTs as the "one best way" to conduct educational research and offer convincing evidence that educational progress can be made by other more pragmatic and incremental means (Burkhardt & Schoenfeld, 2003; Chatterji, 2005; Erickson & Gutierrez, 2002; Maxwell, 2004; Riehl, 2006; The Design Collective, 2003).

Yet such arguments appear to be making little headway. Indeed, even those who get directly involved and collaborate in good faith with the What Works agenda may be censored when their findings do not support an apparently previously decided party line (Schoenfeld, 2006). There is not much science in censorship. Equally, exclusive reliance on RCTs is not only not necessary for policymaking, in many key respects it is not desirable, given the diverse constituencies and interests that policymaking must reconcile, the contingent nature of the process, and the contingent nature of local development and implementation of innovative programs. The NRC Report (2002), subsequent reiterations of its main arguments (Feuer, Towne, & Shavelson, 2002; NRC, 2005; Shavelson et al., 2003), and concomitant legislation (Eisenhart & Towne, 2003) seem more like general attempts to discipline educational research and researchers and to produce a general shift in the problematics and topography of educational research rather than to produce better evidence for policymaking.

The Response of Qualitative Research

To recap, the specific focus on RCTs seems peculiar to the United States; advocacy of RCTs seems directed at many different approaches to educational research, not just qualitative research. Nevertheless, criticism of the quality of educational research, in general, and of qualitative research, in particular, is widespread internationally and can certainly be understood as part of a more general move to reassert the preeminence of a natural science model of causality, what counts as evidence in social science, and the primacy of outcome measures in debates about efficiency and effectiveness in human services (Thomas & Pring, 2005; Yates, 2005). In policy terms, the basic issue is that of justifying the overall level and specific content of government expenditure on public services. How can policymakers come to know which programs to invest in and whether they are effective?

As argued above, research evidence can (and should) only ever be one element of such a policymaking process. Equally, there are many good reasons apart from serving policy for qualitative researchers to continue to reflect on the strengths and weaknesses of their field. Nevertheless, the relationship of research to policy is what seems to be driving current concerns and being manifested in reports such as the NRC (2002, 2005), a recent Workshop on Scientific Foundations of Qualitative Research (Ragin et al., 2004), discussion of doctoral programs (Eisenhart & DeHaan, 2005), the new American Educational Research Association (AERA) "guidelines" for reporting research (see http://www.aera.net/opportunities/?id=1850), and so forth. The response to criticism has been to start trying to set standards in qualitative research, particularly qualitative educational research, to reassure policymakers about the quality of qualitative research, and to reassert the contribution that qualitative research can (and should) make to government-funded programs.

The problem, however, is that the field of "qualitative research" or "qualitative inquiry'" is very large and diverse, and there is unlikely to be easy agreement about core standards. Recent meetings of the International Congress of Qualitative Inquiry (University of Illinois 2005, 2006, 2007, and 2008) have attracted up to 1,000 participants on each occasion from fifty-five different countries, working in and across many different disciplines (anthropology, psychology, and sociology, among others), different applied research and policy settings (education, social work, health studies, etc.), and different national environments with their different policy processes and socioeconomic context of action.

It will be difficult to reach agreement; indeed, it is not self-evident that such agreement is desirable even if possible. Nor is this simply a matter of scope and scale, of what might be termed "practical complexity," whereby agreement might eventually be reached, at least in principle. Different disciplines and contexts of action produce different readings and interpretations of apparently common literatures and similar issues. It is the juxtaposition of these readings, the comparing and contrasting within and across boundaries, that allows us to learn about them and reflect on our own situated understandings of our own contexts. Multiplicity of approach and interpretation, and multivocalism of reading and response, is the basis of quality in the qualitative research community and, it might be argued, in the advancement of science more generally. The key issue is to discuss and explore quality across boundaries, thereby continually to develop it, not fix it, as at best a good recipe, at worst a government-issue straight-jacket.

Experience in the United Kingdom

Some attempt at just such fixing has been made in the United Kingdom, and the results are instructive. Recently, for example, independent academics based at the National Centre for Social Research (a not-for-profit organization) were commissioned by the Strategy Unit of the UK government Cabinet Office to produce a report on *Quality in Qualitative Evaluation: A Framework for Assessing Research Evidence* (Cabinet Office, 2003a). The rationale seems to have been that UK government departments are increasingly commissioning policy evaluations in the context of the move toward evidence-informed policy and practice, and it was considered that guidelines for judging the quality of qualitative approaches and methods were necessary.

The report is in two parts: a seventeen-page summary, including the "Quality Framework" itself (Cabinet Office, 2003a), and a 167-page full report (Cabinet Office, 2003b), including discussion of many of the issues raised by the framework. The summary report states that the framework has been

> designed primarily to assess the *outputs* of qualitative enquiry ...
> and ... It is also hoped that the framework will have a wider
> educational function in the preparation of research protocols,
> the conduct and management of research and evaluation and
> the training of social researchers" (Cabinet Office, 2003a, p. 6,
> emphasis in the original).

So, the framework is a guide for the commissioners of research when drawing up tender documents and reading reports, but it also has ambitions to influence the conduct and management of research and the training of social researchers.

The problem, however, is that in trying to cover everything, the document ends up covering nothing, or at least nothing of importance. The basic "Quality Framework" begs questions at every turn, and the full 167-page report reads like an introductory text on qualitative research methods. Paradigms are described and issues rehearsed, but all are resolved in a bloodless, technical, and strangely old-fashioned counsel of perfection. The reality of doing qualitative research, and indeed of conducting evaluation, with all the contingencies, political pressures, and decisions that have to be made, is completely absent. Thus, in addition to the obvious need for "Findings/conclusions [to be] supported by data/evidence" (Cabinet Office, 2003b, p. 22), qualitative reports should also include:

- detailed description of the contexts in which the study was conducted (p. 23);
- discussions of how fieldwork methods or settings may have influenced data collected (p. 25);
- descriptions of background or historical developments and social/organizational characteristics of study sites (p. 25);
- description and illumination of diversity/multiple perspectives/alternative positions (p. 26); and
- discussion/evidence of the ideological perspectives/values/ philosophies of the research team (p. 27).

And so on and so forth across six pages and seventeen quality "appraisal questions."

No one would deny that these are important issues for social researchers to take into account in the design, conduct, and reporting of research studies. However, simply listed as such, they comprise a banal and inoperable set of standards that beg all the important questions of conducting and writing up qualitative fieldwork: Everything cannot be done; *choices* have to be made; how are they to be made and how are they to be justified?

To be more positive for a moment, it might be argued that if qualitative social and educational research is going to be commissioned, then a set of standards that can act as a bulwark against commissioning inadequate and/or underfunded studies in the first place ought to be welcomed. It might also be argued that this document at least demonstrates that qualitative research is being taken seriously enough within the government to warrant a guidebook being produced for civil servants. This might then be said to confer legitimacy on civil servants who want to commission qualitative work, on qualitative social researchers bidding for such work, and indeed on social researchers more generally, who may have to deal with local research ethics committees [institutional review boards in the United States]) that are predisposed toward a more quantitative natural science model of investigation. But should we really welcome such "legitimacy"? The dangers on the other side of the argument, as to whether social scientists need or should accede to criteria of quality endorsed by the state, are legion. It is not at all clear that, *in principle*, state endorsement of qualitative research is any more desirable than state endorsement of RCTs. *Defining what counts as science is not the state's business.*

Another arena in England where research meets policy is that of systematic reviewing, mentioned above (Oakley, 2003, 2006; Wade et al., 2006). Initially, findings based on RCTs were considered the "gold standard" of systematic reviewing, but this position has been significantly modified as it has encountered considerable scepticism in the United Kingdom and work is now under way to integrate different kinds of research findings, including those of qualitative research, into such reviews. This may be construed as progress of a sort, but it also involves attempts to appraise the quality and thus the "warrant" of individual qualitative research studies and their findings: Are they good enough to be included in a systematic review or not? This, in turn, can lead to absurdly reductionist checklists as the complexity of qualitative work is rendered into an amenable form for instant appraisal. Thus, for example, Attree and Milton (2006) report on a "Quality Appraisal Checklist ... [and its associated] ... quality scoring system ... [for] "the quality appraisal of qualitative research" (p. 125). Studies are scored on a four-point scale:

A. no or few flaws

B. some flaws

C. considerable flaws, study still of some value

D. significant flaws that threaten the validity of the whole study (p. 125)

Only studies rated A or B were included in the systematic reviews that the authors conducted, and in the paper they attempt to exemplify how these categories are operationalized in their work. But, as with the Cabinet Office example above, their descriptions beg many more questions than they answer. Thus, lengthy appraisal (the Cabinet Office report) leads to a counsel of perfection—researchers are extolled to do everything—whereas rapid appraisal (see Attree & Milton [2006] in the context of systematic reviewing) leads to a checklist of mediocrity. Even the most stunning and insightful piece of qualitative work can only be categorized as having "no or few flaws." Again, to try to be fair to the authors, they indicate that "the checklist was used initially to provide an overview of the robustness of qualitative studies ... to balance the rigor of the research with its importance for developing knowledge and informing policy and practice" (Attree & Milton, 2006, p. 119). But this is precisely the issue: Standards and checklists *cannot* substitute for informed judgment when it comes to balancing the rigor of the research against its potential contribution to policy. This *is* a matter of judgment, both for researchers and for policymakers.

Proponents of systematic reviewing still try to insist on expelling judgment from the process, however, and rendering qualitative work in quantitative terms. As their focus of attention has expanded from a concentration on RCT studies, they bemoan the fact that different reporting traditions and practices in different fields restrict their capacity to evaluate studies and extract data easily. Reporting guidelines have come to be produced with which all empirical studies should accord so that they can more easily be assessed for quality: "draft guidelines for the REPOrting of primary empirical Studies in Education (the REPOSE Guidelines) ..." (Newman & Elbourne, 2004, p. 201). Such guidelines are argued to be "relevant to the reporting of any kind of primary empirical research using any type of research design" (Newman & Elbourne 2004, p. 208): an extraordinarily ambitious claim with obvious homogenizing intent. The actual guidelines comprise a two-page checklist of note-type subheadings, including supposedly generic and all-encompassing categories such as "sampling strategy," "data collection," "data analysis," and so forth (p. 211). Individually, they are unobjectionable; taken together, they are yet another counsel of perfection that would require a book-length report to fulfill and, if applied in practice, will always lead to the conclusion that anything short of a book is of poor quality. It is a strange product for a movement ostensibly concerned with utility, as policymakers routinely deal in memos not books.

Developments in the United States

Similar standards and guidelines and checklists are starting to appear in the United States with, I argue, similar results. For example, Ragin et al. (2004) report on a Workshop on Scientific Foundations of Qualitative Research, conducted under the auspices of the National Science Foundation and with the intention of placing "qualitative and quantitative research on a more equal footing ... in funding agencies and graduate training programs" (p. 9). The report argues for the importance of qualitative research and thus advocates funding qualitative research *per se*, but by articulating the "scientific foundations," it is arguing for the commissioning of not just qualitative research, but of "proper" qualitative research. Thus, for example, they argue that

> considerations of the scientific foundations of qualitative research often are predicated on acceptance of the idea of 'cases'. ... No matter how cases are defined and constructed, in qualitative research they are studied in an in-depth manner. Because they are studied in detail their number cannot be great (pp. 9–10).

This is interesting and provocative with respect to the idea of standards perhaps acting as a professional bulwark against commissioning inadequate and/or underfunded studies: A quick and cheap survey by telephone interview would not qualify as high-quality, "scientific" qualitative research. But when it comes to the basic logic of qualitative work, Ragin et al. (2004) do not get much further than arguing for a supplementary role for qualitative methods: "Causal mechanisms are rarely visible in conventional quantitative research ... they must be inferred. Qualitative methods can be helpful in assessing the credibility of these inferred mechanisms" (p. 15).

In the end, their "Recommendations for Designing and Evaluating Qualitative Research" concludes with another counsel of perfection: "These guidelines amount to a specification of the *ideal* qualitative research proposal [original emphasis]. A strong proposal should include as many of these elements as feasible" (p. 17). But again, that's the point, what is *feasible* is what is important, not what is ideal: How are such crucial choices to be made? Once again, guidelines and recommendations end up as no guide at all, rather they are a hostage to fortune, whereby virtually any qualitative proposal or report can be found wanting.

Perhaps the exemplar *par excellence* of this tendency is the AERA "Standards for Reporting on Empirical Social Science Research in AERA Publications." "The 7,000-plus word document is devoted entirely to "educational research grounded in the empirical traditions of the social sciences ... other forms of scholarship ... e.g. history, philosophy, literary analysis, arts-based inquiry ... are beyond the scope of this document" (p. 1). So we are already alerted to what is *really* important. Even this truncated version of what counts as educational research spawns "eight general areas" (p. 2) of advice, each of which is subdivided into a total of forty subsections, some of which are subdivided still further. Yet only one makes any mention of the fact that research findings should be interesting or novel or significant, and that is the briefest of references under "Problem Formulation," which we are told should answer the question of "why the results of the investigation would be of interest to the research community" (p. 2), though intriguingly, in this context, not the policy community. In this case, then, we are confronted by both a counsel of perfection *and* a checklist of mediocrity. The standards may be of help in the context of producing a book-length thesis or dissertation, but no 5,000 word journal article could meet them all. Equally, however, even supposing that they could all be met, the article might still not be worth reading. It would be "warranted" and "transparent," which are the two essential standards highlighted in the preamble (p. 2), but it could still be boring and unimportant.

It is also interesting to note that words such as "warrant" and "transparency" raise issues of trust. They imply a concern for the very existence of a substantial data-set as well as how it might be used to underpin conclusions drawn. Yet the issue of trust is only mentioned explicitly once, in the section of the standards dealing with "qualitative methods": "It is the researcher's responsibility to show the reader that the report can be trusted" (p. 11). No such injunction appears in the parallel section on "quantitative methods" (pp. 10–11); in fact, the only four uses of the actual word "warrant" in the whole document all occur in the section on "qualitative methods" (pp. 11–12). The implication seems to be that quantitative methods are really trusted—the issue doesn't have to be raised—whereas qualitative methods are not. Standards of probity are only of concern when qualitative approaches are involved.

As is typical of the genre, the standards include an opening disclaimer that "the acceptability of a research report does not rest on evidence of literal satisfaction of every standard. … In a given case there may be a sound professional reason why a particular standard is inapplicable" (p. 1). But once again, this merely restates the problem rather than resolves it: We are confronted by fifteen pages of standards that do not offer any *real* guidance on how *actually* to conduct and report empirical research. The issue, each and every time, is how to choose between alternative courses of action and how to justify that choice.

Toward a Different Approach

It is not that qualitative research has no standards, or even poorly articulated standards. Far from it: The library shelves are stacked with epistemological discussion and methodological advice about the full range of qualitative approaches available, along with what is at stake when fieldwork choices are made and what the implications are of following one course of action rather than another. Reading such sources iteratively and critically, in the context of designing and conducting a study and discussing the implications and consequences with doctoral supervisors, colleagues, or project advisory groups is what maintains and develops standards in qualitative research.

Setting standards in qualitative research, however, is a different matter. It implies the identification of universally appropriate and applicable procedures, which, in turn, involves documentary and institutional realization and compliance. And, as we have seen, the results of such efforts are not helpful to a deliberative process such as research. Moreover, it is not that the committees and research teams that produce such documents are incompetent or malicious, rather the discursive nature of the problem is not resolvable in terms of written standards. Language cannot settle matters of judgment. It can only open up more questions (of ambiguity and specificity: "But what do you mean by ...?"). In turn, the impulse of the committee discussion or the policy workshop is to attempt to answer such questions; but all criteria, pursued in this way, simply "multiply like vermin."[5]

Thus, we cannot legislate judgment out of the process of quality control; rather, our judgments must be educated by discussion, debate, and the testing of ideas and findings in public forums, through the various processes of academic life, both formal and informal. Formerly, such processes have been largely internal to the scientific community, producing self-regulated quality over the long term, though with the possibility that any individual study may fall short of appropriate standards at any particular point in time. This is a situation that governments (and some researchers themselves) no longer seem to want to tolerate. Every study must now be "quality assured" by being "standardized."

At the same time, however, it has been recognized from many different perspectives, including that of the empowerment of research subjects on the one hand, and policy relevance and social utility on the other, that an assumption of scientific disinterest and independence is no longer sustainable. Other voices must be heard in the debate over scientific quality and merit, particularly with respect to applied, policy-oriented research. Thus, for example Gibbons et al. (1994) distinguish between what they term "Mode 1" and "Mode 2" knowledge, with Mode

1 knowledge deriving from what might be termed the traditional academic disciplines and Mode 2 knowledge deriving from and operating within "a context of application": "[I]n Mode 1 problems are set and solved in a context governed by the, largely academic, interests of a specific community. By contrast, Mode 2 knowledge is carried out in a context of application" (p. 3). Mode 2 knowledge will thus generate solutions to problems as they emerge, in much the same way as the design experiments or action research approaches reviewed above. Such knowledge is "transdisciplinary ... [and] involves the close interaction of many actors throughout the process of knowledge production" (Gibbons et al., 1994, p. vii). In turn, quality must be "determined by a wider set of criteria which reflects the broadening social composition of the review system" (Gibbons et al., 1994, p. 8).

These arguments have been used to underpin a discussion document commissioned by the ESRC on "Assessing Quality in Applied and Practice-Based Educational Research" (Furlong & Oancea, 2005). Although the document falls into the category of yet another "framework" or set of "standards" and largely retains the distinction between scientific merit defined in terms of theory and methodology and social robustness defined in terms of policy relevance and utility, it nevertheless does not simply retreat into science or, perhaps more accurately, a narrow scientism (as does the U.S. advocacy of RCTs, for example). Its production is an acknowledgment that other sources of legitimacy and criteria of quality are important. Thus, the report articulates four dimensions of quality: epistemic, technological, use value for people, and use value for the economy and argues strongly that a restricted, traditional view of scientific quality is no longer tenable.

In practical terms, this means designing studies with collaborating sponsors and participants, including policymakers, and talking through issues of validity, warrant, appropriate focus, and trustworthiness of the results. A significant amount of such work is under way in the United Kingdom at present (see James, 2006; Pollard, 2005, 2006; Somekh & Saunders, Forthcoming; Torrance & Coultas, 2004; Torrance et al., 2005). The process is not without its problems or critics, but in essence the argument is that if research is to engage with policy, then research and policymaking must progress, both theoretically and chronologically, in tandem. Neither can claim precedence in the relationship. Research should not simply "serve" policy; equally, policy cannot simply "wait" for the results of research. Research will encompass far more than simply producing policy-relevant findings; policymaking will include far more than research results. Where research and policy do cohere, the relationship must be pursued as an iterative one, with gains on both sides.

Governments and some within the scholarly community itself seem to be seeking to turn educational research into a technology that can be applied to solving short-term educational problems, rather than a system of enquiry that might help practitioners and policymakers think more productively about the nature of the problem and how it might addressed. The latter process will be as beneficial to policy as to research. Producing research results takes time, and the results are unlikely to be completely unequivocal in any case. Drawing policymakers into a discussion of these issues is likely to improve the nature of research questions and research design, while also signaling to them that the best evidence available is unlikely ever to be definitive.

The U.S. policy focus on RCTs is all the more puzzling in light of these developments and arguments in the United Kingdom. Similarly, the more general retreat into trying to define the scientific merit of qualitative research simply in terms of theoretical and methodological standards, rather than in wider terms of social robustness and responsiveness to practice, seems to betray a defensiveness and loss of nerve on the part of the scholarly community. We need to acknowledge and discuss the imperfections of what we do, rather than attempt to legislate them out of existence. We need to embody and enact the deliberative process of academic quality assurance, not subcontract it to a committee. Assuring the quality of research, and particularly the quality of qualitative research in the context of policymaking, must be conceptualized as a vital and dynamic process that is always subject to further scrutiny and debate. The process cannot be ensconced in a single research method or a once-and-for-all set of standards. Furthermore, it should be oriented toward risk taking and the production of new knowledge, including the generation of new questions (some of which may derive from active engagement with research respondents and policymakers), rather than supplication, risk aversion, and the production of limited data on effectiveness for system maintenance (what works). Thus, researchers and, particularly in this context, qualitative researchers, must better manage their relationships with policymakers, rather than their research activities per se. This will involve putting more emphasis on interacting with policy and policymakers and less emphasis on producing guidelines and standards that will only ever be used as a stick with which to beat us.

In the conclusion to a new book on *Knowledge Production: The Work of Educational Research in Interesting Times*, my colleague Bridget Somekh argues that "educational research communities ... have been socially constructed as powerless ... and have colluded in this process ... through an impetus to conformity rather than transgressive speculation" (Somekh & Schwandt, 2007, p. 334). She further argues that engagement with policy and policymaking should include the discussion of "speculative knowledge" (i.e., future possibilities emerging out of research), "to improvise the co-construction of new visions" (p. 340). This seems to me to be a much more productive ground for engagement with policymaking. It is not without its threats and challenges, especially with respect to co-option and collusion, but if it is speculative of new policy (and research) and properly cautious about the provisional nature of research knowledge, rather than promising a false certainty and legitimacy for policy, then the dialog could be productive on both sides.

Notes

1. This chapter is based on a paper originally presented to a symposium on Standards of Evidence in Qualitative Inquiry, American Educational Research Association 74th Annual Conference, Chicago, April 9–13, 2007. Direct correspondence to: h.torrance@mmu.ac.uk

2. For example, it is variously argued that the view of knowledge production and accumulation in the social sciences on which systematic reviewing is based is epistemologically flawed and that such reviews are, in any case, not fit for the purpose, taking too long to complete, costing too much, and producing too little by way of useful material for policy. MacLure (2005)

further argues that the technologically driven data-base searches that are employed "degrades the status of reading and writing as scholarly activities" (p. 393) and that the overall approach is animated by a fear of the unknowable (and hence unaccountable) interpretations of researchers inherent in the use of language itself.

3. There are also issues of commercial contracts, government investment in and support of the ICT sector, etc., that need not concern us here, but obviously tie in long-term investment in these and other programs in ways that make a simple "what works" answer untenable and unusable.

4. For a more extensive discussion of these and similar issues, see Hammersley (2005).

5. This exquisitely apposite phrase comes from an article written by Margaret Brown (1988, p. 19) about initial attempts to produce the English National Curriculum and Testing system, which resulted in every member of the subject group writing teams wanting to include everything that they considered important to the subject (see Torrance, 2003).

References

Attree, P., & Milton, B. 2006. Critically appraising qualitative research for systematic review: Defusing the methodological bombs. *Evidence & Policy* 2(1):109–26.

Boaz, A., W. Solesbury, & F. Sullivan. 2004. The practice of research reviewing 1: An assessment of 28 review reports. London: UK Centre for Evidence-Based Policy and Practice, Queen Mary College. http://evidencenetwork.org (accessed November 28, 2007).

Boaz, A., W. Solesbury, & F. Sullivan. 2007. *The practice of research reviewing 2: Ten case studies of reviews.* London: UK Centre for Evidence-Based Policy and Practice, Queen Mary College. http://evidencenetwork.org (accessed November 28, 2007).

Bridges, D. 2005. The international and the excellent in educational research. Paper prepared for the Challenges of the Knowledge Society for Higher Education conference, Kaunus, Lithuania, December 16.

Brown, A. 1992. Design experiments: Theoretical and methodological challenges in creating complex interventions in classroom settings. *Journal of the Learning Sciences* 2(2):141–78.

Brown, M. 1988. Issues in formulating and organising attainment targets in relation to their assessment. In H. Torrance (Ed.), *National assessment and testing: A research response*, pp. 118–34. London: British Educational Research Association.

Brown, S. 2003. Assessment of research quality: What hope of success? Keynote address to European Educational Research Association annual conference, Hamburg, Germany, September 17.

Burkhardt, H., & A. Schoenfeld. 2003. Improving educational research: Toward a more useful, more influential and better-funded enterprise. *Educational Researcher* 32(9):3–14.

Cabinet Office. 2003a. Quality in qualitative evaluation. A framework for assessing research evidence. London: Government Chief Social Researcher's Office. [Report prepared on behalf of the Cabinet Office by L. Spencer, J. Ritchie, J. Lewis, & L. Dillon, National Centre for Social Research.]

Cabinet Office. 2003b. Quality in qualitative evaluation. A framework for assessing research evidence. London: Government Chief Social Researcher's Office. [Report prepared on behalf of the Cabinet Office by L. Spencer, J. Ritchie, J. Lewis, & L. Dillon, National Centre for Social Research.]

Chatterji, M. 2005. Evidence on "What Works": An argument for extended-term mixed-method (ETMM) evaluation designs. *Educational Researcher* 34(5):14–24.

Davies, P. 2004. Systematic reviews and the Campbell Collaboration. In G. Thomas & R. Pring (Eds.), *Evidence-based practice in education*, pp. 21–33. Maidenhead, UK: Open University Press.

Davies, P., & R. Boruch. 2001. The Campbell Collaboration. *British Medical Journal* 323(7308):294–95.

Denzin, N. K., & M. D. Giardina, Eds. 2006. *Qualitative inquiry and the conservative challenge*. Walnut Creek, CA: Left Coast Press.

Design-Based Research Collective, The. 2003. Design-based research: An emerging paradigm for educational enquiry. *Educational Researcher* 32(1):5–8.

Eisenhart, M. 2006. Qualitative science in experimental time. *International Journal of Qualitative Studies in Education* 19(6):697–708.

Eisenhart, M., & DeHaan, R. L. 2005. Doctoral preparation of scientifically based education researchers. *Educational Researcher* 34(4):3–13.

Eisenhart, M., & L. Towne. 2003. Contestation and change in national policy on "scientifically-based" education research. *Educational Researcher* 32(7):31–38.

Elliott, J. 1989. *Action research for educational change*. Buckingham, UK: Open University Press.

Erickson, F., & K. Gutierrez. 2002. Culture, rigor and science in educational research. *Educational Researcher* 31(8):21–24.

Feuer, M., L. Towne, & R. Shavelson. 2002. Scientific culture and educational research. *Educational Researcher* 31(8)4–14.

Furlong, J., & A. Oancea. 2005. *Assessing quality in applied and practice-based educational research.* Swindon, UK: ESRC.

Gibbons, M., C. Limoges, H. Nowotny, S. Schwartzman, P. Scott, & M. Trow. 1994. *The new production of knowledge.* Thousand Oaks, CA: Sage.

Gough, D., & D. Elbourne. 2002. Systematic research synthesis to inform policy, practice and democratic debate. *Social Policy and Society* 1(3):225–36.

Hammersley, M. 2001. On systematic reviews of research literature: A narrative response. *British Educational Research Journal* 27(4):543–54.

Hammersley, M. 2005. The myth of research-based practice: The critical case of educational inquiry. *International Journal of Social Research Methodology* 8(4):317–30.

Hargreaves, D. 1996. Teaching as a research based profession. TTA annual lecture, April, London, TTA.

Hillage, J., R. Pearson, A. Anderson, & P. Tamkin. 1998. *Excellence in research on school.* DfEE Research Report 74: London: DfEE.

House, E., & K. Howe. 1999. *Values in evaluation and social research.* Thousand Oaks, CA: Sage.

James, M. 2006. Balancing rigour and responsiveness in a shifting context: Meeting the challenges of educational research. *Research Papers in Education* 21(4):365–80.

MacLure, M. 2005. "Clarity bordering on stupidity": Where's the quality in systematic review? *Journal of Education Policy* 20(4)393–416.

Maxwell, J. 2004. Causal explanation, qualitative research and scientific enquiry in education. *Educational Researcher* 33(2):3–11.

National Research Council (NRC). 2002. *Scientific research in education.* Washington, DC: NRC.

National Research Council (NRC). 2005. *Advancing scientific research in education.* Washington, DC: NRC.

Newman, M., & D. Elbourne. 2004. Improving the usability of educational research: Guidelines for the REPOrting of Primary Empirical Research Studies in Education (The REPOSE Guidelines). *Evaluation and Research in Education* 18(4):201–12.

Oakley, A. 2000. *Experiments in knowing.* Cambridge: Polity Press.

Oakley, A. 2003. Research evidence, knowledge management and educational practice: Early lessons from a systematic approach. *London Review of Education* 1(1):21–33.

Oakley, A. 2006. Resistances to new technologies of evaluation: education research in the UK as a case study. *Evidence and Policy* 2(1):63–88.

OECD. 2002. *Educational research and development in England*. OECD Review CERI/CD(2002)10, Paris.

Pawson, R., & N. Tilley. 1997. *Realistic evaluation*. London: Sage.

Pollard, A. 2005. Challenges facing educational research. *Educational Review* 58(3):251–67.

Pollard, A. 2006. So, how then to approach research capacity building? *Research Intelligence* 97(November):18–20.

Ragin, C., J. Nagel, & P. White. 2004. *Workshop on scientific foundations of qualitative research*. http://www.nsf.gov/pubs/2004/nsf04219/start.htm (accessed November, 28, 2007).

Riehl, C. 2006. Feeling better: A comparison of medical research and educational research. *Educational Researcher* 35(5):24–29.

Schoenfeld, A. 2006. What doesn't work: The challenge and failure of the What Works Clearinghouse to conduct meaningful reviews of studies of mathematics curricula. *Educational Researcher* 35(2):13–21.

Shavelson, R., D. Phillips, L. Towne, & M. Feuer. 2003. On the science of education design studies. *Educational Researcher* 32(1):25–28.

Slavin, R. 2002. Evidence-based education policies: Transforming educational practice and research. *Educational Researcher* 31(7):15–21.

Somekh, B. C. Lewin, D. Mavers, C. Harris, K. Haw, T. Fisher, E. Lunzer, A. McFarlane, & P. Scrimshaw. 2002. *ImpaCT2: Pupils' and teachers' perceptions of ICT in the home, school and community*. London: Department for Education and Skills

Somekh, B., Underwood, A. Convery, G. Dillion, T. Harber Stuart, J. Jarvis, C. Lewin, D. Mavers, D. Saxon, P. Twinning, & D. Woodrow. 2005. *Evaluation of the DfES ICT TestBed project*. Coventry, UK: BECTA.

Somekh, B., & L. Saunders. Forthcoming. Developing knowledge through intervention: Meaning and definition of "quality" in research into change. *Research Papers in Education*.

Somekh, B., & T. Schwandt, Eds. 2007. *Knowledge Production: The work of educational research in interesting times*. London: Routledge.

Stenhouse, L. 1975. *An introduction to curriculum research and development*. London: Heinemann Books.

St. Pierre, E., & K. Roulston. 2006. The state of qualitative inquiry: A contested science. *International Journal of Qualitative Studies in Education* 19(6):673–84.

Thomas, G., & R. Pring, Eds. 2005. *Evidence-based practice in education*. Buckingham, UK: Open University Press.

Tooley, J., & D. Darby. 1998. *Educational research: A critique.* London: OfSTED.

Torrance, H. 2003. Assessment of the national curriculum in England. In T. Kellaghan & D. Stufflebeam (Eds.), *International handbook of educational evaluation*, pp. 905–928. Boston: Kluwer.

Torrance, H. 2006. Globalising empiricism: What if anything can be learned from international comparisons of educational achievement? In H. Lauder, P. Brown, J. Dillabough, & A. H. Halsey (Eds.), *Education, globalisation and social change*, pp. 88–98. Oxford: Oxford University Press.

Torrance, H., H. Colley, K. Ecclestone, D. Garratt, D. James, & H. Piper. 2005. *The impact of different modes of assessment on achievement and progress in the learning and skills sector.* London: Learning and Skills Research Centre.

Torrance, H., & J. Coultas. 2004. *Do summative assessment and testing have a positive or negative effect on post-16 learners' motivation for learning in the learning and skills sector?* London: Learning and Skills Research Centre.

Wade, C., H. Turner, H. Rothstein, & J. Lavenberg. 2006. Information retrieval and the role of the information specialist in producing high-quality systematic reviews in the social, behavioural and education sciences. *Evidence and Policy* 2(1):89–108.

Yates, L. 2004. *What is quality in educational research?* Buckingham, UK: Open University Press.

Yates, L. 2005. Is impact a measure of quality? Producing quality research and producing quality indicators of research in Australia. Keynote address for AARE Conference on Quality in Educational Research: Directions for Policy and Practice, Cairns, Australia, July 4–5.

2 | On Promoting Rigor in Educational Research

The Example of the UK's Research Assessment Exercise?[1]

Ian Stronach
Manchester Metropolitan University

One shouldn't complicate things for the pleasure of complicating, but one should also never simplify or pretend to be sure of such simplicity where there is none. If things were simple, word would have gotten round, as you say in English.
—Derrida, 1988, p. 119

Introduction

The UK Research Assessment Exercise (RAE) is a periodic high-stakes appraisal of the national and international "quality" of university-based research. It involves profiling individual researchers on a four-point scale, based on their nominated best four outputs in the period under assessment (2001–2007). Thus, hung, drawn, and quartered, researchers are appraised by a discipline-based panel of peers and "users" of research. Research funding is then dispensed according to the overall excellence of each Unit of Assessment (UoA) (department, institute, or whatever), indicated by total scores or grade-point averages. RAE 2008 has not yet indicated how that distribution will be made, or even the global sums involved, but it is certain that a de facto normative spread will reward top performers and penalize low scoring departments (if RAE 2001 is anything to go by). Entry is voluntary for institutions, and many of the teaching-led universities have given up as a result of past failures to secure any such funding (Corbyn, 2007b, p. 8). Such selectivity is accompanied by rhetorics of "capacity building."

The RAE is of much more than parochial importance for a number of reasons. First, it has spawned copies elsewhere, for example, in Hong Kong, Australia, and New Zealand. Second, it is a working example of a certain kind of distinctive governmentality, whereby central government seeks to micro-manage professional activity through procedures that aspire to a form of "quality assurance," based on "objective" league tables of excellence. Third, it expresses a more general instrumentalization of higher education that I have elsewhere criticized as "mythic economic instrumentalism" (Stronach, 2005, Forthcoming). Finally, it is a recognizable international trend, whereby the quantification of quality performs a kind of postmodern alchemy via technicist reduction and coercive collaboration. Such a trend suggests that study of the precise workings of RAE procedures may tell us something about the nature of a kind of creeping totalitarian farce (Fielding, 2007; Stronach, 2005). In North American contexts, it may also be some kind of minatory case study of the future.

I begin this chapter with a deconstruction of the RAE Education sub-panel's rubrics, drawing also on the broader RAE regulations, procedures, and associated documentation and research. I then seek to tease out the sorts of covert epistemologizing that may (or may not) be likely to take place. The theoretical ambition is to take a Derridean approach to acts of translation, reworking that metaphor as a way into the acts of translation that the RAE undertakes in placing numerical values on the quality of research outputs. How do we measure our "pounds of flesh"? As a practical "hermeneutics of suspicion," it seeks a "provocative validity" in that one of its aims is to provoke clarity and reassurance from the authors of such RAE documents. In that ambition it has already had some success, as a response from Margaret Brown, chair of the RAE Education sub-panel, demonstrates (Brown, 2007, pp. 353–56).[2]

The complexity of appraising the international significance of research within and across the full range of disciplines ought to be obvious. But in the UK RAE one might argue that it was the "simple" word that got around. In relation to excellence criteria, the Higher Education Funding Council for England (HEFCE) offered these definitions and scales:

4* Quality that is world-leading in terms of originality, significance, and rigor.

3* Quality that is internationally excellent in terms of originality, significance, and rigor but which nonetheless falls short of the highest standards of excellence

2* Quality that is recognized internationally in terms of originality, significance, and rigor.

1* Quality that is recognized nationally in terms of originality, significance, and rigor.

U/C Quality that falls below the standard of nationally recognised work. Or work which does not meet the published definition of research for the purposes of this assessment. (see http://hefce.ac.uk/research/assessment)

My first purpose here is to deconstruct the categories, criteria, and rubrics of the RAE, particularly as they apply to Panel K, sub-panel UoA 45, Education. I hope that such a critical consideration can help participants of all shades enter a debate that will inform decision-making and critique. I also hope—though probably in vain—that such reconsiderations can help inform future policy development in the area of research performance appraisal more generally. It should be stressed, for the benefit of those unfamiliar with deconstruction, that such an undertaking seeks out the unspoken, the implicit and the contradictory in these rubrics. In so doing, it aims for a "provocative" validity and the performance of alternative interpretations. These do not constitute a new bedrock on which appraisal can confidently be founded. Instead, they unsettle conventional readings in ways that open up new understandings and richer appreciation of the dilemmas of this sort of appraisal, in terms of its ambitions to "correspondence," "consensus," or—as I will eventually argue—"translation," drawing on Benjamin and Derrida. Such an approach has much in common with the recent work of Lather and St. Pierre in the United States (Freeman et al., 2007; Lather, 2005, 2006; St. Pierre, 2002).

• • •

To begin at the beginning, the RAE criteria seem to have emerged more from a political process than an academic one. In identifying criteria that promised to distinguish "world-leading" research (4*) from "internationally excellent" (3*) and work "recognized internationally" (2*), they raised the issue of "internationality" in relation to research. They did so with regard to three categories of evaluation: "originality, significance, and rigor." These were the givens of the RAE process. Cultural outsiders may wonder at the combination of scores and stars—stars are more common in elementary schools than anywhere else in the United Kingdom, reflecting perhaps an unconscious aspect of the ongoing infantilization of educational discourse.

The new criteria reflected government perceptions that previous RAE appraisals had been subject to credentialist inflation, and so replaced the old grades (1, 2, 3b, 3a, 4, 5, 5*).[3] In specifying three grades of internationality, the government met grade inflation with criterial hyperinflation. First of all, there are a number of technical and logical points that need to be made. The criteria were incompetent in that the descriptors gave no indication as to how they might be measured or defined. Subsequent attempts by Panel K to offer "expanded definitions of the quality levels" merely offered further undefined attributes: "highly significant contribution," "significant contribution," "recognized contribution," and the loser's 1* of "limited contribution." The expansion amounted to the displacement of one unspecified performance vocabulary with another. At the same time, the tautological relation is obvious: What's world-leading? Answer: Whatever's highly significant. What's highly significant? Whatever's world-leading.[4] The expansion of the quality levels, in short, is "gaseous" in its rhetorical nature (Novoa & Yariv-Masha, 2003). Finally, the envisaged system was normed in relation to an absolute rather than a distribution: "The definition of each *quality* level relies on a conception of *quality* (world leading *quality*) which is the absolute standard of *quality* in each unit of assessment" (RAE, 01/2005, p. 10, emphases added). So quality "relies on" quality and "is" an absolute in and of itself, shortly before disappearing up its own benchmark.

Indeed, this is the "tautology of redundant specification" (Chambers, 2003, p. 181).

Second, there is an oddity about the categories of excellence, "originality, significance, and rigor." The first two sound like maximum competencies, but the third suggests a minimum competence, which makes peculiar sense if one tries to align it with the evaluation criteria: What would "world-leading rigor" look like? Would it be a good thing, or would it imply the rigidity of a rigor mortis?

Third, research quality was to be appraised in terms of "originality, significance, and rigor." These were the key requirements across the generic RAE documentation and main panel rhetorics.[5] It is noteworthy that Panel K is unusual in that it sometimes reverses this order and refers to "rigor, significance and originality" (pp. 19, 32, 46). The Education sub-panel followed suit (UoA, discipline, or field-based review draft, p. 5; Education sub-panel document, p. 23). There is no such reversal in related subjects (e.g., UoA 41, Sociology). The Education sub-panel also spells out its take on "rigor" quite closely in offering guidance on how each piece of research might present itself to the panel—"in particular how the criterion of rigor is met," along with "methodological robustness" and "systematic approach." Without being oversuspicious, such words as "systematic," "robust," and "rigor" belong most readily to neopositivist forms of research narrative that many have criticized as "scientism" rather than science (Erickson & Gutierrez, 2002; St. Pierre, 2002). One might wonder if the panel is expressing, or being required to express, a coded predilection. The sub-panel is clear elsewhere, however, that there have to be methodological horses for courses, even if it offers this reassurance in a subordinate clause: "But rigor can best be assessed on a case by case basis using whichever dimensions are most appropriate" (RAE/Panel K, 2006, p. 33).

Other, more science-related panels are less concerned with rigor. Engineering does not mention the term and spells out its priorities in terms of advancing knowledge and understanding, originality and innovation, impact on theory, methodology, policy, practice, etc. Physics expects to see some of the following: "agenda-setting, research that is leading or at the forefront of the research area, great novelty in developing new thinking, new techniques or novel results" (RAE/Panel E, 01/2006, p. 42). Again, no mention of rigor. Linguistics, on the other hand, takes that term and disseminates it across a whole range of research qualities: "intellectual coherence, methodological precision and analytical power; accuracy and depth of scholarship; evidence of awareness of and appropriate engagement with other work in the field or sub-field" (RAE/Panel M, 01/2006, p. 97). So the notion of rigor can either be dropped or exploded, and by disciplines more readily called "sciences" than educational research or indeed psychology.

Whence the education sub-panel's additional concern for rigor and the special emphasis expressed in Panel K? Is this the semi-sciences reflecting the same obsessive concern for respectability as the semi-professions? Put provocatively, is Science mobilized as Rigor within the RAE sub-panel process to make an honest woman of Educational Research? Certainly, there are such mobilizations of science both in the United Kingdom and the United States (Freeman, et al., 2007; Lather, 2005;).

• • •

Thus far, in relation to rigor, we have some straws in the wind—no more—a shift in word order, a foregrounding in terms of specification, a hypothetical bias toward particular scientific approaches to social inquiry (a possibility noted by Armstrong and Goodyear [2005]).[6] In the rest of this chapter, I say more about the location and import of this notion of "rigor" in the hope that its opening-up will lead to more clarity for those who orchestrate, execute, or endure the RAE process.

There is a research basis for the RAE categories of appraisal. Wooding and Grant (2003) conducted research on behalf of the HEFCE across a broad range of disciplines to establish the key categories against which the research community would wish to see their work appraised. They did so via a number of workshops across the country. It is reasonable to assume that their work is sufficiently representative across most disciplines concerned in the RAE. In their executive summary, they reported that there was a consensus that high-quality research was based on "*rigor*; international recognition; originality; and the idea that the best research sets the agenda for new fields of investigation" (Wooding & Grant, 2003, p. 3, emphasis added). So there we have a vindication of Panel K's and the Education sub-panel's reprioritizations—rigor *is* the paramount concern. And that reflects a consensus across research communities.

But when we examine the full research text, of which the executive summary claims to be an accurate summary, we find the following statement: "The concept of defining the research agenda by framing new research questions and advancing a field into new areas was seen as *the most important characteristic* of high quality research." (Wooding & Grant, 2003, p. 14, emphasis added).

The enumerations the authors give in their Figure 11 confirm this. The priorities are reported in terms of respondents' views as (1) defining the research agenda (ninety-nine attributions), (2) rigor (seventy-one attributions), (3) international recognition (sixty-six attributions). So rigor is not the leading requirement, as their executive summary claims. Struck by this slip, I thought that an examination of the research annexes might be interesting.

"Defining the research agenda" (DRA) had been one of the HEFCE researchers' emergent categories, and items like "advancement of the field" and "potential to move discipline forward" had typically been included. But an item "advance body of knowledge" was attributed to a separate category called "scholarship," which seemed indefensible as it fitted perfectly into DRA— "advancement of the field" and "advance body of knowledge" are synonymic. Again, the category of rigor had been awarded the response item "depth"—more reasonably attributable to the notion of "originality." Finally, there was a remarkable accident to one of the workshop's appraisal of the importance of originality. Although originality had been highly rated by other workshops, there was a zero score for one workshop. It seemed unlikely that a group of academics would be so uninterested in originality. Further exploration revealed an explanatory footnote, in rather tiny print: "The sticky hexagon fell off the chart and was not available for voting" (Wooding & Grant, 2003, p. 5).

A case of the "hanging chad," as a colleague remarked.[7] An averaging of the other workshop scores for that category (which would have been 7.75) was not undertaken, and instead the presumption of a 0 score was made. Taking these sorts of anomalies into account a reanalysis of the actual workshop data would read as follows:

Defining the research agenda—120

Originality—69

International recognition—66

Rigor—62

So the category of rigor was 1st in the Executive Summary, 2nd in the main text, and 4th in relation to the data in Annex II. Rigor was a shifting if not shifty signifier, whose analysis had certainly not been rigorous. Now, it is almost always a good idea in relation to UK governance to adjudicate cock-up/conspiracy theories in favor of the former, but it does seem *possible* that rigor might be experiencing some unwarranted promotion.

Given the Education sub-panel's unusual concern for rigor, it is worth raising some questions that the panel might want to consider and even address publicly, in a spirit of reassurance. They are: Is there a particular promotion of the notion of rigor? Is that promotion, if such it is, part of paradigmatic prejudice? Will rigor as a minimum competence be used to police the other two categories?[8] Are covertly hegemonic moves being made in relation to RAE documentation?

In relation to all of the above questions, it is relevant to note that the panel has detailed requirements for members to declare interests. All of these are "familial" in nature—same institution, former student, collaborator, etc.; none concerns paradigmatic prejudice, yet as an editor of the *British Educational Research Journal* for eleven years, I know that such bias is far more likely than any other. So why that gap? This is a particularly acute omission, considering how explicitly other panels have marked out excellence as a matter internal to specific fields and concerns: "In view of the diverse nature of the discipline of sociology, the sub-panel understands the quality descriptors to relate to indicators within fields, sub-fields and cognate areas" (RAE, 2006, UoA 41, p. 47). Philosophy, too, invokes imminent criteria: "will judge submissions against the best work in the field" (RAE, 2006, UoA 41, p. 40).

To return to the specifics of the Education sub-panel's

guidelines, they are unusual in that they offer a very specific example of what might count as a justifying rhetoric for any single publication (150 words are permitted to provide evidence of the claim to originality, significance, and rigor). It reads as follows:

Hypothetical Example

Humanities in primary schools—short booklet containing advice to teachers and policymakers based on a synthesis of international research. This provides an innovative conceptualisation of the field and has been referred to by the TDA [Training and Development Agency] for Schools (2007) as the basis for its criteria for CPD [Continuing Professional Development] in this area. The review considered 1250 references of which 41 met the criteria for inclusion. The full review has been accepted by Springer in 2008. The distillation of the implications of the literature was done by a working group of five researchers and five teachers. The draft was refereed by two international referees and piloted by ten teachers and four policymakers to ensure it was appropriate and user-friendly. It is cited by two researchers because of the considerable work involved in its production; they contributed equally and co-directed the project, financed by a £15,000 grant from Tesco [a UK supermarket chain]. (RAE 2006, UoA 45, p. 32)

There are a number of points to be made here. First, this is the only example. In the draft, there were five such examples (RAE, 2006, UoA 45, draft as at 16.7.05, pp. 4–5), and one wonders why that plurality was narrowed down, making the example much more likely to be read as an exemplar or even as a template. Second, the earlier draft had taken a very different tack—emphasizing contributions to theory or methodology, prestigious keynotes, international awards, and so on (RAE, 2006, UoA 45, draft as at 16.7.05, p. 4). Would it be unreasonable to envisage the heavy hand of the state intervening in this peer-led process of consultation, promoting itself and its agencies as the User/Methodologist Who Mattered? Third, the narrative is almost exclusively focused on local and national users and on outlining the detail of a research process in accordance with one particular notion of rigor.

The evidence for originality is very limited (a claim of "innovative conceptualization"), and the significance is clearly circumscribed by the national.

So that's a clear 1*? Yet, it would be a foolish reader who thought that it was included to illustrate the bottom end of the range. It is also hard not to take the methodological orientation of that narrative and associate it with the foregrounding of a particular approach to educational research with its characteristic notions of rigor, robustness, and systematicity—the features we earlier wondered about in relation to panel predilections. If we then ask ourselves "what kind of writing is this?" then there is a simple and clear answer. This is the kind of "structured abstract" that Sebba has been calling for since 1998 and it is currently based on an extension of the work of Hartley (2003). It performs and validates a kind of neopositivism that has been quick to dismiss almost all other approaches to educational inquiry as invalid and above all, lacking in rigor.[9] As in the fictional abstract, non-positivist narratives fail to meet "the criteria for inclusion." And it is rigor that demarcates that exclusion.

• • •

To conclude, the categories and criteria for RAE appraisal in educational research are far from clear. There seems, *prima facie*, to be cause for serious concern in relation to the promotion of certain kinds of research and certain kinds of outcome. No doubt, the panel will argue that they are their own masters and will come to their own judgments—and the element of judicious peer review and consensus will, of course, be present. Indeed, three of the Education sub-panel members said so when an early version of this paper was presented at the British Educational Research Association (BERA) conference in September 2006. Provided they make full disclosure of paradigmatic prejudices, no one will doubt the panel's integrity. But the discourses around which they construct their deliberations also surround them. The extent to which they will be prisoners, warders, or governors remains to be seen: Escapees they will not be.

This brief account began with the claim that the orienting

metaphors of appraisal depended on notions of correspondence and consensus. In the shortest of shorthands, these represent different epistemologies—one could plausibly toss Hammersley into the first box and Habermas into the second, albeit not with the same reverence. But both projects suppress a kind of impossibility. All *translations*, to move to our third metaphor of evaluation, express what Derrida has called "an economy of in-betweenness" (2001, p. 179). In discussing *The Merchant of Venice*, Derrida argues that the economy of translation (ducats/pound of flesh; Christian/Jew) circles through both a "proper meaning" and a "calculable quantity" (Derrida, 2001, p. 179). Letter and spirit are irreconcilable yet inevitable and necessary to each other: "This relation of the letter to the spirit, of the body of literalness to the ideal interiority of sense is also the site of the passage of translation, of this conversion that is called translation" (Derrida, 2001, p. 184).

The RAE process is just such a plural act of conversion/translation. Quite explicitly, it re-expresses the local as a globally normative value, one that invites international appraisal, investment and emulation. That is one version of the fantastic "passage" of translation. It is part of the global phenomenon of "comparison, defining a new mode of governance" (Novoa & Yariv-Mashal, 2003, p. 428; Stronach, 1999). It involves the incommensurable translation of a field into a harvest, a transubstantiation that is no less mystical than that of bread or wine in Christian ritual, to return to Benjamin's analogy for the notion of translation. In addition, it effects the parallel construction of the "self-auditing academic" (McWilliam, 2004, p. 162), and with it another passage, this time of identity rather than status or nature. Of course, one could go on, but already it can be seen that the singular body of a spirit of inquiry is thus translated into sundry commodities of appraisal—individual, institutional, disciplinary, national—and various "pounds of flesh" are weighed and translated in terms of an "impossible but incessantly alleged correspondence" (Derrida, 2001, p. 184).[10] These require certain kinds of passage that cannot be legislated for, any more than law can guarantee justice in any single case. Justice, like mercy, is above the law, and can have no a priori regulatory transparency, any more than can virtues such as tact. The future RAE move (post-2008) to a greater reliance on metrics will inevitably make even more injudicious such translations, by further obscuring the "objectified subjectivity" of the exercise (Velody, cited in Bence & Oppenheim, 2005, p. 151; see also von Tunzelman & Mbula, 2003, p. 15). The translation of our pounds of flesh into RAE ducats is inherently incommensurable, and that is the scandal of assessment that the RAE and even more its future metrification seek to suppress.[11] If such appraisal has an essence, it is the absence of all possible rigor.

There is a deeper scandal, one well parodied by Sparkes, whose fictional account of the RAE expresses the sorts of madness we have been outlining here. His hero condemns the "bollocks" of the RAE (Sparkes, 2007, pp. 521–50). His account made the front page of the *Times Higher Education Supplement*: "Bollocks": RAE Paper Assesses the RAE (Corbyn, 2007a). The problem, as I earlier argued, is one of a lack of "civil courage" (Stronach, 2004, p. 17) in the academic community: "No other era has worn its academic freedom more lightly, nor given it away more readily" (Stronach, Hallsall, & Hustler, 2002, p. 185). RAE Chairperson Margaret Brown, in responding sanely to my criticisms, acknowledges that there is force to some of them, but she reflects a morality that really is about damage limitation in the face of an increasingly illiberal and irrational state. What is so hard to comprehend is why a process that is so clearly flawed, inexpertly researched, ill-thought out, and obviously manipulated by politicians and policymakers can nevertheless achieve acceptance by a research community that should, by its very nature, be the first to criticize and dismiss it. Sell-out, indeed:

> If the problem, the *aporia*, in any of these cases is resolved not through *experience*, through the "ordeal of the undecidable", but through recourse only to calculation or a formula—which is always somebody's formula—then it will have been a sell-out, a set-up by and for one economy, "fixed" from the start. (Derrida, cited in Davis, 2001, 95; see also Derrida, 2005, Richter, 2002)

Derrida (2005) ends his translation argument concerning Shylock and *The Merchant of Venice* (Shakespeare, 1919) by arguing that in the end it is mercy ("It droppeth as the gentle rain from heaven") rather than justice for which we ought to pray. As things stand, that's our only rather than our best hope.

Though justice be thy plea, consider this,
That in the course of justice none of us
Should see salvation: we do pray for mercy
And that same prayer doth teach us all to render
The deeds of mercy.

(*The Merchant of Venice*, Act 4, Scene 1)

Notes

1. An earlier version of this chapter was delivered at the BERA conference, Warwick University, Warwick, UK, September 2006, and was published in 2007 in the *Journal of Education Policy*.

2. In her response (Brown, 2007), the RAE Education panel chair argued that Stronach saw "conspiracies where I don't believe them to exist." She acknowledged that it was a weakness of the overall RAE process that it failed to draw on "assessment expertise" (Brown, 2007, p. 353), and that it would have been "easier and probably more honest to norm-reference" (Brown, 2007, p. 354), but the process was partly political and inevitably "imperfect and imprecise"—"We only do it because for some reason it is seen to be necessary" (Brown, 2007, p. 356). Nevertheless, she was sure that the panel's deliberations would be inclusive methodologically and theoretically speaking and offer no paradigmatic bias in interpreting the criteria of rigor, significance, and originality. Relating to the Shakespearean analogy, she hoped that the panel would dispense "mercy with justice," confessing that "I have always yearned to play the role of Portia, but had not previously connected it with the RAE, so for that, as for several other insights, I am especially grateful to Ian" (Brown, 2007, p. 356).

3. It may seem strange that a simple numerical scale should become so contaminated with letters and stars, but it's important also to read these scales as class markers, in the way that socioeconomic classes are distinguished in the United Kingdom. To joke only a little, 3b/3a might be seen as corresponding to a distinction between "rough" and "respectable" working class. The economic disenfranchisement of 1/2/3b/3a in 2001 thereby enhanced the loading of funding at the top end and widened the gap between the haves and the have-nots in ways that might also be regarded as analogous, particularly as these cuts were conducted under the overall policy banner of "capacity building." There are underlying parallels, it might be argued, with New Labour inclusionary rhetorics.

4. The Hong Kong exercise showed some of the same enthusiasm for tautology: "Quality of research equates to a level of excellence appropriate to the discipline in Hong Kong."

5. There is a longstanding history of "significance" and "originality" in relation to questions of "recognition" in science and its sociology (Merton, 1957). The priority of originality is clear.

6. Armstrong and Goodyear argue: "It would not do for an assessment model to be dominated by advocates of large-scale, randomised control group experiments (or poststructuralist policy critique, for that matter)" (2005, p. 21). Indeed (see also Stronach, 2005).

7. The 2000 U.S. election was decided on some contested Florida votes, counted as ineligible, and provoking legal arguments that addressed the "hanging chad" on a ballot being questionable evidence of whether a vote had or had not been (mechanically) executed.

8. A natural riposte to such questions is to dismiss such possibilities as a slur on the integrity of reviewers. But our recent and highly analogous experience with an ESRC end-of-report review shows that such paradigm warfare does happen. The report and case study (Piper, Stronach, & MacLure., 2006) was reviewed. One reviewer said good things about the research. First, "a qualitative approach is justified." But with some reluctance I have rated this report "problematic" rather than "good." Why? The reviewer's "fairly strong reservations derive from my prejudices against qualitative research." The other three reviewers rated the research "outstanding," which was its overall grade. The example illustrates *both* the possibilities of bias and its correction. It highlights the need for careful moderation across reviewers and the need to take paradigmatic bias into account.

9. Or perhaps we're back to rigor as in rigor mortis. MacLure has criticized the fruits of such systematic reviews as illustrated in the hypothetical example as "tiny dead bodies of knowledge" (MacLure, 2005, p. 394).

10. Benjamin differentiates between the intended object and the mode of intention in making this point in relation to the meaning of bread and wine in different languages (Benjamin, 1973, p. 74). Others might express a similar point in relation to connotative and denotative meanings. The RAE's move from overall institutional assessment to individual item appraisal has its parallels in the practices of risk management: "The so called asset-by-asset approach dominates the scene over the portfolio-theoretical approach" (Kalthoff, 2005, p. 75).

11. In discussion at the BERA presentation of an earlier version of this paper, I argued that the RAE was like the "pool's panel"—which meets in the United Kingdom to decide the result of postponed football matches so that gambling results are available. But that was the 2001 RAE. There is a difference in the 2008 RAE exercise. This time, the panel's wisdom is far greater: No longer content to decide the outcome of a match that was never played, it also decides how well each player performed.

References

Armstrong, D., & P. Goodyear. 2005. Implications of external research quality for local research leadership: Learning from the UK RAE experience. Paper presented at the AARE Focus Conference, Cairns, Australia, July 4–5.

Benjamin, W. 1973. *Illuminations*. H. Arendt, Ed., H. Zohn, Translator, Glasgow: Fontana/Collins.

Bence, V., & C. Oppenheim. 2005. The evolution of the UK's research assessment exercise: Publications, performance and perceptions. *Journal of Educational Administration and History* 37(2):137–55.

Brown, M. 2007. On promoting rigour: A response. *Journal of Educational Policy* 22(3):353–356.

Chambers, R. 2003. The war of the words: The rhetoric of "Operation Iraqi Freedom" (an informal survey). *Culture, Theory, Critique* 44(2):171–81.

Corbyn, Z. 2007a. "Bollocks": RAE paper assesses the RAE. *Times Higher Education Supplement*, December 7, p. 1.

Corbyn, Z. 2007b. Teaching institutions draw on smaller cohort for RAE. *Times Higher Education Supplement*, December 7, p 8.

Davis, K. 2001. *Deconstruction and translation*. Manchester, UK: St Jerome Publishing.

Derrida, J. 1988. *Limited Inc*. Evanston, IL: Northwestern University Press.

Derrida, J. 2001. What is a relevant translation? *Critical Inquiry* 27(2):174–200.

Derrida, J. 2005. Justices. *Critical Inquiry* 31(3):689–721.

Erickson, F., & K. Guitierrez. 2002. Culture, rigor, and science in educational research. *Educational Researcher* 31(8):21–24.

Fielding, M. 2007. Personalisation, education and the totalitarianism of the market. London: Institute of Education, mimeo.

Freeman, M., K. deMarrais, J. Preissle, K. Roulston, & E. St. Pierre. 2007. Standards of evidence in qualitative research: An incitement to discourse. *Educational Researcher* 36(1):25–32.

Hartley, J. 2003. Improving the clarity of journal abstracts in psychology: The case for structure. *Science Communication* 24(3):366–379.

Higher Education Funding Council for England (HEFCE). *The research assessment exercise*. Bristol, UK. http://hefce.ac.uk/research/assessment (accessed June 8, 2007).

Kalthoff, H. 2005. Practices of calculation. Economic representations and risk management. *Theory, Culture & Society* 22(2):69–97.

Lather, P. 2005. Foucauldian scientificity: Rethinking the research, policy, practice nexus. Paper delivered at the American Educational Studies Association. Charlottesville, VA, November 4.

Lather, P. 2006. Foucauldian scientificity: Rethinking the nexus of qualitative research and educational policy analysis. *International Journal of Qualitative Studies in Education* 19(6):783–91.

MacLure, M. 2005. "Clarity bordering on stupidity": Where's the quality in systematic review? *Journal of Education Policy* 20(4):393–416.

McWilliam, E. 2004. Changing the academic subject. *Studies in Higher Education* 29(2):151–63.

Merton, R. K. 1957. *Social theory and social structure.* New York: Free Press of Glencoe.

Novoa, A., & T. Yariv-Mashal. 2003. Comparative research in education: A mode of governance or a historical journey? *Comparative Education* 39(4):423–38.

Piper, H., I. Stronach, & M. MacLure. 2006. Touchlines: The problematics of touching between children and professionals. Economic and Social Research Council, England (RES-000-22-0815).

Research Assessment Exercise (RAE). 2006. Criteria and working methods, Panel E. Physics.

Research Assessment Exercise (RAE) Panel M. 2006. Criteria and working methods, Unit of Assessment 58, Linguistics.

Research Assessment Exercise (RAE). 2006. Sub-panel criteria and working methods, Unit of Assessment 45, Education.

Research Assessment Exercise (RAE). 2006. Sub-panel criteria and working methods, Unit of Assessment 41, Sociology.

Research Assessment Exercise (RAE). 2006. Panel criteria and working methods: Panel K.

Richter, G. 2002. Sites of indeterminacy and the spectres of Eurocentrism. *Culture, Theory, Critique* 43(1):51–65.

Roberts' Review, The. 2003. Joint funding bodies' review of research assessment. Higher Education Funding Council (HEFCE), May 19. http://www.ra-review.ac.uk/reports/roberts.asp (accessed July 16, 2007).

Sebba, J. 1998. Improving the quality of research publications: What has been learned from systematic reviewing? Paper presented at the American Educational Research Association conference, San Diego, California, April 14.

Shakespeare, W. 1998. *The merchant of Venice.* Oxford: Oxford University Press.

Sparkes, A. 2007. Embodiment, academics and the audit culture: A story seeking consideration. *Qualitative Research* 7(4):521–50.

St. Pierre, E. 2002. "Science" rejects postmodernism. *Educational Researcher* 31(8):25–27.

Stronach, I. 1999. Shouting theatre in a crowded fire: "Educational effectiveness" as cultural performance. *Evaluation* 5(2):173–93.

Stronach, 2004. Ending educational research, countering dystopian futures. In J. Satterthwaite, E. Atkinson, and W. Martin (Eds.), *The disciplining of education: New languages of power and resistance*, pp. 3–20. Oakhill, UK: Trentham

Stronach, I. 2005. "International" criteria for RAE judgements. *Research Intelligence* 92(1):16–17.

Stronach, I. 2007. On promoting rigour in educational research: The example of the RAE? *Journal of Education Policy* 3:343–54.

Stronach, I. Forthcoming. *Globalising the educational, educating the global. How method made us mad.* London: Routledge.

Stronach, I., R. Halsall, & D. Hustler. 2002. Future imperfect: Evaluation in dystopian times, In K. Ryan & T. Schwandt (Eds.), *Exploring evaluator role and identity*, pp. 167–92. Greenwich, CT: IAP.

Von Tunzelman, N., & E. Mbula. 2003. Changes in research assessment practices in other countries since 1999: Final report, HEFCE, February. Brighton: University of Sussex, SPRU Science and Technology Policy Research.

Wooding, S., & J. Grant. 2003. Assessing research: The researchers' view. MR-1698-HEFCE, May, vols. 1 and 2. RAND: Europe.

3 | Isolating Science from the Humanities

The Third Dogma of Educational Research

Kenneth R. Howe
University of Colorado, Boulder

Introduction

A half century ago, C. P. Snow decried the isolation of the sciences and humanities from one another in his celebrated *The Two Cultures* (1959). The divide has only grown wider in the intervening years as the relevance of the humanities to defining and addressing the public's problems has continued to diminish.[1] The humanities are now largely relegated to the role of edification.

Ellen Condliffe Lagemann aptly depicted the parallel development in educational research as follows: "Edward L. Thorndike, the Teachers College psychologist, 'won' and the philosopher John Dewey 'lost'" (2000, p. xi). But despite Thorndike's victory, the educational research community remained relatively receptive to—at least indulgent of—humanities-oriented research, particularly following the explosion of qualitative research associated with the "interpretive turn"[2] of the latter quarter of the 20th century. Things have changed in recent years, however, in response to the perceived crisis in public education. A demand for evidence-based education policy and practice took shape in the U.S. Congress early in the 21st century. Evidence based quickly became identified with "scientifically based," and in 2002 the Office of Educational Research and Improvement (OERI) was reorganized and renamed the Institute of Education Sciences (IES).[3]

Also in 2002, the National Research Council (NRC) formed a panel of distinguished scientists and education researchers to more precisely specify the characteristics of scientific educational research. The result was the report *Scientific Research in Education* (SRE), which, although not without critics,[4] has done much to define a new methodological orthodoxy that fosters a dualism between empirical science and the humanities. NRC's subsequent report, *Advancing Scientific Research in Education* (2004), imports the dualism into doctoral programs in education (Bullough, 2006). Finally, as a consequence of the same general thrust to render educational research scientific that led to SRE, the American Educational Research Association (AERA) promulgated "Standards for Reporting on Empirical Social Science in AERA Publications" (2006). By including only research that fits with a rather narrow conception of empirical, the standards further reinforce the empirical science/humanities dualism.[5]

I call this dualism the "third dogma of educational research" because of its close relationship to the first two dogmas: the quantitative/qualitative incompatibility thesis and the fact/value dichotomy (Howe, 1985, 1988, 2003). In what follows, I discuss critical examinations of the original two dogmas that I have provided previously and then connect them to the new orthodoxy. Next, I critically examine the third dogma. I conclude with some suggestions regarding a more fruitful and defensible conception of the role of the humanities vis-à-vis scientific research in education.

The Quantitative/Qualitative Dogma

The quantitative-qualitative incompatibility thesis holds that quantitative and qualitative research methods are incompatible with one another and thus cannot be coherently combined (Howe, 1988, 2003). The source of the incompatibility is typically not located at the level of research "methods" (Guba, 1987) or "techniques and procedures" (Smith & Heshusius, 1986), but in the more comprehensive epistemological paradigms in which the methods find their roots. Quantitative methods are traced to positivism, and qualitative methods are traced to interpretivism, broadly construed. Because positivism and interpretivism are incompatible epistemological paradigms, so, too, are quantitative and qualitative research methods.

Proponents of the incompatibility thesis contend that justifying "compatibilism" by decoupling epistemological paradigms from research methods in deference to "what works" ignores the deeper incompatibility in the underlying epistemological paradigms (e.g., Smith & Heshusius, 1986; Yanchar & Williams, 2006). Some theorists justify compatibilism by simply decoupling epistemology from research methods (e.g., Firestone, 1987; Reichardt & Cook, 1979). I call this move the "autonomy thesis" (Howe, 1988) and join incompatibilists in judging it an inadequate way of addressing the question of the compatibility of research methods. Among other problems, it unavoidably presumes some epistemological view itself, without explicating or justifying it. But contrary to the way compatibilism has often been pigeonholed, including in Yanchar and Williams's (2006) recent attempt to rescue a "soft" version of the incompatibility thesis, decoupling epistemology from research methods in favor of "what works" is not the only way to justify compatibilism. In particular, it is not the justification I provide.

I argue that quantitative and qualitative methods are compatible in spite of the fact that the general epistemological paradigms, positivism and interpretivism, are not. My tack has been to critically evaluate, not merely describe, underlying epistemological paradigms. The incompatibility of underlying epistemological paradigms signals that one or both are flawed and, generally speaking, it is positivism that comes up short. Positivism has been long since repudiated in philosophy of science: It is "dead … or as dead as a philosophical movement ever becomes" (Passmore, 1967). My argument decouples research methodology from epistemological paradigms only in the sense of jettisoning positivism.

Positivism failed to work out its principle of reductionism, which required explicating the criteria by which genuinely scientific claims could be identified and used to mark the boundary between science and metaphysics—speculative conceptual pursuits not tied directly to unadulterated empirical data (Quine, 1951).[6] The kind of inert, empirically pure "sense data" or "observation sentences" required of reductionism do not exist. The alternative view made prominent by Kuhn (1962) is that the empirical data of science are "theory laden," shaped by the paradigms scientists bring to observation. Because the empirical and conceptual-metaphysical are intertwined in this way, the boundary between science and other intellectual work defies explication in terms of distinct conceptual-metaphysical versus empirical domains of knowledge.

A related principle of positivism that also faltered is the "unity of science," whereby physics served as the model of science to be emulated, including the social sciences. The embrace of this principle led social researchers to attempt to develop their own unadulterated observational vocabulary—"behaviorese"— which aspired to eliminate metaphysical entities such as minds, thoughts, intentions, and the like. The behaviorist school called into question methods (e.g., introspection) that depend on the testimony of individuals regarding what's going on in the *subjective* nether world of the mind (e.g., Mackenzie, 1977).

The embrace of the unity of science also underpinned the view that, to be scientific, social research should adopt the kind of formalized mechanisms for causal inference, explanation, and prediction that characterized physics. Consistent with this, precise quantitative data were to be obtained and plugged into the inferential machinery. Testing of scientific hypotheses was reserved for formalized inference vis-à-vis the "context of justification." Less formalized, qualitative data and inference were relegated to the "context of discovery," where tentative hypotheses might be invented and mulled but not verified or falsified.

In social research, the classic statement on formalized inference can be found in Campbell and Stanley's *Experimental and Quasi-Experimental Designs for Research* (1963), in which they describe the experimental methods as "the *only* means for settling disputes regarding educational practice, as the *only* way of verifying educational improvements, and as the *only* way of establishing a cumulative tradition" (1963, p. 2, emphasis added). Campbell and Stanley were generally critical of qualitative methods, attributing to them the "fallacy of misplaced precision" and characterizing the "one-shot case study" as so methodologically flawed as to be "well-nigh unethical" to use (1963, p. 7).

The collapse of reductionism undermined the justification for limiting the vocabulary of social research to behaviorese. It became increasingly recognized that social science research requires an overall interpretivist framework that includes a central place for an "intentionalist" vocabulary suitable for understanding and explaining the norm-regulated behavior in which humans, unlike molecules in motion, engage.[7] It also became increasingly recognized that confinement to the mechanism of formalized quantitative inference was ill suited to social research. Indeed, Donald Campbell recanted his criticisms of qualitative methods, partly in response to growing dissatisfaction with experimentalist research and partly in response to developments in the philosophy of science.

> The polarity of quantitative-experimental versus qualitative approaches to research on social action remains unresolved, if resolution were to mean a predominant justification of one over the other. ... Each pole is at its best in its criticisms of the other, not in invulnerability of its own claims to descriptive knowledge. ... If we are to be truly scientific, we must reestablish the qualitative grounding of the quantitative. (Campbell, 1974, pp. 29–30)

The idea that social research should look to physics as the model to emulate had run its course. As Anthony Giddens remarked in 1976, "[T]hose who are still waiting for a Newton of social science aren't only waiting for a train that won't come in, they're waiting in the wrong station altogether" (p. 13). Because positivism is not a tenable epistemological view, particularly for social research, to include it among the epistemological perspectives in which research methods may be grounded frames the question of compatibilism in the wrong way. That positivism and interpretivism are incompatible epistemological frameworks is true, but it is also irrelevant. Properly framed, the question of compatibilism is whether quantitative and qualitative methods are compatible once positivism is removed from the picture. And, if so, in terms of what epistemological framework?

Beginning with Dewey, and continuing through Williard Van Orman Quine, Richard Rorty, Hilary Putnam, Richard Bernstein, Catherine Elgin, and Nancy Fraser, to name only a few, pragmatists and neopragmatists have been persistent and effective critics of positivist and positivist-inspired philosophy of science. In the process, pragmatists developed an alternative epistemological framework—sometimes referred to as a post- or anti-epistemological framework—based on the central premise, consistent with abandoning reductionism, that humans do not stand apart from and "map" the empirical world. Rather the empirical world and human constructions of it are inextricably woven. In the pragmatist view, *"[W]hat we call 'language' or 'mind' penetrate so deeply into what we call [empirical] 'reality' that the very project of representing ourselves as being 'mappers' of something 'language–independent' is fatally compromised from the very start"* (Putnam, 1990, p. 28, emphasis in original).

In a related vein, pragmatists characterize research methodology as being developed and refined in an ongoing fashion, by a back-and-forth process of mutual adjustment between research methods and general methodological-epistemological principles (Howe, 1988, 2003). The pragmatic approach makes no prior commitments to the general merits of quantitative versus qualitative methods or to any abstract, once-and-for-all epistemological framework that dictates methods. Pragmatism is committed to a thoroughgoing experimentalism that includes not just substantive scientific questions within its purview, but also the methodology used to frame and answer such questions (Howe, 2004). As Larry Laudan explains, "[M]ethodology [is] every bit as precarious epistemically as science itself. ... [O]ur knowledge about how to conduct inquiry hangs on the same thread from which dangle our best guesses about how the world is" (1996, p. 141).

The Fact/Value Dogma

The idea that facts and values occupy separate epistemic domains is deeply entrenched. And it underpins the admonition to social researchers to keep their investigations purged of values or to at least declare them as biases. Notwithstanding how this positivist-inspired ideal is almost universally disavowed, the belief that the subject matter to which social research applies its tools, as well as the findings it produces, can and ought to remain free of values remains pervasive among social researchers. As Michael Scriven warned, it continues to "rise from the ashes" (1983, p. 81).

The fact-value dichotomy is actually shorthand for a long list of dichotomies that includes the known versus felt, the cognitive versus noncognitive, the objective versus subjective, the rational versus emotional, the descriptive versus prescriptive, and the scientific versus political, among others. Claims that fall into the epistemic domain associated with the right side of the above pairs cannot satisfy reductionism's requirement that their truth conditions be specifiable in terms of purified empirical observation. But the idea that there is a dichotomy between facts and values representing two fundamentally different epistemic domains is but a corollary of reductionism. Following reductionism's collapse, "*the whole argument for the classical fact/value dichotomy was in ruins*" (Putnam, 2002, p. 30, emphasis in original). And so was the argument for value-free social research.

Social research is laden with values in two fundamental ways. First, the quasi-technical concepts social researchers use often have a significant value dimension, as in "literacy," "achievement," "accountability," "at risk," and "oppressed." Such concepts are "two-edged" (Howe, 1985, 2003), meaning that they roll facts and values into one claim. Because two-edged concepts are routinely and unavoidably incorporated into the descriptive vocabulary of social research, the values of certain subcommunities of researchers, policymakers, program designers, and so on are routinely and unavoidably woven into the fabric of social research.

The nature of these concepts may be illustrated by comparing the three descriptors "attends a high school of 500 students," "at risk," and "oppressed." There is no real evaluative edge to "attends a high school of 500 students."[8] By contrast, "at risk" and "oppressed" do have evaluative edges. Both evaluate the educational prospects of the students to whom they refer unfavorably. "Oppressed" also evaluates the social-cultural conditions at work against these students' prospects unfavorably. Placed on a continuum of value-ladenness, "attends a high school of 500 students" is at one end, "at risk" is in the middle, and "oppressed" is at the other. But, and this is the crux, claims that use "oppressed" are not less factual, or nonfactual, than are claims that use "at risk" or "attends a high school of 500 students," respectively. Rather, compared to these other two, claims that use "oppressed" provide thicker descriptions that require different empirical evidence to support, descriptions that can be true or false. Once we shake free of the fact/value dogma, there should be nothing odd or startling about evaluative claims being true or false: "[W]e need no better grounding for treating 'value judgments' as capable of truth and falsity than the fact that we can and do treatment them as capable of warranted assertibility and warranted deniability" (Putnam, 2002, p. 110).

In addition to being incorporated into the descriptive vocabulary of social research via two-edged concepts, values—political values, in particular—are also incorporated into its general methodological frameworks. Indeed, it is best to think not in terms of methodologies per se but in terms of political methodologies (Howe, 2005), for political commitments are unavoidable.

The scope and complexity of prospective interventions are determined by what is taken as given, or "fixed," which has discernable political import (Root, 1993). For example, where existing socioeconomic status (SES) stratification is construed as part of the fixed background against which reading remediation programs are implemented, it is beyond the purview of educational researchers to critically examine SES stratification in relation to obstacles faced by students in keeping pace with their peers in reading. Under these conditions, the task of researchers is to determine the best means of reading remediation within the maneuver space associated with status quo social-political-economic conditions. An experimental-quantitative approach is well suited for this kind of investigation. By contrast, where SES stratification is not taken as part of a fixed background but is included among the causes of the outcomes to be investigated, an interpretivist-qualitative approach is required, which includes methods that permit, for example, analyzing the effects of broad social structures and giving voice to research participants. Although the relationship between methodology and political commitments is neither straightforward nor universal, the above contrast captures a quite common feature of experimental-quantitative versus interpretivist-qualitative approaches. The contrast illustrates how, in "fixing" much of the political-economic status quo, the experimental-quantitative approach tends to be politically conservative compared to the interpretivist-qualitative approach.

In terms of its relationship to general political frameworks, any social research methodology must adopt some conception of the moral status of the human beings it engages in interactions (e.g., as *data sources* versus *interlocutors*); some procedure for drawing conclusions from the research process (e.g., *expert authority* versus *joint deliberation*); and some conception of what these conclusions are for (e.g., to be *implemented* versus *proffered*). How a social research methodology handles these determines its conception of the relationship between social research and democratic politics. Though much research would occupy places between the poles in the above contrasts, for purposes of illustration, the first member of each pair may identify with a technocratic conception of the role of educational research in democratic politics; the second, with a deliberative conception. I'll have more to say later about what kind of conception is best. My point here is that *some* conception of the relationship between social research and democratic politics is associated with any social research methodology—whether recognized and acknowledged or not—by virtue of assuming *some* stance on the moral status of research participants, procedures for drawing conclusions, and what conclusions are for—whether recognized and acknowledged or not. Moreover, what that conception is goes into determining the extent to which a given social research methodology—*political-methodology*—is adequate.

The Two Dogmas and the New Orthodoxy

As I indicated in the beginning of this chapter, the 2002 NRC Report *Scientific Research in Education* (SRE) is exemplary of the new orthodoxy. I use SRE because it is a very clear and comprehensive statement, produced by an impressive group of scholars.[9]

The view articulated in SRE, "mixed methods experimentalism," is moderate compared to the "neoclassical experimentalism" of the Campbell-Stanley tradition, which openly disdains qualitative methods (Howe, 2004). Like neoclassical experimentalism, however, SRE's mixed-methods experimentalism puts quantitative-experimental research methods and determining what works at the center of education science. Also like neoclassical experimentalism, it adopts randomized experiments as the methodological ideal for education science and calls for their increased use.

SRE divides scientific questions into three kinds—descriptive, causal relationship, and causal mechanism—and supports tailoring research methods to fit the question(s) at issue. Programs of education research proceed cumulatively: from describing and conjecturing, to establishing causal relationships, to understanding the mechanisms underlying such relationships. Within this cumulative process, SRE is receptive to a role for qualitative methods (part of a larger class of descriptive methods) but assigns them a subsidiary role. In particular, qualitative methods may suggest hypotheses to test and may suggest alternative hypotheses from "outside the study," but causal inference pertaining to what works falls within the exclusive purview of experimental methods (NRC, 2002, p. 108). SRE elevates experimental-quantitative methods to the top of a methodological hierarchy, adopting randomized experiments as the "ideal" (NRC, 2002, p. 109). In the language of positivism, quantitative methods do the real work of science in the "context of justification"; qualitative methods are relegated to the "context of discovery."

The high epistemic status SRE affords experimental methods complements its *regularity* conception of causation. A rudimentary example of a causal relationship that fits this conception is "T works to produce O, under C" (where T is some treatment, O is some outcome, and C is some set of conditions). SRE provides no response to the kinds of criticisms that historically dogged experimentalism's emphasis on investigating these kinds of relationships. For example, fixating on the search for regularities accessible via experimental methods results in myopia regarding the tradeoff between internal validity and external validity. Given the kind of flux that characterizes the social world, identified regularities within it are unstable. As Cronbach (1975) observed, such regularities "decay," which seriously limits the extent to which education science advanced by accumulating a stock of them.

A more fundamental problem with SRE's treatment of causation is its silence on the concept of "intentional causation." Intentional causation is required to explain human behavior in the form of norm-regulated *practices*—marrying, for example. Such practices cannot be rendered intelligible as mere regularities. They proceed from the *inside* in the sense that they must be understood in terms of the successful interpretation of norms and expectations by *agents*.[10] For example, the concept of a "resistance culture" provides a set of norms and expectations that explain how and why marginalized groups may defy school authority (Willis, 1977). Similarly, the "culture of romance" provides a set of norms and expectations that explains why college women may compromise their initial educational aspirations (Holland & Eisenhart, 1990). Since positivism gave way to the "interpretive turn," the idea that intentional causation is fundamental to the explanation of human behavior has become a widely shared premise in philosophy of social science.

For its part, SRE construes the intentional (volitional) features of human behavior as simply a problem for experimental research design: "Education is centrally concerned with people: learners, teachers, parents, citizens and policy makers. The volition, or will, of these individuals decreases the level of control that researchers can have over the process" (NRC, 2002, p. 86). The difference between causal inference in physics and education is thus construed along one dimension, that of the precision with which regularities can be determined. Because people behave more erratically than protons, educational research has to cope with the increased sources of "noise" and larger "error limits" compared to physics (NRC, 2002, p. 83).

According to SRE, the focus of education science is on establishing causal relationships about what works. But "What works?" is elliptical for "What works to produce valued outcomes?" And the valued outcomes of interest—the Os in "T works to produce O, under C"—are picked out by the kind of two-edged concepts described earlier: literacy, achievement, citizenship, cooperativeness, and so on. Again, by using such concepts, education researchers routinely—and unavoidably—introduce the values of certain subcommunities of education researchers, policymakers, curriculum designers, and so on, into the descriptive vocabulary of *scientific* education research. Value commitments are uniformly woven into the fabric of investigations of what works, notwithstanding how infrequently they may be actually identified and carefully examined.

With respect to the relationship between education research and democratic politics, SRE mildly protests how education research is often buffeted by changes in political winds and recommends that it be better shielded. Otherwise, SRE has little to say about the issue. The conception of the role of education research in democratic politics that may be attributed to SRE is the technocratic conception briefly alluded to earlier. At the heart of this conception is the idea that education science and democratic politics occupy separate domains: investigating relationships of whether, to what extent, at what monetary cost, etc.

"T works to produce O, under C" is in the domain of education science; what Os should be investigated and pursued or not in light of the information provided by education researchers is in the domain of democratic politics.

SRE's conception of the role of education research in democratic politics aligns with "aggregative democracy," a theory that has increasingly come under criticism as a consequence of the reemergence of "deliberative democracy" (e.g., Gutmann & Thompson, 2004). Below, I briefly characterize aggregative versus deliberative democracy and suggest why educational research should be aligned with the latter.

In investigating the relationship between social research and democracy in the early 20th century, John Dewey (1973) maintained that social research should be applied in human concerns, not *to* them. By this he meant two things: (1) Political import is *internal* to the conduct of social research, not something that can be culled and dealt with exclusively by people in roles other than social researcher; and (2) social research should have as its aim contributing to the formation of intelligent public opinion, not manipulating public opinion to serve more narrow "pecuniary" or political interests. The political theory in which Dewey embeds his view of social research is a forerunner of today's deliberative democratic theory.

Deliberative democratic theory places special emphasis on inclusive and fair participation in the political process. It requires participants to engage in good-faith critical dialog, whereby they (1) use "public reason," avoiding reasoning that others could not find acceptable, for example, sectarian reasoning; and (2) are open to revising their initially preferred policies and practices as a result of deliberating with others. The ideal goal of the process is to reach conclusions that will be accepted as reasonable (not necessarily as correct) by all concerned.

The principle of inclusion is paramount in deliberative democratic theory. Two types should be distinguished: "external" and "internal" (Young, 2004). External inclusion is *formal*, as in ensuring that marginalized groups are included in local face-to-face democratic forums. External inclusion is clearly a necessary condition of genuinely democratic procedures. But it is not sufficient. Internal, or *substantive*, inclusion is also required to ensure that, once admitted to the dialog, individuals are taken seriously—or afforded "recognition"[11]—rather than ignored, dismissed, patronized, or outmaneuvered by those with greater power and savvy.

This deliberative democratic conception of decision making contrasts sharply with the conception associated with "aggregative democracy" (e.g., Guttmann & Thompson, 2004). The aggregative conception takes initial preferences as given and exempts them from the need for justification. In contrast to a process of critical dialog that characterizes deliberative democracy, democratic decision making consists in merely aggregating preferences to produce collective decisions.[12] To the extent that dialog is a part of the process in aggregative democracy, it is *strategic* rather than *deliberative*; it is a process whereby individuals and groups attempt to win assent to their initial preferences using whatever gambits prove successful. The idea of subjecting initial preferences to critical evaluation and being open to revising them, central to deliberative democracy, is foreign to the aggregative conception of democratic decision making.

The technocratic conception of the relationship between education research and democratic politics is vulnerable to versions of two general criticisms parallel to criticisms of the broader idea of aggregative democracy. First, exempting the sought-after outcomes of education (the Os in "T works to produce O") from criticism and revision serves to entrench status quo distributions of goods and powers, which are by and large unjust. Such unjust distributions, in turn, preclude the possibility of effective participation in the education research process on the part of many citizens and, thus, the possibility of getting their voices heard in education policymaking and program development. Second, the technocratic conception needs to be defended rather than presumed. That such a defense could succeed is unlikely. The possibility—and desirability—of culling political values from educational research is grounded in moribund positivist principles.

Working out the relationship between educational research and democratic politics in any detail is more than I can undertake here (but see House & Howe, 1999; Howe, 2003). My aim in this section has been to use deliberative democratic theory to challenge the rigid science/politics dichotomy and associated technocratic conception of the political role of the educational research presumed by the new orthodoxy. I could be mistaken in my attribution or, perhaps, a technocratic conception is more defensible than I would have it. Still, it is telling that rather than addressing questions of value in specifying what good educational research is, the new orthodoxy has opted to take them off the table.

In summary, SRE endorses a *weak* form of compatibilism vis-à-vis the quantitative/qualitative dogma, in which interpretive-qualitative methods play a subsidiary role with respect to experimental-quantitative methods. This is quite consistent with positivism; it mirrors the epistemic difference between the "context of justification" and the "context of discovery," neglecting the true epistemic contribution to be made by interpretive-qualitative methods. SRE assumes a posture vis-à-vis the fact/value dogma also quite consistent with positivism. Values are not amenable to (reductionist) empirical tests, SRE's "Scientific Principle 1." Values are thus beyond the purview of science, to be hammered out in political forums and mused about by philosophers using non-(un-?) scientific methods.

The Third Dogma of Educational Research

Educational researchers in the humanities tradition are more likely to be concerned about and conversant with values issues when attempting to specify the features of "good educational research" (Hostetler, 2005) than are researchers in the empirical social science tradition. But the new orthodoxy excludes the content and methods of humanities-oriented research from the conversation. SRE distinguishes scientific research in education from other kinds of scholarship in terms of the criterion of empirical testability—a criterion interpreted so as to exclude philosophy and history, humanities-oriented research in general, from the domain of scientific research, isolating them from the intellectual activity identified as the key to improving education policy and practice. Whereas SRE alludes to the idea that scientific research in education may be informed by the humanities, its failure to in any way elaborate it renders this but lip service.

The dualism between the humanities and empirical social research—the third dogma—is a positivist throwback, just like the first two dogmas. The idea that empirical testability may serve as the criterion to draw a line of demarcation separating science from non-science is a version of the central tenet—reductionism—on which positivism foundered. In the social sciences, the line of demarcation became especially blurred with the advent of interpretivist methodology, in which the aims, requisite skills, and vocabularies of the humanities and empirical social science significantly overlap.

Research in the humanities has important empirical dimensions and is thus not properly conceived as exclusive of, or as an alternative to, empirical research. The array of humanities research in education engages the empirical world by assuming general empirical premises, by appealing to existing empirical research, and by employing its own methods of empirical investigation. There is a continuum here that is suggestively captured by distinguishing humanities-*oriented* from empirically *oriented* research. Humanities-oriented questions differ from empirically oriented questions in large part by the ease with which they are verified or falsified by relatively straightforward empirical testing. For instance, the question of whether No Child Left Behind serves to enhance the health of our democracy is farther removed from straightforward empirical testing than the subsidiary question of whether it serves to narrow achievement gaps. But an answer to the first question is not independent of an answer to the second.

There is no epistemological justification for setting up the dualism between empirically oriented and humanities-oriented research in education. In turn, there is no justification for culling humanities-oriented concerns, particularly the critical investigation of values, from the conduct of empirical research and policy analysis and, in the process, externalizing them from the content and methodology of scientific research in education.

Concluding Observations

To say that the line between the humanities and empirical social research cannot be drawn on fundamental epistemological grounds is not to say that the disciplines cannot be distinguished from one another in significant ways. But the way the new orthodoxy isolates humanities-oriented research from empirically oriented research in education obscures rather than illuminates how the disciplines

function. The varieties of education research are better characterized in terms of a continuum that ranges from evaluation based to
discipline based (Howe, 2005). Evaluation-based research focuses
on determining what works (and doesn't work) at both the level
of policy (e.g., school choice) and pedagogy (e.g., reading instruction). The disciplines are often interwoven into evaluation-based
research as appropriate (e.g., philosophy and economics in the case
of school choice; cognitive psychology and anthropology in the
case of reading instruction). Evaluation-based research may not
explicitly enlist any disciplines at all but simply ascertain the effectiveness of given education interventions to produce given outcomes. Discipline-based research focuses on pursuing questions in
education as framed by a discipline (e.g., in anthropology, how the
concept of culture can be used to illuminate the behavior of children in schools). Such research is abstract and theoretical by comparison to the evaluation-based variety. It may (arguably, should)
ultimately help frame and answer what works questions but is not
pursued with that aim immediately in mind.

Specialization in the disciplines is a deeply rooted, probably permanent feature of scientific research and may be justified in terms of the different issues and methods that distinguish
the humanities from empirically oriented social research. Indeed,
numerous disciplinary subdivisions are legitimate within both
humanities-oriented and empirically oriented research in education. But deference to specialization goes too far when it results
in the kind of isolation of empirically oriented from humanities-
oriented research that goes with the third dogma. What is called
for under these circumstances is a much greater emphasis on
interdisciplinary collaboration between empirically oriented and
humanities-oriented educational researchers.

Interdisciplinary collaboration comes in different forms. Much
interdisciplinary research consists of a "juxtaposition of monodisci-
plines" (Sperber, 2003), each addressing the same question(s) from
a different vantage point. This form is an advance over balkaniza-
tion, but the ideal form of interdisciplinarity, particularly in evaluation-based educational research, would consist of a thoroughgoing
form of collaboration across humanities- and empirically oriented
education research. It would start with problem formulation and
continue through analysis and interpretation of results.

Some of my own research approximates this ideal (e.g., Howe & Ashcraft, 2005; Howe, Eisenhart & Betebenner, 2001), and I suspect many other examples could be found. But redirecting the design of a substantial number of individual educational studies so that this approach becomes the norm is probably not in the offing. In general, the organizational and reward structure of the profession, particularly specialization and the imperative to demonstrate one's status as recognized expert by publishing in specialized journals, constitutes a significant impediment to this kind of research. This is not to suggest that specialization is a bad thing per se, only that it needs to be kept in better balance. Short of close collaboration within education studies becoming the norm, then, an *interdisciplinary spirit* could—and should— be infused into the educational research community, in which exchanges across the line currently isolating humanities-oriented from empirically oriented lines would become much more a commonplace. A good place to begin is with doctoral programs that prepare educational researchers (Bullough, 2006).[13] The alternative path is the one prescribed by the third dogma: Divide educational researchers into "two cultures" and police the borders.

Notes

1. The idea of a "crisis in the humanities" has some currency. A Google search of the exact expression on June 2, 2007 produced 1,140 hits.

2. "Interpretive turn" is attributed to Rabinow and Sullivan (1979).

3. IES was mandated by the Education Sciences Reform Act (H.R. 3801 [2002]).

4. Several prominent journals have devoted entire issues or special sections to the topic. Examples include a major section on "scientific research in education" in *Educational Researcher* 31(8), 2002; the entire issue of *Qualitative Inquiry* 10(4), 2004; a symposium on "the education science question" in *Educational Theory* 55(2), 2005; and an issue of *Teacher's College Record* 107(1), 2005, devoted to the implications of scientific research in education for qualitative inquiry. In addition to the special section in *Educational Researcher* referred to above, a series of articles in various ways critical of the new orthodoxy have appeared, including Bullough (2006), Freeman et al. (2007), Johnson and Onwuegbuzie (2004), and Hostetler (2005).

5. I do not believe this problem with the AERA standards is necessarily irremediable. Recognizing that the array of approaches in the field of educational research is broader than that encompassed by the standards for empirical research, AERA subsequently organized a task force charged with developing standards for humanities-oriented research. I am a member of this task force; deliberations were ongoing during the writing of this chapter.

6. Quine's critique targeted the empiricist tradition generally, but I avoid that complication here. Positivism is a paradigm version of empiricism.

7. I use "interpretivism" in an expansive way, to include a variety of postpositivist views, which insist that social research requires a special "intentionalist" vocabulary and an associated array of qualitative methods. The kind of (pragmatic) view in which I anchor interpretivism (Howe, 1988, 1998, 2003) denies that social research should be interpretivist where that means excluding the general kinds of methods and vocabularies used in natural science.

There is a large and established literature in this vein in the theory and philosophy of social science that has yet to be brought to bear on the education science question. It finds its contemporary roots in seminal work such as Jurgen Habermas's *Knowledge and Human Interests* (1971) and Anthony Giddens's *New Rules of Sociological Method* (1976). More recently, feminist philosophers such as Lorraine Code and Sandra Harding, among others, have joined the conversation. See, for example, Harding's *Social Science and Inequality: Feminist and Postcolonial Issues* (2006) and the collection by Linda Alcoff and Elizabeth Potter, *Feminist Epistemologies* (1993). Feminist social researchers have also joined in. See, for example, Mary M. Fonow and Judith A. Cook, *Beyond Methodology: Feminist Scholarship and Lived Research* (1991).

8. Of course, it would routinely occur in claims that do have an evaluative edge, for example, "A student who attends a high school with 535 students will get a better education than one who attends a high school of 2,000." It could also acquire a positive evaluative edge through association with small high schools.

9. I should make clear that the document is the target of my criticisms, not members of the NRC committee. They went about their task in a politically charged situation and, no doubt, made many compromises. As far as I know, none of them is completely satisfied with the result.

10. This general idea has a long history in the social sciences and is associated with challenges to the unity of science. It can be found as early as the 18th century, in the work of Italian philosopher Giambattista Vico, who argued that human behavior is inherently historical and thus not subject to the kind universality and certainty attributed to natural science by leading philosophers such as Descartes. The German philosopher Wilhelm Dilthey's echoed Vico's view in the 19th century, employing a distinction between *Naturwissenshaften* (natural science) and *Giesteswissenshaften* (social science). *Giesteswissenshaften* is characterized by the goal of "understanding," which is achieved through empathy with other human beings. *Naturwissenshaften*,

by contrast, is characterized by the goal of (causal) "explanation," which is achieved by documenting regularities in the occurrence of events.

In the 20th century, central work in the vein includes Peter Winch's *The Idea of a Social Science and Its Relation to Philosophy* (1958); Georg Henrik von Wright's *Explanation and Understanding* (1971/1997); John Searle's *Minds, Brains and Science* (1984) and *The Construction of Social Reality* (1995); and Daniel Dennett's *The Intentional Stance* (1987). The references cited in note 6 are also germane.

11. Charles Taylor (1994) brought the concept of "recognition" to prominence in political theory. It remains a central concept, even as deliberative theorists such as Benhabib (2002) and Young (2004) challenge Taylor's analysis of it, which, they believe, too sharply distinguishes recognition from matters of distribution.

12. The general characterization of aggregative democracy here parallels quite closely how I have elsewhere criticized "emotive democracy" (House & Howe, 1999; Howe, 2003).

13. In our doctoral program at Boulder we have made an effort to provide students with a more well-rounded experience and to facilitate interaction across disciplinary and methodological boundaries. Its seven required core courses are made up of two in quantitative methods, two in qualitative methods, and one each in three substantive areas, teaching and learning, education policy and research, and multicultural education. Several issues are examined in both the methodological and substantive courses. Bullough might be encouraged to know that the policy and research course emphasizes historical and philosophical contexts. It includes Tyack's *One Best System* and several readings from Dewey on political and educational theory.

References

Alcoff. L., & E. Potter, Eds. 1993. *Feminist epistemologies*. New York: Routledge.

American Educational Research Association (AERA). 2006. Standards for reporting on empirical social science research in AERA publications. http://aera.net/opportunities/?id=1480 (accessed March 12, 2007).

Benhabib, S. 2002. *The claims of culture*. Princeton, NJ: Princeton University Press.

Bullough, R. 2006. Developing interdisciplinary researchers: Whatever happened to the humanities in education? *Educational Researcher* 35(8):3–10.

Campbell, D. (1974). Qualitative knowing in action research. Kurt Lewin Award address, Society for the Psychological Study of Social Issues, presented at the 81st annual meeting of the American Psychological Association, New Orleans, September 14.

Campbell, D., & J. Stanley. 1963. *Experimental and quasi-experimental designs for research*. Chicago: Rand McNally.

Condliffe Lageman, E. (2000). *An elusive science: The troubling history of education research*. Chicago: University of Chicago Press.

Cronbach, L. (1975). Beyond the two disciplines of scientific psychology. *American Psychologist* 30(2):116–27.

Dennett, D. (1987). *The intentional stance*. Boston: The MIT Press.

Dewey, J. (1973). Search for the great community. In J. McDermott (Ed.), *The philosophy of John Dewey*, pp. 620–42. Chicago: University of Chicago Press.

Firestone, W. 1987. Meaning in method: The rhetoric of quantitative and qualitative research. *Educational Researcher* 16(7):16–21.

Fonow, M., & J. Cook, Eds. 1991. *Beyond methodology: Feminist scholarship and lived research*. Bloomington: Indiana University Press.

Freeman, M., K. deMarrais, J. Preissle, K. Roulston, & E. St. Pierre. (2007). Standards of evidence in qualitative research: An incitement to discourse. *Educational Researcher* 36(1):25–32.

Giddens, A. 1976. *New rules of sociological method*. New York: Basic Books.

Guba, E. (1987). What have we learned about naturalistic evaluation? *Evaluation Practice* 8(1):23–43.

Gutmann, A., & D. Thompson. 2004. *Why deliberative democracy?* Princeton, NJ: Princeton University Press.

Habermas, J. 1971. *Knowledge and human interests*. Boston: Beacon Press.

Harding, S. 2006. *Social science and inequality: Feminist and postcolonial issues*. Urbana: University of Illinois Press.

Holland, D., & M. Eisenhart. 1990. *Educated in romance: Women, achievement and college culture*. Chicago: University of Chicago Press.

Hostetler, K. 2005. What is "good" education research? *Educational Research* 34(6):16–21.

House, E., & K. Howe. 1999. *Values in evaluation and social research*. Thousand Oaks, CA: Sage.

Howe, K. 1985. Two dogmas of educational research. *Educational Researcher* 14(8):10–18.

Howe, K. 1988. Against the quantitative-qualitative incompatibility thesis (or dogmas die hard). *Educational Researcher* 17(8):10–16.

Howe, K. 1998. The interpretive turn and the new debate in education. *Educational Researcher* 27(8):13–20.

Howe, K. 2003. *Closing methodological divides: Toward democratic educational research*. Dordrecht, Netherlands: Kluwer.

Howe, K. 2004. A critique of experimentalism. *Qualitative Inquiry* 10(4):42–61.

Howe, K. 2005. The question of education science: Experimentism versus experimentalism. *Educational Theory* 55(3):307–22.

Howe, K., & C. Ashcraft. 2005. Deliberative democratic evaluation: Successes and limitations of an evaluation of school choice. *Teachers College Record* 7(10):2274–97.

Howe, K., M. Eisenhart, & D. Betebenner. 2001. School choice crucible: A case study of Boulder Valley. *Phi Delta Kappan* 83(2):137–46.

Johnson, R., & A. Onwuegbuzie. 2004. Mixed methods research. A research paradigm whose time has come. *Educational Researcher* 33(7):14–26.

Kuhn, T. 1962. *The structure of scientific revolutions*. Chicago: University of Chicago Press.

Laudan, L. 1996. *Beyond positivism and relativism*. Boulder, CO: Westview Press.

Mackenzie, B. 1977. *Behaviorism and the limits of scientific method*. Atlantic Highlands, NJ: Humanities Press.

National Research Council (NRC). 2002. *Scientific research in education*. Washington, DC: National Academy Press.

National Research Council (NRC). 2004. *Advancing scientific research in education*. Washington, DC: National Academy Press.

Passmore, J. 1967. Logical positivism. In P. Edwards (Ed.), *The encyclopedia of philosophy*, vol. 5, pp. 52–57. New York: The Free Press.

Putnam, H. 1990. *Realism with a human face*. Cambridge, MA: Harvard University Press.

Putnam, H. 2002. *The collapse of the fact/value dichotomy*. Cambridge, MA: Harvard University Press. Quine, W. V. O. 1951. Two dogmas of empiricism. *The Philosophical Review* 60(1):20–43.

Rabinow, P., & W. Sullivan. 1979. The interpretive turn: Emergence of an approach. In P. Rabinow & W. Sullivan (Eds.), *Interpretive social science*, pp. 1–21. Los Angeles: University of California Press.

Reichardt, C., & T. Cook. 1979. Beyond qualitative versus quantitative methods. In T. Cook & C. Reichardt (Eds.), *Qualitative and quantitative methods in evaluation research*, pp. 7–32. Beverly Hills, CA: Sage.

Root, M. 1993. *Philosophy of social science*. Cambridge, MA: Blackwell.

Scriven, M. 1983. The evaluation taboo. In E. House (Ed.), *Philosophy of evaluation*, pp. 75–82. San Francisco: Jossey-Bass.

Searle, J. 1984. *Minds, brains and science*. Cambridge, MA: Harvard University Press.

Searle, J. 1995. *The construction of social reality*. New York: The Free Press.

Smith, J. K., & L. Heshusius. 1986. Closing down the conversation: The end of the quantitative-qualitative debate among educational researchers. *Educational Researcher* 15(l):4–12.

Snow, C. P. 1959. *The two cultures*. Cambridge: Cambridge University Press.

Sperber, D. 2003. Why rethink interdisciplinarity? http://www.interdisciplines.org/interdisciplinarity/papers/1 (accessed March 12, 2007).

Taylor, C. 1994. The politics of recognition. In A. Gutmann (Ed.), *Multiculturalism: Examining the politics of recognition*, pp. 25–74. Princeton, NJ: Princeton University Press.

Willis, P. 1977. *Learning to labor: How working class kids get working class jobs.* Farnborough, UK: Saxon House.

Winch, P. 1958. *The idea of a social science and its relation to philosophy*. London: Routledge.

Wright, G. H. von. 1971/1997. *Explanation and understanding*. Ithaca, NY: Cornell University Press.

Yanchar, S., & D. Williams. 2006. Reconsidering the compatibility thesis and eclecticism: Five proposed guidelines for method use. *Educational Researcher* 35(9):3–12.

Young, I. M. 2004. *Inclusion and democracy*. New York: Oxford University Press.

4 | A Fine Line

Positioning Qualitative Inquiry in the Wake of the Politics of Evidence[1]

Julianne Cheek
University of South Australia

Setting the Scene

Life as a qualitative researcher is a constant struggle: in the academy, workplace, or wherever qualitative researchers are found. Daily, qualitative inquirers are assaulted by the increasing pursuit of certainty with respect to research quality, impact, or other measures of research output. Such a quest is evident from the ever-present desire of governments, administrators, universities, and the like to control, predict, and erase the messiness of our existence, including that of our research. Yet, at the same time, we live and research in uncertain times, both globally and in a multitude of different ways at our local levels. Consequently, we work and exist in contradictory spaces.

For example, we hear much about vigorous, innovative, and cutting-edge qualitative inquiry. We celebrate the continued expansion and development of this field as it continues to push methodological and substantive boundaries, thereby moving into new and exciting spaces (see, e.g., Denzin & Lincoln, 2005; Denzin, Lincoln, & Giardina, 2006). But paradoxically, we also hear a loud and clear message about the continued contraction of spaces for both qualitative research and researchers. These contracted spaces are bounded by narrowing understandings about research and what constitutes research evidence. Such a contraction is an outworking of the politics of evidence.

This is a politics focusing on contested notions of evidence. It is both about the way we do our research (the methods or procedures used to produce the evidence) and concomitant ways of thinking about what form(s) evidence must take for it to be considered valid, acceptable, and therefore useful. It is a politics that seeks to insert the certain into all aspects of research endeavors, and it is fueled by understandings largely driven by policies and guidelines developed by neoliberal agencies and governments. In turn, such policies and guidelines derive from notions of the research marketplace, and researchers as commodities in that place. Such thinking overtly links politics, research, and evidence. Ironically, it does so using the rhetoric of scientism with its reification of so-called objective and value-free measures of the quality of research evidence. Yet, the politics of evidence is anything but objective and value free. As Goldenberg (2006, pp. 2630–31) points out, the "appeal to the authority of evidence that characterizes evidence-based practices does not *increase* objectivity but rather *obscures* the subjective elements that inescapably enter all forms of human inquiry."

This political climate creates a paradox that confronts us all. On the one hand, there appears to be the promise of a seemingly certain future for the continued development of robust, innovative, and cutting-edge qualitative inquiry. On the other hand, there has never been a more uncertain time, given the rise of the evidence-based movements, with their colonization, prescription, and determination of what constitutes rigor, evidence, and even research. These movements embody normative assumptions about not only "what is supposedly objectively 'true' but also what is 'good' and demands our dutiful obedience" (Murray et al., 2007, p. 516). This paradox affects research and researchers in general, including some who may not be qualitative researchers but who may not be dutifully obeying by, for example, researching nonpolitically sanctioned substantive focuses, not denigrating qualitative studies on the basis of hierarchies of evidence, or choosing to publish in places not on a prescribed list of so-called top-tier journals developed for the purpose of research assessment exercises (Mylonopoulos & Theoharakis, 2001). It is with this context in mind that the following discussion enfolds regarding the positioning of qualitative inquiry and inquirers in the wake of the politics of evidence.

A Call for a Re-view?

As qualitative researchers, we often talk about the need to consider our place in the research process; where we are coming from in terms of our assumptions and understandings; and how these might impact on our choice of topics, approaches, and analyses. But perhaps we have not done as much of that sort of thinking as we might regarding the issues and questions we raise, which seem to occupy our time and thinking, and regarding qualitative research and the politics of evidence. What are the things we choose to highlight and focus on in that debate, and conversely, what do we choose to ignore? Do our assumptions and understandings frame, and even determine, what is discussed? After all, it is not just proponents of the evidence-based orthodoxies who are setting parameters in this political arena. As qualitative researchers, we are doing so as well.

Put another way, I am suggesting that rather than simply being an assumed position or a starting point from which our discussion of the positioning of qualitative research proceeds, the issues and questions *themselves* that we identify to shape this discussion are an integral part of that positioning. If we only react and respond to questions, without really thinking about, for example, if these are *the* questions to ask, what these questions do, if these questions might change over time, or whether there are others that could be, but are not being asked, then the subsequent discussion and answers will, and can only ever be, the ones that the questions enable in the first place. This creates the possibility for a situation in which we continue to be buffeted in the spaces that the questions, rather than the answers, create. For it is the question that is asked that creates the possibilities for what answers can be given. Yet it is to the answers that our focus is inexorably drawn, and often variants of the same old answers are given so that the questions, with all their assumptions and baggage, remain intact.

This has the potential to lead to a static and conservative

positioning of qualitative research and researchers. Even so-called radical discussions might be viewed as delimited radical discussions because they occur only within what are essentially conservative parameters, derived, in turn, from taken-for-granted assumptions about qualitative research and the boundaries that operate both within and without of itself theoretically and methodologically. So, do we assume a homogeneous or static definition of qualitative inquiry? Do we assume an absolute incommensurability of thought and nonpermeability in terms of the lines that are drawn between scientific agencies and the qualitative community? And does this put us in danger of being open to the charge of fundamentalist tendencies, albeit with respect to qualitative inquiry itself? Schwandt (2006, p. 809) has something to say about this when he posits that it is far less important to be identifying enemies and threats to qualitative inquiry than to be developing and pursuing activist qualitative inquiry agendas. Drawing on Topper (2005, pp. 181, 215), he asks what if we were:

> to endorse a conception of inquiry that is at once "scientific *and* critical" rigorous *and* heterodox, structured *and* patchwork ... what if we were less concerned with defining QI as the binary opposite of some other way of knowing and more concerned with developing an ongoing commitment to forms of critical pluralism that sustain communication across theoretical and methodological boundaries?

It is therefore *the questions* concerning the positioning of qualitative inquiry in the wake of the politics of evidence that I want to focus on here: What questions are being asked, by whom, when, and why? *And, crucially, what questions are being asked from within qualitative inquiry itself, not simply of it by others?* My aim is to stimulate ideas for developing new and different questions, thus opening up the possibility for new and different strategies, thinking, and action as to the positioning of qualitative research. What follows are some thoughts about how we might think and act differently or "as well as" in relation to the very fine, or perhaps the very thin, line that we walk and talk when positioning ourselves and our forms of inquiry. Put another way, I am trying to try to write *against* the questions we ask. I am drawing here on an idea of Judith Butler's when she talks about "disobedience to the principles by which one is formed" (Butler, 2002, p. 20). This is an idea that has been picked up in a number of contexts and used for a number of substantive focuses. It asks us to:

> rethink critique as a practice in which we pose the questions of the limits of our most sure ways of knowing ... because one has run up against a crisis within the ... field in which one lives. The categories by which social life are ordered [read our questions about qualitative inquiry] produce a certain incoherence or entire realms of unspeakability. And it is from this condition ... that the practice of critique emerges, with the awareness that no discourse is adequate here or that our reigning discourse [e.g. framing of the issues/questions and the subsequent answers/types of discussion] have produced an impasse. (Butler, 2002, p. 5)

It is time for us, as qualitative researchers, to begin to write against ourselves a little more in relation to the questions, and, concomitantly, the so-called answers we promulgate with respect to the positioning of our research and ourselves in the wake of the politics of evidence. We have to take a long hard look at ourselves and our practices and refuse (or at least challenge) the world, both as it is handed down to us and as we hand it down among ourselves and to others. Is it really a matter of polemics—either we sell out or remain "pure" but irrelevant? Is there some sort of middle ground or even middle grounds? If so, what might they be?

Toward Writing against Ourselves

I was reading an article by Denzin, Lincoln, and Giardina (2006) called "Disciplining Qualitative Research." At the end of the article is a section titled Coda. Here, the authors note a level of growth over the past two decades in the practice and development of qualitative inquiry as well as in the training of new inquirers in qualitative inquiry. At the same time, what they term "centripetal forces" are "attempting to return us to a central and unified discourse around what constitutes 'science'" (p. 778). They write that despite these forces:

> Still, students sign up in large numbers for whatever training they can get. Qualitative methods books, particularly those that demonstrate some innovation in qualitative research methods, such

as work on Internet research, or visual methods, or documentary usage, sell extremely well. Such signs seem to indicate that against all odds, qualitative research is mature and thriving, and inquirers-in-training want to know all they can about how to practice such arts and sciences. (Denzin, Lincoln, & Giardina, 2006, p. 778)

Such a statement is full of optimism and hope for the future of qualitative inquiry. However, I felt myself troubled by it. I couldn't seem to connect with it at all and I wondered why. Why didn't I feel the same positive things about these particular signs? What was troubling me?

An e-mail I received while I was reading this article provided me with a way of exploring this sense of unease. It helped me focus on not only the paradoxes and the consequent fine line that confronts us all but also on the way in which, by asking slightly different questions of such paradoxes, we can begin to write against ourselves in relation to our positioning in the wake of the politics of evidence. The e-mail was from a researcher in Canada whom I have never met but who had read some of the things I had written about the politics and practice of research. The e-mail detailed his experiences when submitting what he termed exploratory proposals for ethics and scientific review and his concern over these review processes, particularly as, and now I use his words, "we all know, ethics and scientific review often direct what gets considered for funding and what does not and therefore it has been a crucial step for me to consider." He went on to ask me the question that is central to this discussion. Again I use his words:

> How do you find the middle ground between (appearing to be) complaining, and saying to heck with it all? I have been trying to address this issue by inviting a discussion of the framing of research, particularly what is implied and assumed in the conventional definition of research. Any suggestions you might have from your experience would be greatly appreciated. (personal communication, February 16, 2007)

Two things struck me about this e-mail. The first was the need to make sure qualitative inquirers can obtain help in a very practical, down-to-earth way to navigate the apparatuses (in this case, ethics and review committees) that have been built up around the evidence movement. Such assistance has to be grounded in the reality of the everyday and be cognizant of the pressures that face researchers in terms of having to gain and retain a job, get promoted, and so forth. In other words, we need strategies for moving the talk about positioning ourselves into action—but it must be realistic action. The second thing that struck me from the e-mail was that it did not seem that such help was readily accessible and/or available. So I decided to do a little research myself. I tried to put myself in the position of a researcher in a fairly isolated working environment, not necessarily geographically but perhaps methodologically, who is confronting these types of gatekeeping mechanism. Where would I go for help? What would I find? Then what would I do?

Searching the literature, I pulled up a few articles with ideas about, or examples of, how to practically navigate ethics committees, review boards, funding bodies, citation indices, or research assessment exercises. Of these, very few were written with qualitative research as the organizing frame for the discussion. In other words, *we* (qualitative researchers) are not writing them! Our writing still seems to be a step removed from the actual in this regard. We do have incisive and considered contributions to the debate and literature by a number of prominent qualitative researchers who expose the issues and the agendas behind the evidence movement (Denzin & Giardina, 2006).

We have calls to action including the need to defend ourselves from the fall out of the evidence-based agendas (e.g., Lincoln & Cannella, 2004; Murray et al, 2007). But we have few contributions, at the level of how to actually *do* this, that would be useful to a person in the situation that the author of the e-mail found himself in. And this begs the question: Why is this the case? Qualitative researchers who sit on review panels, boards, and so on have a wealth of experience in this regard, and although we may well be sharing this expertise as much as we can both locally and more formally, this expertise is not easy to find and not readily available for others to use. As qualitative researchers, we do not seem to be capturing and therefore building our collective expertise and wisdom in this regard in a systematic or readily accessible way.

I then returned to the observation made in the article by

Denzin, Lincoln, and Giardina (2006) that there has been an explosion of workshops and training courses, and inquirers-in-training want to know all they can about how to practice such arts and sciences. So I attempted to find these courses and workshops and see what they were about. What did I find? Most of the qualitative-related workshops were about specific methods or approaches. Some were about theories and some about writing. But very few were about aspects of navigating the positioning of qualitative inquiry in the wake of the politics of evidence and surviving as a qualitative researcher in such a context. In fact, I found practically none.

What I did find, though, were numbers of this type of workshop for a general audience run by either administrators, such as research office personnel, or by scientists who had no background in qualitative methods. Such workshops included ones about how to do something for a defined, particular need, such as preparing proposals for specific funding schemes (e.g., Australian Research Council workshops, Framework 7 workshops[2]), how to compile your individual researcher portfolio for the Research Quality Framework (RQF),[3] and even workshops about how to apply for promotion, usually run at local levels. Not surprisingly, the promotional material and content (where stated) of such workshops/sessions was replete with assumptions about research and evidence that a qualitative researcher would need to challenge in the workshop or run the risk of not fitting at all and therefore being viewed as irrelevant as a participant. Such a situation, of course, heightens the risk of it seeming that qualitative researchers are always complaining, perverse, difficult, or different.

Further, in such a scenario, fitting into the workshop and fitting research-related outcomes to what is being discussed becomes the researcher's problem—an individual problem that diverts attention from the bigger underlying issues. Would it not be better, in fact is it not absolutely crucial, for us to start developing and conducting this type of workshop in a way in which qualitative inquiry is a valid starting point, and guidelines for funding schemes, portfolios, or promotion are recognized as problematic? *But also* (and this is the middle ground), shouldn't qualitative researchers be devising workshops for which the outcome is a practical guide on *how* to meet the requirements for reporting and presenting our work? We should be developing these skills in a way that we can live with, one that does not require us to sell out on our beliefs and that enables us to know what we are doing and why so that we can start thinking about how to change things through understanding how best to work with them and on them. This is part of the engagement of qualitative research with "the intellectual, historical, social, cultural and political landscapes" (Schwandt, 2006, p. 803) in which it is situated.

For example, I may not be able to avoid having to compile an individual research portfolio[4] for the RQF. *But* in doing it, I can learn everything there is to know about this portfolio and how to navigate it so that I can both meet its requirements and work from a strong and inside position to change it. To do so is to explore such practices from a qualitative inquiry viewpoint; it is no longer trying to fit qualitative inquiry into existing frames only to be perceived as inherently problematic. In this way, the discussion has a different frame—it is the guidelines or requirements that are problematic, and the discussion is therefore about what we must do (pragmatics) and why (politics of evidence), rather than what we must not do (qualitative inquiry) and why not (because it is not science, it does not fit).

This is not just playing with words—it is a matter of strategy and a way of thinking that turns the issue upside down. This inversion strategy has worked for me and enables me to try to change things—but usually from the inside and from the front foot, rather than from an external position and constantly on the back foot. At worst, it can promote tolerance; at best, it nurtures understanding and acceptance of qualitative inquiry. It is to build on and extend the observation that inquirers-in-training want to know all they can about how to practice such arts and sciences. Such practice, I believe, is as much about learning how to navigate the politics of research as it is about learning methods.

Given this way of thinking, a new and different set of questions emerges: Why are we not systematically developing and conducting workshops and writing about these sorts of things? Why, for example, in Australia, are we not having systematic and coordinated discussions about how qualitative researchers can best organize and present individual researcher portfolios? Why do we not work out who could best advocate our position on strategic committees, such as RQF panels, work with each other to make it happen, and then ensure that those people share all that they have learned? Is it because at times a subtle (or not so subtle) form of competitive individualism or institutionalism seems to collide with, and maybe even cloud, the collective working for the common good? Or is it because we have thought of middle ground too much, or even exclusively, in terms of developing methods and techniques that try to incorporate/integrate a variety of approaches, such as mixed methods? Maybe we aren't progressing because we haven't really given enough thought to the idea of a middle ground at all.

Toward a Middle Ground?

Implications for the positioning of qualitative inquiry in the wake of the politics of evidence arise from this notion of a middle ground. How can we think of this middle ground in new and different ways? How can we position ourselves in this place? Despite the undoubted advances that have been made, we have a huge gap in the development of qualitative research and researchers, and it is a gap of our own, not others', making. It is all very well for us to bemoan the effects of the politics of evidence and know that it represents a serious and sustained attack on us and our research approaches. We do act by critiquing it at every turn to expose its fundamentalist tendencies and inherent flaws. But this, although absolutely crucial, is not enough. I am suggesting that there is a need for a new type of action—dare I even say activism. As qualitative researchers, it is entirely possible that we, too, can become very comfortable, even satisfied, with the almost routinized positions that we take up in relation to, or the rules of engagement we have with, the politics of evidence. Is it possible that many of us, myself included, slip into the safe and comfortable position within a space from which we can critique and attack, but from which we never have to venture out?

Certainly we need to be talking about the effects of the politics of evidence and tearing apart the flawed assumptions underpinning much of the talk and action associated with it. But surely, equally, we need to be building—not only building our lines of defense and/or attack, but also building common ground where communication and even clearly delimited collaboration with this movement (and I know that for some this is unpalatable) might exist. Otherwise, how are we going to get our voices heard beyond our own networks? It is absolutely no use if what we discuss or read and write among ourselves goes nowhere as a result. Certainly, it is crucial that we enjoy such communication as offering us both time to reflect and a place where we can comfort, sustain, nourish, and support each other. But equally we need to be building our strategy, building our development, working out the way(s) *we will engage* the politics of evidence, rather than *having* to engage with it, or worse, have *it constantly engage us* and use our time and energy destructively. That is the material of despair—for then it truly will have positioned us! And we could be seen as complicit in that positioning by virtue of our inaction in terms of the way we position ourselves.

We need to be alert to the opportunities that sometimes the quest for, and pursuit of, evidence create for us. We may find allies in unlikely places. Of course, the challenge for us in all of this is that we are clear about what the impact of our work has been or putting it another way, can point to some of the benefits (be they clinical, societal, theoretical, methodological, and so on) of us having done that research. Because if we cannot do that, then there is another set of serious questions that need to be asked, including why do that research in the first place? And why should we not have to justify what we do? We cannot use qualitative inquiry as something to hide behind—for to do so has the potential to be just as a potent form of methodolatry and fundamentalism as those forms we so strenuously critique as arising from, and creating, the wake of the politics of evidence. Some of the assumptions underpinning what may be considered the most sacred of qualitative rituals and practices are challenged in a witty and incisive article in *Qualitative Health Research* written by Thorne and Darbyshire (2005). They assert that it is time to rediscover some of the lost art of critique. Not the brand of critique that is no more than picking fault and quarrel with positions other than your own, but the more nostalgic notion of critique, which recognizes that as qualitative researchers, our own practices, positions, and pronouncements might merit some of the same caustic scrutiny usually reserved for the methodological or philosophical Other.

So, where to from here?

For all of us, living and researching as we do in a world replete with contradictions and uncertainty, a key question is whether we can deal with and live with uncertainty in every aspect of research and research practice. How can we ensure our research reflects such uncertainty and can thrive despite such contradictions? How can we think less of polar oppositions or dichotomies such as good/ bad practices or having/not having voice in research, methods, or research assessment? Can we as qualitative researchers instead tolerate what Agamben terms "zones of indecidability," thereby perhaps providing a way into the seemingly elusive middle ground, "where it is impossible to draw a line clearly" (see Raulff, 2004, p. 612)? Can we tolerate ambiguity? How can our research reflect the ambiguity and uncertainty of our wider contemporary contexts, or capture this with respect to the individuals who are part of our research endeavours? In our research, how can we remain faithful to the tenets of qualitative inquiry, yet be mindful of connections and disconnections, contradictions, and paradoxes with and within the macro contexts in which we operate?

To some extent, these ideas abandon the safe, the comfortable, and the expected and challenge and encourage qualitative inquirers while making them think about the fine line that we pursue daily with regard to qualitative research in the wake of the politics of evidence. In so doing, they have deliberately sought to destabilize aspects of the present we find ourselves in, to challenge what otherwise may become the obvious, the ordinary, the normal, the taken for granted, and the seemingly inevitable. Reflecting on issues and questions such as these causes me to hesitate when thinking about qualitative research, the conduct or assessment of that research, the positions constructed for me within and without of qualitative research endeavors, and how I act on and within those positions. As a qualitative researcher, I am challenged to consider what all this means for the way I conceptualize and do my research. I am challenged to approach my research with an open mind but not an empty head. Theory and context can sensitize me to see things I might not have seen and caution me against complacency and the seemingly obvious.

In summary, this discussion has been about exploring how to avoid bad short answers to complex problems and issues—in this case, the positioning of both qualitative research and qualitative researchers in the wake of the politics of evidence. In so doing, I am drawing on an assertion made by Hacking (1991) on the oversimplification of complex theoretical problems and the shallow way in which they are sometimes thought, written, and spoken about. The desire for the short answer is a symptom of the world in which we all live. It is one of instant communication, instant gratification, and instant responses, where quick solutions are the new mantra with respect to all aspects of our lives. Impatience is rife; hesitation is seen as weakness; and pausing to think deeply has become a casualty in the quest for the instant. Yet, more than ever, there is great need for patience, hesitation, and deep thinking with respect to qualitative inquiry and our position as researchers.

Action must be taken decisively with regard to the fine lines we are constantly straddling when positioning ourselves as researchers, and qualitative inquirers more specifically, in the wake of the politics of evidence. We need to make sure that we are clear about the existence of these lines; we must consider who and what is constructing them, how they might be problematized, where they might intersect, and how we can ensure that it is we who are drawing the lines—not others. It is for each of us to explore what kinds of assumptions, what kinds of familiar, unchallenged, unconsidered modes of thought (Foucault, 1988) might impact on the way we think about and speak about our research and research practices. Then we will be much further along the path toward ensuring the paradoxical continuation of the growth, development, and expansion of qualitative inquiry at the very time that the spaces for that inquiry are assaulted incessantly and seem to contract in the wake of the politics of evidence.

Notes

1. An earlier version of this chapter was presented as a keynote address at the 3ʳᵈ International Congress of Qualitative Inquiry, University of Illinois, Urbana-Champaign, May 3, 2007.

2. The Australian Research Council advises the Australian government on research matters and manages the National Competitive Grants Program, a significant component of Australia's investment in research and development (http://www.arc.gov.au). Framework 7 is a new funding scheme launched as part of the European Union's Programme for Research (http://ec.europa.eu/research/future/index_en.cfm).

3. The Research Quality Framework is an initiative of the Australian government to assess the quality and impact of Australian research.

4. An Individual Research Portfolio is a summary of a researcher's DEST-approved research activity that occurred between 01/01/01 and 31/12/06. It requires research-active staff to identify their top four research publications and enables staff to demonstrate their contributions to the research environment during the six-year period (www.unisa.edu.au/eas/research/Research%20Quality%20Framework/IRP%20FAQs%20(2).doc).

References

Butler, J. 2002. What is critique? An essay on Foucault's virtue. http://www.law.berkeley.edu/centers/kadish/what%20is%20critique%20J%20Butler.pdf (accessed August 12, 2007).

Denzin, N. K., & M. D. Giardina, Eds. 2006. *Qualitative inquiry and the conservative challenge: Confronting methodological fundamentalism*. Walnut Creek, CA: Left Coast Press.

Denzin, N. K., & Y. S. Lincoln. 2005. Introduction: The discipline and practice of qualitative research. In N. K. Denzin & Y. S. Lincoln (Eds.), pp. 1–32. *Handbook of qualitative research*, 3ʳᵈ ed. Thousand Oaks, CA: Sage.

Denzin, N. K., Y. S. Lincoln, & M, D. Giardina. 2006. Disciplining qualitative research. *International Journal of Qualitative Studies in Education* 19(6):769–82.

Foucault, M. 1988. *Politics, philosophy, culture and other writings 1977–1984*. New York: Routledge.

Goldenberg, M. J. 2006. On evidence and evidence-based medicine: Lessons from the philosophy of science. *Social Science and Medicine* 62(1):2621–32.

Hacking, I. 1991. The archaeology of Foucault. In D. Hoy (Ed.). *Foucault: A critical reader*, pp. 235–40. Oxford: Basil Blackwell.

Lincoln, Y. S., & G. S. Cannella. 2004. Dangerous discourse: Methodological conservatism and governmental regimes of truth. *Qualitative Inquiry* 10(1):5–14.

Murray, S. J., D. Holmes, A. Perron, & G. Rail. 2007. No exit? Intellectual integrity under the regime of "evidence" and "best-practices." *Journal of Evaluation in Clinical Practice* 13(4):512–16.

Mylonopoulos, N. A., & V. Theoharakis. 2001. Global perceptions of IS journals. *Communications of the ACM* 44(9):29–33.

Raulff, U. 2004. An interview with Giorgio Agamben. *German Law Journal* 5(5):609–14.

Schwandt, T. 2006. Opposition redirected. *International Journal of Qualitative Studies in Education* 19(6):803–10.

Thorne, S., & P. Darbyshire. 2005. Land mines in the field: A modest proposal for improving the craft of qualitative health research. *Qualitative Health Research* 15(8):1105–13.

Topper, K. 2005. *The disorder of political inquiry.* Cambridge, MA: Harvard University Press.

Theoretical and Methodological Interruptions

5 | The Evidentiary Narrative

Notes toward a Symbolic Interactionist Perspective about Evidence

David L. Altheide
Arizona State University

Introduction

People believe the strangest things. Many believe that the earth is flat, that the earth is 5,000 years old, that angels (real creatures with wings) are all around us. Many people, including twelve jurors, believed that "O.J. didn't do it" (kill his wife and her friend). Some Americans even believe that the Bush administration orchestrated the 9/11 attacks. A poll in September 2007, found that 33% of Americans believed that Saddam Hussein and his Iraqi friends were heavily involved in the planning and support of those attacks (Davies 2007), in spite of several official commission reports showing that this was not true. Moreover, many people in the Middle East, especially Iran, believe that the Bush administration actually conspired with al-Qaeda to attack the United States (*Frontline*, October 23, 2007).

Why do people believe such things, and what evidence would convince them otherwise? I wish to address the problem of knowledge and evidence from a symbolic interactionist perspective. This will entail offering a distinctive view of evidence-as-process, or what I call the "evidentiary narrative." But it also draws our attention to the ways in which credible information and knowledge are buffered by symbolic filters, including distinctive "epistemic communities," or collective meanings, standards, and criteria that govern sanctioned action, including talk (e.g., scripts, accounts, disclaimers).[1] As such, this exploratory chapter seeks to join identity/membership, information/knowledge/evidence, and propaganda/social control. More specifically, it offers a conceptual formulation of the evidentiary narrative, which emerges from a reconsideration of how knowledge and belief systems in everyday life are tied to epistemic communities that provide perspectives, scenarios, and scripts that reflect symbolic social and moral orders. Part of my task is to show the relevance of epistemic communities—and cultures—to and for evidence.

It is important to note that viewing evidence as part of a communication process suggests that evidence is not about facts per se, but about an argument, a narrative that is appropriate for the purpose-at-hand. That means it is contextualized and part of a bounded project, with accompanying assumptions, criteria, rules of membership, participation, etc. Moreover, what is meant by evidence can be viewed as "information that is filtered by various symbolic filters and nuanced meanings compatible with membership." From a radical sociology of knowledge perspective, the active reception of a point of information is contingent on the "media logic," of legitimacy (acceptability) of the information source, the technology, medium, format, and logic through which it is delivered (Altheide & Snow, 1979). Only then can the information be interpreted as evidence in juxtaposition with an issue, problem, or point of contention. Conversely, information that is not suitably configured and presented is likely to be resisted, if not rebuffed, within a prevailing discourse, typically guided by a folk concept that "applies material against which people judge whether what they see looks like [right]" (Turner, 1969, p. 818) or is pertinent to the topic at hand (Altheide & Gilmore, 1972; Turner, 1957).

The symbolic meaning filters that are called forth all stem from various memberships. Ultimately, evidence is bound up with our identity in a situation. I argue that the multiple memberships we hold in various epistemic communities are contextually and situationally shuffled and joined for a particular purpose (e.g., when an assumption or value is challenged or called into question). I further suggest that documents (i.e., anything that can be retrieved or recorded for subsequent analysis about social meanings) provide a window into collective sentiments, preferences, and identity pronouncements about epistemic communities. To

Figure 1
The Evidentiary Narrative Process: From Information to Evidence

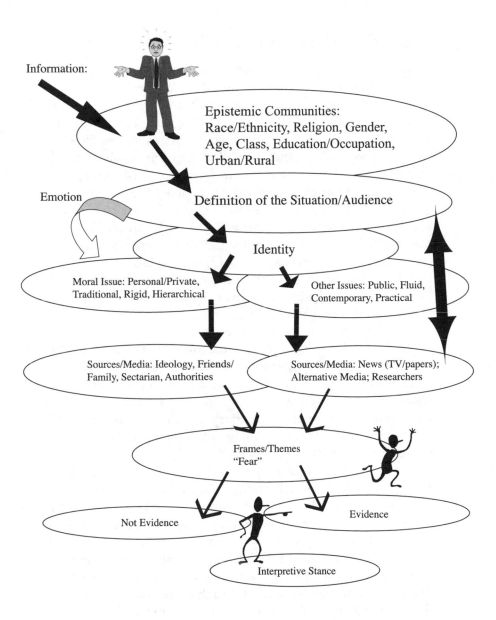

that end, I will use examples from various aspects of and relating to the Iraq War to illustrate how evidence is meaningfully joined to such communities.

The Evidentiary Narrative in Perspective

I go back to my fundamentalist religious background. My brothers and I had long rejected the fundamentalist evidence for the existence of God. When my brother Duane and I were college freshmen, we liked to hone our reasoning and logical skills by competing against easy pickings: None were easier, we thought, than the people who staffed the "Christian Businessmen" booth at the Western Washington Fair in Puyallup, Washington, near our home. We liked to argue with them about fundamental religious questions, (e.g., does God exist, and if so, does He care, and if so, why does He permit evil, or maybe an intellectually respectable God doesn't want us to fall for just anything). During one conversation, a dear old man said, "Son, if God doesn't exist, then how can a brown cow eat green grass and make white milk." Well, he had me. I still puzzle over the ease with which people find confirming or disconfirming evidence.

Since that time, I have reflected on the problem and conclude that evidence is processual and hinges on what might be termed an "evidentiary narrative," which is reflexive of an ecology of knowing, or the spatial/temporal interaction of background assumptions or what the anthropologist Lind (1988) refers to as the "culture stream."[2] The evidentiary narrative is built on several arrays of meaning. Figure 1 attempts to capture the contributors to the evidentiary narrative process.[3]

The evidentiary narrative is informed by work that John Johnson and I did on criteria of validity for evaluating qualitative research (Altheide & Johnson, 1994). We argued that a more encompassing view of the ethnographic enterprise would clearly delineate the process by which the ethnography occurred must be clearly delineated, including accounts of the interaction between the context, researcher, methods, setting, and actors. The broad term that we offered, "analytic realism," is based on the view that the social world is an interpreted world, not a literal world, always under symbolic construction (even decon-struction!). We can also apply this perspective to understand how situations in everyday life are informed by social contexts and uses of evidence. This application illuminates the process by which evidence is constituted. I mention a few of these later in the chapter and will show their relevance for issues and dis/agreements pertaining to the Iraq War.

A brief overview of analytic realism can help us approach evidence in a new way. It is useful to consider the following when trying to understand evidence that is stated or affirmed:

1. the relationship between what is observed (behaviors, rituals, meanings) and the larger cultural, historical, and organizational contexts within which the observations are made (the substance);

2. the relationship between the observer, the observed, and the setting (the observer);

3. the issue of perspective (or point of view), whether the observer's or the member(s)', used to render an interpretation of the ethnographic data (the interpretation);

4. the role of the reader in the final product (the audience); and

5. the issue of representational, rhetorical, or authorial style used by the author(s) to render the description and/or interpretation (the style).

Each of these areas includes questions or issues that must be addressed and pragmatically resolved by any particular observer in the course of his or her research. As originally formulated, these five dimensions of qualitative research include problematic issues pertaining to validity. Indeed, we argued that the "ethnographic ethic" calls for ethnographers to substantiate their interpretations and findings with a reflexive account of themselves and the process(es) of their research (Altheide & Johnson, 1993).

I wish to shift the focus to what people regard or take for granted as validity or truth and what relevance this has for evidence. Please note that my approach is quite different from classical varieties (i.e., evidence and the law) (Anderson, Twining, &

Wigmore, 1991). Just as ethnographers honor the perspective of their subject, so, too, should we affirm the process of how people interpret the world vis-à-vis what we might term "evidence." My focus, then, is on how social order—indeed a social cosmology— is reflected in symbolic communication in everyday life. Mary Douglas's view is similar, although she argues that worldviews are shaped by the dimensions of "individuation" and "social incorporation":

> This means that the social environments in which all individu- als operate have two characteristics: First, all social environments have, to some extent, external constraints. They typically stem from hierarchical structures and the regulations associated with such social constructions (grid). ... Second, all social environments are characterized by the extent to which the individuals are part of demarcated social entities (group). The more closely individuals are incorporated into such social entities, the more likely their deci- sions will be affected by group norms. (Douglas, 1982, p. 190)

These worldviews are taken for granted and widely shared and can be illustrated with examples of the views about the United States initiating the terrorist attacks of 9/11, or the idea that many citizens in a host of Middle Eastern countries take for granted that the U.S.'s pro-Israel policy, which they see as opposed to the welfare of Palestinians and others, governs most actions involved with the Middle East. Indeed, there is a vast historical record of the role of U.S. interference in the affairs of many nations in this region, much of this captured in various news media (Adams, 1982). That many citizens have a quasi-conspiratorial view of Middle Eastern life at the hands of the United States is hardly surprising, nor are most observers surprised that worldviews are colored by this taken-for-granted understanding of world affairs.

Epistemic Communities and the Evidentiary Narrative

Evidence is aligned with epistemic cultures/communities. What people regard as evidence is contingent on symbolic processes and meanings that shape, guide, and deflect as well as construct boundaries (Schwalbe et al., 2000). These are associated, acquired, and accompanied with various memberships (and identities) and components, some explicit, (e.g., occupations and education), but most are implicit, if not tacit (e.g., region, class, religion, ethnicity, religion, family structure, and functioning). These provide an evidentiary narrative through which people define, create, share, recognize, and reject information as relevant for a purpose at hand, including a topic that might be considered.

The situation and occasion is partially set by the audience, which calls forth the appropriate membership/identity (Blumer, 1962), and very importantly, a proper performance (Goffman, 1959, 1963b) (see Figure 1—Definition of the Situation/Identity). But if people have multiple memberships and presumably an array of evidentiary narratives that can be used singularly or in combination, which ones will be used? For example, will "science" and rational reflection be appropriate, or will one's childhood perspective apply?[4] The key is the interaction process, wherein two or more people are engaged in arriving at and sustaining a definition of the situation. Such definitions usually reflect the context of the interaction and assumptions about order, reality, and normalcy.

People who are communicating count on each other in a cooperative fashion, rather than in an evaluative or competitive one. They work at presenting themselves in a convincing way to affirm an identity. It is important to note that people in everyday life seldom focus on evidence per se; they just say and do what seems appropriate for the situation at hand. In this sense, evidence is very pragmatic and very interactionist; if it works with an audience at a specific place and time, it is not likely to be challenged. People do not respond merely to facts; rather, it is the meaning and context that make a difference. People draw on epistemic cultures that provide the taken-for-granted perspective, knowledge, and frames. Moreover, information and facts are not the same as evidence; what matters is what is accepted as facts-for-the-purpose-at-hand.[5]

Although it is certainly the individual who displays the agency of epistemic claims, I argue below that the perspective, orientation, social support, and standpoint from which individuals address information-as-evidence are decidedly collective and social. This part looms much larger when we examine mediated documents about the Iraq War that demonstrate the deadly playfulness of logic-in-use by the powerful ideologues.

The Evidentiary Narrative and the Iraq War

The Iraq War offers numerous examples of the importance of what we see and call things—of the synthesis of context, situation, and stance—but we could use others. The following pages provide examples of how evidence is constructed and interpreted by epistemic communities that share basic assumptions about the moral superiority and righteousness of the United States. Scientific rationality or critical thinking is subordinate to absolutist thinking (Douglas, 1971). The role of the news in defining, selecting, and framing reports is critical (see Figure 1: "Issues," Media Sources, and Framing).

Fear tends to dominate the mass media. Evidentiary narratives susceptible to doom and gloom from the news media could find ample support for hostile views about the "Arabs," along with reassurance that steps would be taken to protect citizens from the objects of fear. Visuals of the falling towers on September 11, 2001, sustained an evidentiary narrative about the heartless enemies of the United States and the necessity to make war against Iraq and do whatever was necessary to prevent such attacks in the future (Altheide, 2006). Evidence was set forth to support the false claims about Iraq (Denzin, 2007). Opinion poll data showed that for at least six years after this event, a third or more of the American people believed that Saddam Hussein and Iraq were responsible for these attacks. It is what they saw—the destruction—that mattered. The repeated showing of the visuals, an unprecedented propaganda campaign, and the emotional appeals of the Bush administration about the ongoing threats to the United States added to the pervasive discourse of fear that permeated our national culture (Altheide, 2002).

Let us look to an example that involves the extensive use of more than 180,000 contract workers to cook and build structures and roads in Iraq, plus an estimated 50,000 former military people who work for rapidly growing security-for-hire companies that have received billions of dollars in government contract work. One of these, Blackwater (Silverstein, 2006), came under scrutiny after its employees—who are largely autonomous from U.S. military control—killed seventeen Iraqi citizens, in what came to be understood as an unprovoked attack (Johnston & Broder, 2007). Despite operating in the shadows for several years, and engaging in numerous questionable shootings and attacks, the mass shooting attracted a lot of attention. What would the evidence be? Who would hear it? What would it look like? The director of Blackwater (Erik Prince) quickly grasped the importance of rhetoric and the evidentiary narrative via the mass media. He knew that what we call things matters for what will be taken as evidence, what will be scrutinized, so he had to take a stance. When challenged, Blackwater's director countered:

> He forcefully rejected the characterization of Blackwater from some members of the committee as a mercenary army. He said that contractors had served with the United States military since Revolutionary times and that mercenaries were soldiers who fought with foreign armies for money. *"They call us mercenaries,"* he said. *"But we're Americans working for America protecting Americans."* (Broder, 2007, emphasis added)

Upon further questioning by congressional committee members, Mr. Prince acknowledged that his company employed "third country nationals" from Latin America and Eastern Europe, while also providing security in other countries, presumably by nonnative workers. But these were only facts, and not relevant vis-à-vis an evidentiary narrative that would be connected to broader themes. Whatever evidence might be uncovered would be polished through the dominant cultural narrative of patriotism. Mr. Prince acknowledged that "crazy things" had happened, that they had fired some zealous and violent individuals, but the organization and service was sound. And they had "compensated" families of the numerous civilians they killed with $2,500–$5,000. (This was consistent with what the U.S. military paid for "collateral damage.")

To help drive home this message that they were a sound useful and patriotic operation, Mr. Prince quickly hired a stable of attorneys and public relations people to help "manage" and define the situation, including, of course, exclusive interviews to "set the record straight." The strategy involved redirecting the charges away from the single shooting—and avoiding discussion of dozens of other provocations—to the broader purpose of being patriotic and defending the United States and its troops, boasting that their main charge, to protect diplomats, had been 100% successful; not one had been injured by the enemy! The aim was to move discussion away from prosecuting any Blackwater employee—and certainly not Mr. Prince—because they, after all, had been granted immunity by the former head of the Coalition Provisional Authority (CPA), L. Paul Bremer. Thus, Blackwater employees and the tens of thousands of other hired guns were not officially accountable to anyone: not to the United States government, the military, or Iraqis. The discussions focused on changing some rules to make the mercenaries accountable to military authority in the future. Thus, frames, in the Lakoffian sense, were skillfully manipulated to resonate with audiences attuned to the patriot games.

Let's look at this more closely: Dominant evidentiary narratives are not displaced easily because their standpoint is all-encompassing and do not accommodate detractors. Thus, Blackwater was not a rogue organization: It was headed by a former U.S. soldier—a S.E.A.L.—who was quite wealthy and had supported Republican candidates. Moreover, it had a contract with the United States to help fight terrorists in a war zone. This was part of the cultural narrative that guided the evidentiary narrative. The problem was that the evidence about inappropriate and shocking killing of civilians was not likely to be considered as long as the cultural narrative remained unchallenged. After all, our cultural narrative is that troops and soldiers are fighting for us and in a fundamental sense represent us and "are us." There is always a subtext of sacrifice, including loss of life. But highly paid mercenaries, who are not under our military's command, are another thing altogether. Both narratives are intertwined and difficult to offset in the context of numerous images and claims about troops and the insurgents, who will stoop to anything. I will return to this scenario below.

• • •

Consider two further incidents about people being killed. The first occurred in Pakistan in January 2006, when a U.S. drone was programmed to fire ten missiles at several houses where an al-Qaeda leader was believed to be. Eighteen people were killed, including women and children. The target escaped. Note the way that cultural narratives are embedded about "them" and "us" in the following material.

One foreign journalist challenged the evidentiary narrative and questioned why the civilian deaths in Pakistan were treated much differently:

> What makes the latest gory incident more abhorrent is that at least 18 Pakistani citizens, including eight women and five innocent children, were torn into pieces by the deadly missiles. This is nothing but sheer terrorism. As per US version, some foreign elements, especially Ayman al-Zawahiri, were the real target of the aggression. However, even if there were some foreign figures, the saner approach would have been to pass on the information to Pakistani authorities to carry out necessary operation against them. (Staff Editorial, 2006, 1)

At least one U.S. publication, *The Christian Science Monitor*, suggested that some remorse might be shown for the Pakistani civilians, further stating that this would help U.S. interests:

> The attack was meant to kill Al Qaeda's deputy leader, Ayman al-*Zawahiri*. It appears to have missed its target, though it killed some of his aides. It certainly killed a dozen Pakistani villagers, including women and children. This is the second such attack on *Pakistan* in a fortnight, and the previous one also caused eight civilian deaths. … The *Bush* administration, however, has yet to express regret to the Pakistani government and people over the deaths of women and children. It would also be a good thing if the US media recognized just how much damage this kind of silence does to the US image and US interests … not only has the administration failed to make a gesture that would have cost it nothing, members of Congress have rubbed salt in Pakistani wounds by affirming that the strike was justified but failing to express equally clearly about their sorrow about the "collateral" deaths of innocent *civilians*. (Lieven & Menon, 2006, 9, emphasis added).

About a week later, President Bush traveled to Pakistan and did not refer to the civilian killings: "With Pakistan's prime minister, Shaukat Aziz, at his side, Mr. Bush spoke about areas of agreement, like trade and fighting terrorism, in four minutes of public remarks in the Oval Office. The president called the countries' relationship "vital," whereas Mr. Aziz called it "multifaceted" (Bumiller, 2006).

Grief is tied to legitimacy: Grief is for "us," not "them." But our empathy seems to be essential to raise, if not to listen to or even to "see" evidence; it is the evidentiary narrative that helps frame information, giving it the essential meaningful dimension that can make it significant. President Bush's lack of concern is telling, but it tells it a lot louder when it is compared with the shooting of faculty and students at Virginia Tech University in April 2007. These deaths were not justified and certainly not ignored. This is what the president stated about the Virginia Tech shootings that took the lives of thirty-one students: "It's impossible to make sense of such violence and suffering," Bush said, "Those whose lives were taken did nothing to deserve their fate. They were simply in the wrong place at the wrong time. Now they're gone, and they leave behind grieving families and grieving classmates and a grieving nation" (President Bush, April 17, 2007). It should be added, of course, that no one implied that the students did anything to "deserve their fate."

There is a striking contrast with death as collateral damage in fighting terrorism. The "vital" concern with terrorism informs what is relevant and what is not relevant. For all practical purposes, evidence that does not fit with the evidentiary narrative is not relevant because it is not symbolically enclosed in context of meaning. When all that matters is support for "our fight against terrorism," then loss of civilian lives, or even the Pakistani leader General Musharraf suspending the constitution and imprisoning his opposition as well as international human rights workers—as he did in November, 2007—does not matter a great deal, as long as our fight against terrorism can continue. So how did the United States officially respond to this crude smashing of dissent and democracy in a country very dependent on U.S. aid? Note the reference to being "cognizant" and, presumably, examining "evidence":

> Secretary of State Condoleezza Rice said that while the United States would "have to review the situation with aid," she said three times that President Bush's first concern was "*to protect America and protect American citizens by continuing to fight against terrorists.*"
>
> "That means we have to be very *cognizant of the counterterrorism operations* that we are involved in," she said. "We have to be very cognizant of the fact that some of the assistance that has been going to Pakistan is directly related to the counterterrorism mission."

In Islamabad, aides to General Musharraf—who had dismissed pleas on Friday from Ms. Rice and Adm. William J. Fallon, the senior military commander in the Middle East, to avoid the state-of-emergency declaration—said they had anticipated that *there would be few real consequences.* ...In unusually candid terms, they said *American officials supported stability over democracy.* (Sanger & Rohde, 2007, A1, emphasis added)

• • •

When leaders are consumed by ideology and take actions that are consistent with beliefs, then we have ideologically informed decisions that may or may not work out. They usually do not, but then again, that is the same problem: How do we know that things aren't working out? What evidence would we accept? That question quickly becomes "whose evidence," which implies, of course, that all evidence is linked to perspective, not truly objective and bias free. And there is considerable truth to that. This point can be illustrated by the ways in which staff was appointed for the CPA in Iraq. This is a good case study because it is recent (2008) and because it is one of the most ideologically driven crusades in modern history.

The concern of the Bush administration was to have key workers in Iraq who were loyalists to a narrow party line. It is quite common for politicos to appoint "fellow travelers" to positions; however, they usually prefer that such appointees have a modicum of competence in the appointed area. (There are many instances in the appointment of ambassadors, of course, where this is not the case.) This did not happen in Iraq. Several journalists and government officials familiar with the process in Iraq have commented that people were selected for positions there based more on their conservative politics and loyalty than on experience and competence in the subject area. A former officer explained how people were appointed:

> All of these factors seemed to combine, but to try to figure out exactly how they weighed on Vice President Cheney is very difficult. What you can say is he was the first vice president to create a large foreign policy staff, and it was the most ideologically rigid and biased staff possible. *You can't find one name there that was*

not part of this neoconservative structure. (Anthony Cordesman, interview. http://www.pbs.org/wgbh/pages/frontline/yeariniraq/interviews/cordesman.html [accessed October 19, 2007], emphasis added)

Similarly, *The Washington Post* Baghdad bureau chief discussed how far ideology reached substantive areas of expertise:

What happened was that the hiring was done by the White House liaison to the Pentagon, an office of the Pentagon political appointee. This office served as the gatekeeper. Instead of casting out widely for people with knowledge of Arabic, knowledge of the Middle East, knowledge of post-conflict reconstruction, they went after the political loyalists and canvassed the offices of Republican congressmen, conservative think tanks and other places where they knew they would find people who would be unfailingly loyal to the president and to the president's mission in Iraq. ...

The hiring process involved questions that would have landed a private-sector employer in jail. They asked people what their views on *Roe v. Wade* were, whether they believed in capital punishment. A man of Middle Eastern descent was asked whether he was Muslim or Christian. People were asked who they voted for for president. (*Frontline* interview. http://www.pbs.org/wgbh/pages/frontline/yeariniraq/interviews/rajiv.html [accessed October 19, 2007])

Membership informs what is taken for granted about reality as well as what is not likely to be questioned and challenged. This is true of executing a war as well.

• • •

The way in which civilian killings in Iraq was presented illustrates the context of meaning that produces and reflects evidentiary discourse and language of "we do no wrong." It is a language of membership. Although the U.S. military has prosecuted some 200 cases of violent crimes in Iraq, the contexts of war, combat, ideology, and beliefs about the "enemy" make this a very rare—and difficult—task. Much of the problem involves the language and discourse that we use to refer to acts (van Dijk, 1985). However, we can learn from these cases, particularly about the nature, process, and context of definitions and uses of "evidence."

The evidentiary narrative of wrongdoing and brutality encompasses certain symbols within its discursive frame. One example is "gunmen," usually associated and framed with crime and criminals. There are several pieces to this: the context, the purpose, the use of a gun (weapon), who uses it, and on whom is it used (e.g., an innocent party). Use of the word "gunmen" illustrates the relationship between evidence, symbolism, and context. Research indicates that the word "gunmen" is seldom used by journalists (narrators) on your side to refer to soldiers or other violent agents on your side who commit acts or violence. For example, a police officer, who accidentally or intentionally shoots a civilian or a suspect is not referred to as a "gunman." Gunmen is almost always used for the Other, someone on the "other" side. We can look at this in a couple of examples. After former Secretary of State Colin Powell stated in September 2006 that the Iraq War was not helpful to the U.S.'s moral reputation, President Bush stated, growing animated as he spoke: "It's unacceptable to think there's any kind of comparison between the behavior of the United States of America and the action of *Islamic extremists who kill innocent women and children to achieve an objective*" (http://www.msnbc.msn.com/id/14848798/, emphasis added).

The enemy was presented routinely as "insurgents," and more typically as "gunmen" in press reports. This is consistent with crime coverage as well as the enemy. Here's an excerpt from a news report in 2001 about Palestinians and Israelis. When the former kills, it is by gunmen, but not so the latter: "The Israeli Army said it *attacked in reprisal* for the killing on Saturday of an Israeli motorist by *Palestinian gunmen* in Jerusalem" (Bennett, 2001, 1, emphasis added).

One account illustrates the "barbarism" attributed to Iraqi "gunmen," whereas the killing by U.S. soldiers is described as simply "killed."

BAGHDAD, Iraq–U.S. forces ... recovered the bodies of two American soldiers reported captured by insurgents last week. An Iraqi defense ministry official said the men were *tortured and "killed in a barbaric way."* ... Maj. Gen. Abdul-Aziz Mohammed, said the bodies showed signs of having been tortured. "With great regret, they were killed in a barbaric way," he said. ... Also, just hours before the two soldiers went missing Friday, a *U.S. airstrike killed a key al–Qaida in Iraq leader described as the group's "religious emir," he said.*

Mansour Suleiman Mansour Khalifi al-Mashhadani, or *Sheik Mansour, was killed* with two foreign fighters in the same area where the soldiers' bodies were found, the U.S. spokesman said. The three were trying to flee in a vehicle.

… seven masked *gunmen,* one carrying a heavy machine gun, killed the driver and took the two other U.S. soldiers captive. (Gamel, 2006, 1, emphasis added)

The Haditha slaughter, in which twenty-four Iraqis were executed, is the single example located (thus far) of U.S. journalists referring to U.S. soldiers as "gunmen." Following a road-side bombing that killed a U.S. soldier on November 19, 2005, U.S. troops entered several houses nearby and shot twenty-four Iraqi citizens, ranging in age from a child of four to an eighty-nine-year-old man in a wheel chair. And this was the reference to gunmen:

Everybody was at home when the *gunmen* arrived. Except for one 12-year-old daughter, the family was wiped out. Four girls and one boy, ranging in age from 4 to 15, were shot dead by the Marines, neighbors and the surviving child said. According to 12 year old Safa, The Marines yelled in the faces of her family members before they shot them, she said. After they were shot, they kicked them and hit the bodies with their guns. "I feel sorry. I was wishing to be alive," Safa said. "Now I wish I had died with them." Survivors say Marines went house to house in a rage. (Stack & Salman, 2006, A1, emphasis added)

Other writers and publications did not refer to the U.S. soldiers as "gunmen," despite the large amount of corroborating information about the calculated shootings in Haditha. Indeed, in dozens of follow-up reports on the incident, "gunmen" was only used to refer to others—insurgents—who allegedly fired at the U.S. troops, thus leading them to attack the Iraqi civilians. Even subsequent legal investigations of the soldiers involved would not use the term. Instead, other terms and phrases were used to contextualize the discourse of war (e.g., men under stress, grieving, loss of judgment, etc.).

The term "gunmen" did not suit the cultural narrative for the journalists nor quite likely most of the U.S. news audience. The word "gunmen," usually reserved for enemies, was not used in this massacre because the evidentiary narrative was not appropriate for it: After all, the dead were associated with the enemy, and the alleged killers were our troops. Evidence involves process in a context, for the purpose at hand. Ironically, people who supported one of the accused cited the lack of solid evidence for conviction (within an adjudication framework):

> In interviews, organizers and contributors said they believed that many prosecutions were based on *feeble evidence* and gauzy recollections of Iraqis sympathetic to the insurgency and hostile to the U.S. military mission in Iraq.
>
> They note the case against Lance Cpl. Justin L. Sharratt, charged with killing three unarmed Iraqi men at point-blank range in Haditha in 2005. A Marine lawyer investigating the charges recommended dismissing them this month, for *lack of evidence*, and warned that pressing flimsy cases against *combat troops* "sets a dangerous precedent" that *eroded public support for the war* and could cause troops to hesitate when fighting a *determined enemy*. (Von Zielbauer 2007, emphasis added)

It is important to stress that the evidentiary narrative being set forth in the above appeal to "lack of evidence" and "flimsy evidence" joined the implicit connections between witnesses—who were sympathetic to insurgents (although no evidence is presented about this), to the public support for the war, as well as causing "combat troops" to "hesitate"—and perhaps be endangered by a "determined enemy." In short, to use the word "gunmen" would weaken and invalidate the evidentiary narrative that sustains the definition of "combat troops" and even "public support for the war." But there is more.

The importance of membership and orientation toward outsiders is common in war contexts. The situational and very opportunistic perspective about evidence can be illustrated by news reports about the murder of a disabled Iraqi man by several U.S. Marines in the village of Hamdania in April 2006. The news report explicates what was implicit: The evidentiary narrative is apparent: "They" are all bad. The Marines real target was a suspected "insurgent," Saleh Gowad, but they could not find him, so they grabbed another man because they were intent on killing someone in the area, because they believed that most residents were insurgents or were friendly to them.

According to the testimony, an eight-man squad decided to kill a known insurgent named Saleh Gowad. Unable to find Gowad, the Marines snatched Hashim Ibrahim Awad, a disabled police officer, from a nearby house, bound him and marched him about a half mile to a bomb crater, where they placed a shovel and a rifle and then killed him in a way that made it look like they'd been in a firefight with a man planting a bomb. (Perry, 2007)

Some 200 military personnel have been prosecuted for illegal assault and murders in Iraq, but most of the military attacks on Iraqi civilians apparently go unreported (Badkhen, 2005; Stack & Salman, 2006); this one got some attention and charges were filed against the eight-man squad.

The role of membership for evidence is particularly apparent when it comes to justice. Justice in a war context is quite problematic, especially when different audiences have widely disparate contexts and frameworks for recognizing an injustice and then holding someone or something accountable. My focus is not on different opinions but on what people use and refer to as evidence. I am particularly interested in how different criteria are brought to bear on the general situation as well as the specific matter. By the general situation, I refer to perceptions of right and wrong, killing the enemy or "any of them," and how prosecutors of such deeds as well as the news media might be viewed. For example, numerous groups emerged to provide defense funds and other support for any soldiers who were charged with crimes. The implicit meaning of many supporters' statements is that combat operations bring specific pressures and problems that cannot be understood by outsiders, those who are not actually in the combat situations. Notes posted on websites illustrate how some conservative Christians and military veterans oppose prosecution of soldiers:

"I wonder if you are supposed to check out each enemy to see if they have a gun or wait for them to shoot first," wrote a 98-year-old woman from Grand Junction, Colo., who recently sent $25 to the Military Combat Defense Fund, a Boston-area group that has provided more than $85,000 to smaller funds set up for individual Marines accused of murder and other crimes in Haditha and Hamdania, Iraq. "Bible says that the country will always be fighting. We have been praying for all you boys and girls." ... A Marine lawyer investigating the charges recommended dismissing them this month, for *lack of evidence*, and warned that pressing flimsy cases against combat troops "sets a dangerous precedent" that eroded public support for the war and could cause troops to hesitate when fighting a determined enemy. (Von Zielbauer, 2007, emphasis added)

Basically, the supporters take the position that the military cannot be held accountable for any misdeeds because they are in a war. Although some sites do not support cases that appear to be premeditated, others include messages by parents and friends of soldiers charged with such crimes:

Terry Pennington, a former Air Force technician whose son, Lance Cpl. Robert Pennington, was among the Hamdania Marines who pleaded guilty, said: "Many of these people see this country as not having the guts anymore to fight a war. They're outraged really all the way up to the White House" (Von Zielbauer, 2007.)

The evidence to support one's contribution to a website is more conceptual and abstract, except perhaps for family members who have a loved one who is being charged with a crime. However, a more specific scenario arises when individuals are charged, tried, and judged by their peers, who presumably would share the evidentiary narrative, which essentially would disavow acts of brutality as evidence. Thus, attorneys for individuals charged in military courts with heinous crimes are eager to demand that juries of "peers" include many individuals with combat experience in Iraq. Cpl. Trent Thomas, who was convicted of kidnapping and conspiracy to commit murder in conjunction with the murder in Hamdania discussed above, was sentenced to the fourteen months that he had already served, along with a bad conduct discharge.

All nine jurors were combat veterans of Iraq, seven of them from infantry battalions. Of the three officers on the jury, two had experience as enlisted Marines. Five of nine jurors were black, like Thomas.

After the verdict, Thomas' civilian and military lawyers told reporters that they wanted to thank Lt. Gen. James Mattis for making sure Thomas had "a true jury of his peers." (Von Zielbauer, 2007)

The importance of "membership" and being evaluated by criteria and perspectives shared by one's judges was apparent when it could not be guaranteed. Cpl. Robert Pennington accepted an eight-year sentence as part of a plea bargain when his attorney could not guarantee a friendlier jury:

> Deanna Pennington, the mother of Cpl. Robert Pennington, who pleaded guilty in the same incident and accepted an eight-year prison sentence, said later that her son took a plea bargain because his jury pool contained few combat veterans. Her son, a former resident of Snohomish County, feared that Marines who had not been to Iraq would never understand what happened in Hamdania that night in April 2006. (Von Zielbauer, 2007)

Clearly, there was a sense that the support and tacit knowledge/experience of combat veterans in Iraq would help one's case, even when certain facts about premeditated killing were uncontested. It was the meaning and justification of such acts (e.g., stress and anger) that apparently mitigated the other evidence by providing a context of membership, brotherhood, and a moral order. As noted in one account:

> Looking at his fellow Iraq veterans on the jury, Thomas, in an unsworn statement before the sentencing deliberations, talked of the kind of experience they have in common: the grief of seeing buddies killed in combat. After losing friends in Fallujah, he said he decided, "I'm getting cheated on life. This ain't right." (Von Zielbauer, 2007)

Conclusion

This exploratory analysis of the evidentiary narrative, which symbolically joins an actor, an audience, a point of view, assumptions, and a claim about a relationship between two or more phenomena, focuses on evidence as process to provide another way to understand how everyday life perspectives inform what we see as relevant, confirming, or disconfirming of various beliefs, assumptions, and theories. I suggested that applying our understanding of how researchers approach ethnographic data and methods could illuminate a fresh look at the conundrums implicit in formulating and justifying courses of action ranging from domestic violence to state warfare.

I do not think that this is a complete statement about evidence, nor do I contend that all the major issues have been identified. I simply suggest that taking into account how people in epistemic communities locate their lives, identities, and projects in interaction with others and how these are understood and communicated can contribute to more understanding and possibly more tolerance. I am convinced that unless we can understand how contexts of meaning are constructed and enacted—and taken for granted—we cannot promote more communication so that we are at least talking about the same things. If information does not become relevant as evidence to be considered, there can be no hope of dialog-based change. This, then, is the problem of evidence: It is less important to convince or change someone's mind than it is to apprehend what they mean, what the source of it is, and how this was communicated.

The mass media play a critical role in contemporary evidentiary narratives, which are reflected in numerous documents that can be retrieved and analyzed. What we know, see, and believe is interactively shaped, affirmed, and perhaps even revised as audience members interpret, discuss, and reframe messages, representations, and images of reality, including images and issues. Language, especially discourses and scripts, reflects the media processes, including the technology, formats, and style and action that are presented. Although the information is transformed into meanings through numerous filters, there is more evidence that certain themes (e.g., fear) become more embedded and taken for granted, which, in turn, shapes future interpretive frameworks. Fortunately, more journalists are reflecting on the role that they play in this new media, where spin and frames are studied, promoted, and skillfully used to misinform and deceive. One editor has called for a "rhetoric beat" to signal public attention to this process in specific events:

> Still, the consequences of the decision to describe 9/11 as the beginning of a war rather than a criminal investigation drive home the importance of political language in a way that a similar semantic debate over "death tax" versus "estate tax" cannot. In the years since that decision, language—its uses and abuses—has emerged as a central issue in our political culture. ... It's too late

to adjust the war frame that was constructed after the attacks on 9/11. But there is another monumental framing debate looming. For the first time since Vietnam, the U.S. is stuck in an increasingly unpopular foreign conflict with no clear way out. It is undeniable that bad information, ushered into the realm of "fact" in some cases by rhetorical malfeasance, played a central role in getting us there. Now the nation's focus is shifting to how and when to get out and, more important for our purposes, there is a corollary need to describe the getting out. (Cunningham, 2007, p. 39)

I suggest that developing our skills and sensitivity to analysis of documents can illuminate methodological stances and approaches for mining the incredibly rich record of evidence gained, lost, and, more typically, completely overlooked.

These materials, in the context of the discussion about evidence, point to cracks in the dominant evidentiary narrative, which asserts that evidence is reflexive of truth and will be recognized according to certain criteria. But how do criteria change? What role do new communities that speak and honor different narratives play? How are we to evaluate evidence outside of the evidentiary narrative? Who shares the narrative, how does it change, who gets to change it, evaluate it, and so on? What should be the standard for evidence in a disciplinary discourse? I suggest that applying the logic of analytic realism to research and claims making about data and method is a fruitful way to explicate discourse and permit all interactants—the researchers, the subjects, and the audience—to participate. Perhaps these exploratory remarks can help in that project.

Notes

1. I borrow the term "epistemic communities" to capture the shared perspectives that promote evidentiary narratives (Miller & Fox, 2001; Roth, 2007). Not all encounters illustrate the evidentiary narrative, but many do. Evidentiary narratives are constituted by memberships—epistemic communities—that I will discuss in more detail, but they remain as binding, even if they are not as well articulated across the board, varying, say, between a scientific review of a colleague's paper, or a conversation with one's mother. And not all communication affirms or reflects an evidentiary narrative within a community. In general, an evidentiary narrative is called into question during interaction between people from dissimilar epistemic communities.

During such encounters, one person's commentary or observations are likely to be noticed as different—even contrary—to one's own view, thus they are "topicalized" and treated as referential, rather than evocative; relatedly, there may ensue a question, more information seeking, or especially a challenge or disagreement with an assertion. Likewise, different evidentiary narratives are at work when a journalist scrutinizes a public official's proclamation and questions the veracity and relevance for a topic at hand.

2. Lind explores cultural continuities and change, reflecting on the "mechanisms" and "institutional forms" that permit the past to be remembered in the present and passed along and then built on—even changed—in the future. The focus turns to cultural processes that are discovered, tested, altered, instituted, and then reified and soon taken for granted (Berger & Luckmann, 1967; Schutz, 1967).

3. The aim is to illustrate how information becomes interpreted and meaningful for a situation such that it is recognized as evidence-worthy or not. Please note that this is offered as a distinctively social model, regardless of psychological processes.

4. With exceptions, as Jack Douglas argued, the evidentiary narratives that accompany moral meanings in one's life are likely to trump less salient meanings (Douglas, 1971, 1976; Douglas et al., 1988; Douglas & Johnson, 1977). Douglas suggested that our general cultural understandings learned in childhood, about life and morality, are often modified by specific cultural understandings gleaned from occupational and other experiences (Douglas, 1976).

5. Our task is compounded by research findings that suggest that the interaction performance informs audience perceptions of veracity and competence (Goffman, 1959, 1963a, 1963b). This poses serious problems for social analysts because a plethora of available popular culture offerings assures that almost any position or belief will receive some support, if not overwhelming approval! Still, this begs the question about evidence as "belief," "an argument," or even a position. Most of the time, it is simply taken for granted, unless someone who matters to a person in an interaction sequence raises some question about a statement or practice. So this is where analytic realism can be helpful in understanding the process and social construction of evidence: Analytic realism assumes that the meanings and definitions brought to actual situations are produced through a communication process. Researchers and observers need to be aware that the categories and ideas used to describe the empirical (socially constructed) world are also symbols from specific contexts. We must attend to the specific context and situation if we wish to understand how people perceive inconsistency, and in effect, understand the "logic in use."

References

Adams, W. C. 1982. *Television coverage of international affairs*. Norwood, NJ: Ablex.

Altheide, D. L. 1996. *Qualitative media analysis*. Newbury Park, CA: Sage.

Altheide, D. L. 2002. *Creating fear: News and the construction of crisis*. Hawthorne, NY: Aldine de Gruyter.

Altheide, D. L. 2006. *Terrorism and the politics of fear*. Lanham, MD: AltaMira Press.

Altheide, D. L., & K. DeVriese. 2007. Perps in the news: A research note on stigma. *Crime, Media, Culture* 3(3):382–89.

Altheide, D. L., & R. P. Gilmore. 1972. The credibility of protest. *American Sociological Review* 37(1):99–108.

Altheide, D. L., & J. M. Johnson. 1993. The ethnographic ethic. In N. K. Denzin (Ed.), *Studies in symbolic interaction*, pp. 95–107. Greenwich, CT: JAI Press.

Altheide, D. L., & J. M. Johnson. 1994. Criteria for assessing interpretive validity in qualitative research. In N. K. Denzin & Y. S. Lincoln (Eds.), *Handbook of qualitative methodology*, pp. 485–99. Newbury Park, CA: Sage.

Altheide, D. L., & R. P. Snow. 1979. *Media logic*. Beverly Hills, CA: Sage.

Anderson, T. J., W. L. Twining, & J. H. Wigmore. 1991. *Analysis of evidence: How to do things with facts, based on Wigmore's science of judicial proof*. Boston: Little Brown.

Badkhen, A. 2005. Colonel's toughest duty. Battalion commander pays his respects, apologizes to Iraqis whose civilian relatives have been killed by anonymous GIs in passing patrols and convoys. *The San Francisco Chronicle*, October 14, p. A1.

Bennett, J. 2001. Israel wants cease-fire to precede truce talks. *The New York Times*, September 16, p. 1.

Berger, P. L., & T. Luckmann. 1967. *The social construction of reality: A treatise in the sociology of knowledge*. New York: Doubleday.

Blumer, H. 1958. Race prejudice as a sense of group position. *Pacific Sociological Review* 1(1):3–7.

Blumer, H. 1962. Society as symbolic interaction. In A. M. Rose (Ed.), *Human behavior and social processes*, pp. 179–92. Boston: Houghton Mifflin.

Broder, J. M. 2007. Chief of Blackwater defends his employees. *The New York Times*, October 3. http://www.nytimes.com/2007/10/03/washington/03blackwater.html (accessed October 4, 2007).

Bumiller, E. 2006. Bush meets with premier of Pakistan. *The New York Times*, January 25, p. A13.

Cunningham, B. 2007. The rhetoric beat: Why journalism needs one. *Columbia Journalism Review* (November/December):36–39. http://www.cjr.org/essay/the_rhetoric_beat.php (accessed November 21, 2007).

Davies, F. 2007. Many Americans believe there was a link between Iraq, Sept. 11. *San Jose Mercury News*, September 11, p. 1.

Denzin, N. K. 2007. The secret Downing Street memo, the one percent doctrine, and the politics of truth: A performance text. *Symbolic Interaction* 30(1):447–64.

Douglas, J. D. 1971. *American social order; social rules in a pluralistic society.* New York: Free Press.

Douglas, J. D. 1976. *Investigative social research: Individual and team field research.* Beverly Hills, CA: Sage.

Douglas, J. D., F. C. Atwell, & J. Hillebrand. 1988. *Love, intimacy, and sex.* Newbury Park, CA: Sage.

Douglas, J. D., & J. M. Johnson. 1977. *Existential sociology.* Cambridge: Cambridge University Press.

Douglas, M. 1982. *In the active voice.* London: Routledge & K. Paul.

Frontline. 2007. Showdown with Iran. PBS. October 23.

Gamel, K. 2006. Two captured U.S. soldiers killed in "barbaric way." *The Seattle Times*, June 20, p. 1. http://seattletimes.nwsource.com/html/nationworld/2003073487_webiraq20.html (accessed June 29, 2006).

Goffman, E. 1959. *The presentation of self in everyday life.* Garden City, NY: Doubleday.

Goffman, E. 1963a. *Behavior in public places; notes on the social organization of gatherings.* New York: Free Press of Glencoe.

Goffman, E. 1963b. *Stigma; notes on the management of spoiled identity.* Englewood Cliffs, NJ: Prentice-Hall.

Johnston, D., & J. M. Broder. 2007. F.B.I. says guards killed 14 Iraqis without cause. *The New York Times*, November 14, p. A1. http://www.nytimes.com/2007/11/14/world/middleeast/14blackwater.html?_r=1&th&emc=th&oref=slogin (accessed November 14, 2007).

Lieven, A., & R. Menon. 2006. The US should express regret for lives lost in Pakistan airstrike. *Christian Science Monitor*, January 19, p. 9.

Lind, J. Dyste. 1988. Toward a theory of cultural continuity and change: The innovation, retention, loss and dissemination of information. In D. R. Maines & C. J. Couch (Eds.), *Communication and social structure*, pp. 173–94. Springfield, IL: Charles C. Thomas.

Marcus, G. E., J. Clifford, & School of American Research. 1986. *Writing culture: The poetics and politics of ethnography: A School of American Research advanced seminar.* Berkeley: University of California Press.

Miller, H. T., & C. J. Fox. 2001. The epistemic community. *Administration & Society* 32(6):668–85.

Perry, T. 2007. Defense, jury makeup likely spared Marine from prison. *The New York Times* July 23. http://seattletimes.nwsource.com/html/nation-world/2003801642_hamdania23.html (accessed August 30, 2007).

Roth, C. 2007. La reconstruction en sciences sociales: Le cas des réseaux de savoirs. *Nouvelles Perspectives en Sciences Sociales* 2(2):40–74.

Sanger, D. E., & D. Rohde. 2007. U.S. is likely to continue aid to Pakistan. *The New York Times* November 5, p. A1. http://www.nytimes.com/2007/11/05/washington/05diplo.html?th&emc=th (accessed December 24, 2007).

Schutz, A. 1967. *The phenomenology of the social world*. Evanston, IL: Northwestern University Press.

Schwalbe, M., S. Godwin, D. Holden, D. Schrock, S. Thompson, & M. Wolkomir. 2000. Generic processes in the reproduction of inequality: An interactionist analysis. *Social Forces* 79(2):419–52.

Silverstein, K. 2006. Revolving door to Blackwater causes alarm at CIA. *Harpers*, September 12. http://www.harpers.org/archive/2006/09/sb-revolving-door-blackwater-1158094722 (accessed December 24, 2007).

Stack, M. K., & R. Salman. 2006. Survivors say Marines went house to house in a rage. *The Seattle Times*, June 2, p.A1. http://seattletimes.nwsource.com/html/nationworld/2003031922_hadithatale01.html (accessed December 24, 2007).

Staff, Editorial. 2006. Editorial. *Pakistan Observer*, January 15, p. 1.

Tatman, L. 2001. *Knowledge that matters: A feminist theological paradigm and epistemology*. London: Sheffield Academic Press.

Turner, R. H. 1957. The normative coherence of folk concepts. *Research Studies of the State College of Washington* 25(1):127–36.

Turner, R. H. 1969. The public perception of protest. *American Sociological Review* 34(6):815–31.

van Dijk, T. A. 1985. *Discourse and communication: New approaches to the analysis of mass media discourse and communication*. Berlin: W. de Gruyter.

Von Zielbauer, P. 2007. Groups rally to aid accused troops. *The New York Times*, July 22. http://seattletimes.nwsource.com/html/nationworld/2003800480_abuse22.html (accessed December 24, 2007).

⌗ The Value of a Realist Understanding of Causality for Qualitative Research

Joseph A. Maxwell
George Mason University

Until a few years ago [causal claims] were in disrepute in both philosophy and economics alike and sometimes in the other social sciences as well. Nowadays causality is back, and with a vengeance ... methodologists and philosophers are suddenly in intense dispute about what these kinds of claims can mean and how to test them.

—Cartwright, 2007, p. 1

Although I think that Cartwright downplays the extent to which questions of causality and causal explanation have been important in the philosophy of science over the last forty years, following the demise of logical positivism and of the "deductive-nomological model" as a credible theory of scientific explanation (Kitcher & Salmon, 1989; Salmon, 1984, 1998), her statement clearly identifies the current ferment over issues of causality. I believe that current realist approaches to causality provide a valuable conceptual framework both for doing and for justifying qualitative research that aims to draw causal conclusions. In this chapter, I will first provide some background on contemporary realism and how this has been viewed by qualitative researchers. I will then focus specifically on causality, discussing how a realist perspective differs from positivist views of causality, and how qualitative researchers can use this perspective in their work.

What Is Realism?

Philosophic realism in general is defined by Phillips (1987, p. 205) as "the view that entities exist independently of being perceived, or independently of our theories about them." Schwandt adds that "scientific realism is the view that theories refer to real features of the world. 'Reality' here refers to whatever it is in the universe (i.e., forces, structures, and so on) that causes the phenomena we perceive with our senses" (1997, p. 133).

In the philosophy of science, including the philosophy of the social sciences, realism has been an important, if not the dominant, approach for over thirty years (Baert, 1998, pp. 189–90; Suppe, 1977, p. 618); realism has been a prominent position in other areas of philosophy as well (Kulp, 1997). The proliferation of realist positions led one realist philosopher to claim that "scientific realism is a majority position whose advocates are so divided as to appear a minority" (Leplin, 1984, p. 1). The idea that there is a real world with which we interact, and to which our concepts and theories refer, has proved to be a resilient and powerful one that has attracted increased philosophical attention following the demise of positivism.

In the social sciences, the most important manifestation of realism is the "critical realist" tradition most closely associated with the work of Roy Bhaskar (1978, 1989; compare Archer et al., 1998; Harre, 1975; Manicas, 1987, 2006; Sayer, 1992, 2000). However, I also draw substantially from other versions of realism that I see as compatible with the key ideas of the critical realist tradition and that provide additional insights and alternative perspectives for using realism in qualitative research. These include the work of philosophers Cartwright (1999, 2007), Davidson (1980, 1993, 1997), Haack (1998, 2003), McGinn (1999), Putnam (1990, 1999), and Salmon (1984, 1989, 1998); linguist Lakoff (1987; Lakoff & Johnson, 1999); evaluation researchers Pawson and Tilley (1997), Henry, Julnes, and Mark (1998), and Mark, Henry, and Julnes (2000); and qualitative researchers Hammersley (1992), Huberman and Miles (1985), and Miles and Huberman (1994).

There have been a variety of terms used for such versions

of realism, including "critical" realism (Bhaskar 1989; Cook & Campbell 1979), "experiential" realism (Lakoff, 1987), "subtle" realism (Hammersley, 1992), "emergent" realism (Henry, Julnes, & Mark, 1998), "natural" realism (Putnam, 1999), and "innocent" realism (Haack, 1998, 2003). I will use the phrase "critical realism" in a broad sense to include all of these forms of realism.

A distinctive feature of all of these forms of realism is that they deny that we can have any objective or certain knowledge of the world and accept the possibility of alternative valid accounts of any phenomenon. All theories about the world are seen as grounded in a particular perspective and worldview, and all knowledge is partial, incomplete, and fallible. Lakoff states that this form of realism "assumes that 'the world is the way it is,' while acknowledging that there can be more than one scientifically correct way of understanding reality in terms of conceptual schemes with different objects and categories of objects" (1987, p. 265).

Critical realists thus retain an ontological realism while accepting a form of epistemological constructivism and relativism (Smith & Deemer, 2002). This position has achieved widespread, if often implicit, acceptance as an alternative both to naive realism and to radical constructivist views that deny the existence of any reality apart from our constructions. Shadish, Cook, and Campbell (2002) argued that "all scientists are epistemological constructivists and relativists" in the sense that they believe that *both* the ontological world and the worlds of ideology, values, etc., play roles in the construction of scientific knowledge (p. 29).

Conversely, Schwandt (1997) stated that "many (if not most, I suspect) qualitative researchers have a common-sense realist *ontology*, that is, they take seriously the existence of things, events, structures, people, meanings, and so forth in the environment as independent in some way from their experience with them" (p. 134); he also noted that most social constructivists in the sociology of science "do not conclude that there is no material reality 'out there'" (Schwandt, 1997, p. 20; see also Shadish, Cook, & Campbell, 2002, pp. 28–31). Ezzy (2002, pp. 15–18) argued similarly that although some postmodernists deny that reality exists, others simply want to problematize our assumptions about reality in light of the complexity of our process of understanding it, citing

Kvale's claim that although moderate postmodernism rejects the idea of universal truth, it "accepts the possibility of specific, local, personal, and community forms of truth with a focus on daily life and local narrative" (Kvale, 1995, p. 21).

Given the prominence of realist views in philosophy and the prevalence of a common-sense realist ontology in qualitative research, it is puzzling that realism has not had a more explicit influence on qualitative researchers. Despite the early advocacy of an explicitly realist approach to qualitative research by Huberman and Miles (1985; Miles & Huberman, 1994) and others (Hammersley, 1992; Maxwell, 1990a, 1990b, 1992), critical realism has been largely unnoticed by most qualitative researchers. When it *has* been noticed, it has generally been dismissed as simply positivism in another guise (Mark, Henry, & Julnes, 2000, p. 166).

This lack of attention is now starting to change. Smith and Deemer (2000), in their chapter in the second edition of the *Handbook of Qualitative Research*, devoted considerable space to refuting Hammersley's and my arguments for realism. Noting that the epistemology of critical realism is relativist rather than realist in that it rejects the possibility of objective knowledge of the world and accepts the existence of multiple legitimate accounts and interpretations, they asserted that combining ontological realism and epistemological relativism is contradictory and that the ontological concept of a reality independent of our theories can serve no useful function in qualitative research because there is no way to employ this that will avoid the constraints of a relativist epistemology. They concluded that "Maxwell is unable to show us how to get reality to do some serious work" (p. 883). Similarly, Denzin and Lincoln (2005), in their introduction to the third edition of the *Handbook of Qualitative Research*, discussed critical realism as a possible "third stance" distinct from both naive positivism and poststructuralism. However, they ended up rejecting most of what critical realists advocate and stated: "We do not think that critical realism will keep the social science ship afloat" (p. 13).

In this chapter, I contend that realism *can* do useful work for qualitative methodology and practice if it is taken seriously and its implications for qualitative research systematically developed. One of the most important contributions that realism can make derives from a realist understanding of causality. In what follows, I will not attempt to give a detailed philosophical justification for this understanding (for this, see Manicas, 2006; Maxwell, 2004a, 2004c), but focus on its value for qualitative research.

I am not arguing that realism is the "correct" philosophical stance for qualitative research, only that it brings a valuable perspective to the discussion of what kinds of claims and understandings qualitative research can produce. My model for this discussion is the "dialectical" perspective espoused by Greene (2007, pp. 79–82; see also Bernstein, 1992, pp. 8 ff., 225) for integrating qualitative and quantitative research paradigms. Such a perspective values the multiple insights that different paradigms and "mental models" bring to the discussion and the generative potential of an engagement with these different viewpoints.

Realism and Causality

Although there are many differences between positivism and realism (see Schwandt, 1997, pp. 133–34), one of the most important of these for social science research is their divergent views of causality. The positivist view derives from David Hume's analysis of causality. Hume argued that we cannot directly perceive causal relationships, thus we can have no knowledge of causality beyond the observed regularities in associations of events; this position is often called the "regularity view" of causality. It was given its most systematic form by Hempel and Oppenheim (1948) in what they called the "deductive-nomological" theory of causation, which saw causal explanation of events as the subsumption of these events under some general law. This "covering law" approach was the standard view of causality in the philosophy of science for much of the 20th century (Salmon, 1989).

Mohr (1982) labeled this approach to causal explanation "variance theory"; it sees causality as fundamentally referring to a consistent relationship between variables. It treats the actual process of causality as unknowable—a "black box"—and focuses on establishing a correlation between inputs and outputs. In this view, causal inference requires both some sort of systematic comparison of situations in which the presumed causal factor is present or absent, or varies in strength, and the implementation of controls on other possible explanatory variables.

Some qualitative researchers accepted the strictures that this approach to causality entails, and denied that they were making causal claims that were more than speculative (e.g., Lofland & Lofland, 1984, pp. 100–2; Patton, 1990, pp. 490–91). Becker has described the detrimental effect that Hume's theory has had on sociological writing, leading researchers to use vague or evasive circumlocutions for causal statements, "hinting at what we would like, but don't dare, to say" (1986, p. 8).

However, other qualitative researchers reacted to the hegemony of the "regularity" approach by denying that causality is a valid concept in the social sciences. A particularly influential statement of this position was by Lincoln and Guba (1985), who argued that "the concept of causality is so beleaguered and in such serious disarray that it strains credibility to continue to entertain it in any form approximating its present (poorly defined) one" (p. 141). They later grounded this view in a constructivist stance, stating that "there exist multiple, socially constructed realities ungoverned by natural laws, causal or otherwise" (Guba & Lincoln, 1989, p. 86), and that "'causes' and 'effects' do not exist except by imputation" (p. 44).

These two reactions to the regularity view were so influential that the 1,000-page second edition of the *Handbook of Qualitative Research* (Denzin & Lincoln, 2000a) had no entries in the index for cause or explanation. The only references to causality were historical and pejorative: a brief mention of "causal narratives" as a central component of the attempt in the 1960s "to make qualitative research as rigorous as its quantitative counterpart" (Denzin & Lincoln, 2000b, p. 14), and a critique of the "causal generalizations" made by practitioners of analytic induction (Vidich & Lyman, 2000, pp. 57–58).

Both of these reactions identified causality with the regularity theory of causation and ignored the existence of an alternative, realist approach to causality, one that saw causality as fundamentally referring to the actual causal mechanisms and processes that are involved in particular events and situations. For the philosophy of science in general, this approach was most systematically developed by Salmon (1984, 1989, 1998), who referred to it as the "causal/ mechanical" view. In this approach, explanatory knowledge opens up the black boxes of nature to reveal their inner workings. It exhibits the ways in which the things we want to explain come about (Salmon, 1989, p. 182).

In the philosophy of the social sciences, very similar views were developed by those calling themselves "critical realists." Sayer (1992) argued that:

> much that has been written on methods of explanation assumes that causation is a matter of regularities in relationships between events, and that without models of regularities we are left with allegedly inferior, "ad hoc" narratives. But social science has been singularly unsuccessful in discovering law-like regularities. One of the main achievements of recent realist philosophy has been to show that this is an inevitable consequence of an erroneous view of causation. Realism replaces the regularity model with one in which objects and social relations have causal powers which may or may not produce regularities, and which can be explained independently of them. In view of this, less weight is put on quantitative methods for discovering and assessing regularities and more on methods of establishing the qualitative nature of social objects and relations on which causal mechanisms depend. (pp. 2–3)

These mechanisms are seen not as universal laws but as situationally contingent; they are inherently involved with their actual context, which is inextricably part of the causal process.

Mohr (1982) called this approach to causal explanation "process theory," in distinction from variance theory. Similar distinctions to that between variance theory and process theory include Blumer's distinction between variable analysis and the process of interpretation (1956), Ragin's between variable- and case-oriented approaches (1987), and Yin's between factor theories and explanatory theories (1993, pp. 15 ff.).

Both regularity/variance theory and process theory are forms of causal explanation. Process theory is not merely descriptive, as opposed to explanatory variance theory; it is a different *approach* to explanation. Variance theory, which is the dominant approach in experimental and survey methods, typically involves a blackbox approach to the problem of causality in the social sciences.

Lacking direct access to social and cognitive processes, variance theory must attempt to correlate differences in output with differences in input and control for other plausible factors that might affect the output. In contrast, process theory, which is much more suitable for qualitative methods, can often directly investigate these causal processes though observation of social settings and interviews with participants.

This process approach to causation has been advocated by a significant number of qualitative researchers (e.g., Britan 1978, p. 231; Erickson 1986, p. 82; Fielding & Fielding 1986, p. 22), and Schwandt (1997) asserted that "it is irresponsible and untrue to say that qualitative inquiry as a whole eschews causal analysis" (p. 14). Weiss argued that:

> In qualitative interview studies the demonstration of causation rests heavily on the description of a visualizable sequence of events, each event flowing into the next. ... Quantitative studies support an assertion of causation by showing a correlation between an earlier event and a subsequent event. An analysis of data collected in a large-scale sample survey might, for example, show that there is a correlation between the level of the wife's education and the presence of a companionable marriage. In qualitative studies we would look for a process through which the wife's education or factors associated with her education express themselves in marital interaction. (1994, p. 179)

Similarly, Miles and Huberman claimed that:

> Until recently, the dominant view was that field studies should busy themselves with description and leave the explanations to people with large quantitative data bases. Or perhaps field researchers, as is now widely believed, can provide "exploratory" explanations—which still need to be quantitatively verified.
>
> Much recent research supports a claim that we wish to make here: that field research is far *better* than solely quantified approaches at developing explanations of what we call *local causality*— the actual events and processes that led to specific outcomes. (1984, p. 132)

Sayer likewise argued that "[causal] explanation requires mainly interpretive and qualitative research to discover actors' reasoning and circumstances in specific context—not in abstraction from them" (2000, p. 23).

I think that there are two sorts of important work that the realist concept of causality I have described can do in qualitative research. First, there is the work of supporting the use of qualitative research for causal explanation and defending this against the criticisms of quantitative researchers. Second, there is the critical and sensitizing work that realism can do in helping qualitative researchers to further develop their theoretical understanding of, and methods for, developing causal explanations.

Supportive and Defensive Work

A realist understanding of causality provides philosophical justification for the ways in which qualitative researchers typically approach explanation, whether they explicitly use the term "cause" or not. There are three specific aspects of qualitative research that are supported by this understanding.

First, a realist approach justifies qualitative researchers' claims to be able to identify causality in single case studies, without necessarily employing control groups or formal pre/post comparisons. This claim has been defended by many philosophers (e.g., Cartwright, 2000; Davidson, 1997; Putnam, 1999, pp. 140–41; Salmon, 1998, pp. 15–16), but has largely been ignored by quantitative methodologists (an important exception is Shadish, Cook, & Campbell, 2002, p. 465). The ability of qualitative methods to directly investigate causal processes is a major contribution that this approach can make to scientific inquiry and to mixed method research. The view that causal processes can be observed, not just inferred, is supported by experimental research suggesting that humans, as well as other animals, engage in two distinct types of cognitive activity in these two forms of causal comprehension (Dickinson & Shanks, 1995; Kummer, 1995; Premack & Premack, 1995, pp. 653–54).

Second, critical realism's insistence on the inherently contextual nature of causal explanation (Huberman & Miles, 1985; Pawson & Tilley, 1997; Sayer, 1992, pp. 60–61, 2000, pp. 114–18) supports qualitative researchers' emphasis on the importance of context in understanding social phenomena. This is not simply a claim that causal relationships vary across contexts; it is a more fundamental claim that the context within which a causal process occurs is intrinsically involved in that process and often cannot be controlled for in a variance-theory sense without misrepresenting the causal mechanisms involved (Blumer, 1956). Miles and Huberman (1994, pp. 151–65) provided detailed advice on the development and testing of "causal maps" for single-case studies and argued that "the components of a causal map are of a different nature than a disembodied beta coefficient or partial correlation; they are not probabilistic, but specific and determinate, grounded in understanding of events over time in the concrete local context" (p. 159). In this view, causality is basically *local* rather than general, and general causal claims must be grounded in valid site-specific causal explanations.

Third and finally, critical realists insist that meanings (including beliefs, values, and intentions) are just as real as physical phenomena and are essential to the explanation of social and cultural phenomena. Sayer (1992), in a critical realist approach to research methods, stated that "social phenomena are concept-dependent. ...What the practices, institutions, rules, roles, or relationships *are* depends on what they mean in society to its members" (p. 30). Seeing emotions, beliefs, values, and so on as part of reality supports an interpretivist approach to understanding social phenomena without entailing a radical constructivism that denies the existence or causal relevance of a physical world.

The view of meanings as causes is fundamental to our common-sense explanations of people's actions and has been accepted by most philosophers (Robb & Heil, 2003; see also Davidson, 1980, 1993, 1997; McGinn, 1991) and social scientists (e.g., Menzel, 1978). Putnam (1990, 1999) has argued for the legitimacy of both mental and physical ways of making sense of the world and for a distinction between mental and physical *perspectives* or languages, both referring to reality, but from different conceptual standpoints. He stated that "the metaphysical realignment I propose involves an acquiescence in a plurality of conceptual resources, of different and mutually irreducible vocabularies ... coupled with a return not to dualism but to the 'naturalism of the common man'" (Putnam, 1999, p. 38).

Critical realism thus provides a consistent grounding for

accepting a causal role for meanings and does not assume a forced choice between realism, on the one hand, and interpretivism or constructivism, on the other. This point is often misunderstood or missed, because there is a widespread view that realism is the doctrine that "the world is independent of the mental" (Callinicos, 1995, p. 82). The versions of realism discussed here treat mental phenomena as *part of* reality, not as a realm separate from it, although it is a part that is understood by means of a different conceptual framework from that used for the physical world.

Combining this view with a process-oriented approach to causality can resolve the long-standing perceived contradiction between reason explanations and cause explanations, and integrate both in explanatory theories. However, Weber's sharp distinction between causal explanation and interpretive understanding (1905; see Layton, 1997, pp. 184–85) had a profound influence on qualitative research, obscuring the importance of reasons as causal influences on actions and thus their role as essential components of any full explanation of human action. Realism can deal with the apparent dissimilarity of reason explanations and cause explanations by showing that reasons can plausibly be seen as real phenomena in a causal nexus leading to the action.

In combination, these components of a realist approach to causality provide a powerful strategy for addressing causal explanation in qualitative research, allowing qualitative researchers, in many circumstances, to develop causal explanations independently of quantitative, variance-theory strategies. In addition, this strategy complements the strengths of quantitative research and emphasizes the potential contribution of qualitative methods to mixed-method research. Sayer (1992) argues that "All too often the qualitative investigation is abandoned just at the point when it is most needed—for deciding the status and the causal (as opposed to statistical) significance of whatever patterns and associations are found" (p. 115).

These three supportive functions of a realist concept of causality are also valuable in defending qualitative research from the dismissive and marginalizing attacks of science-based research, which seeks to impose a quantitative, variance-theory standard on all social research. I have elsewhere (Maxwell, 2004a, 2004b) presented specific ways in which qualitative researchers can use a critical realist concept of causality to challenge the assumptions on which these attacks are based and to argue that that it is possible for qualitative researchers to be fully "scientific" in the sense of being able to systematically develop and validate causal explanations for the phenomena they study. (Of course, not all qualitative researchers aspire to do this; much qualitative research is explicitly grounded in the arts and humanities rather than the sciences.)

Critical, Theoretical, and Sensitizing Work

In addition to this supportive and defensive work, a realist understanding of causality can also perform important critical work in qualitative research, challenging assumptions and stimulating rethinking of central issues in the social sciences. I see two areas in which a realist concept of causality can make such a contribution.

First, a realist perspective can provide a framework for better understanding the relationship between actors' perspectives and their actual situations. This issue has been a prominent concern in the philosophy of social science for many years (e.g., MacIntyre, 1967; Menzel, 1978), and is central to critical approaches to qualitative research. Critical realism treats both actors' perspectives and their situations as real phenomena that causally interact with one another. In this, realism supports the emphasis that critical theory places on the influence that social and economic conditions have on beliefs and ideologies. Sayer (1992, pp. 222–23) stated that the objects of interpretive understanding (meanings, beliefs, motives, and so on) are influenced both by the material circumstances in which they exist and by the cultural resources that provide actors with ways of making sense of their situations. However, critical realism approaches the understanding of this interaction without assuming any *specific* theory of the relationship between material and ideational phenomena, such as Marxism.

A realist perspective also legitimates and clarifies the concept of "ideological distortion"—that cultural forms may obscure or misrepresent aspects of the economic or social system or the physical environment—while affirming the causal interaction between the physical and social environment and cultural forms. In particular, realism is compatible with what have been called "ideological" or "non-reflectionist" approaches to culture, in which cultural forms that contradict aspects of social structure may serve ideological functions sustain the social system or constitute adaptive responses to the physical or social environment (e.g., Maxwell, 1978; McKinley, 1971a, 1971b; Murphy, 1967). An emphasis on causal processes, rather than regularities or laws, in explaining sociocultural phenomena, also allows explanations to be tailored to single cases and unique circumstances, so that different individuals or social groups may have different responses to similar situations, depending on differences in specific personal or cultural characteristics that are causally relevant to the outcome.

Second, a realist conception of causality highlights issues of validity in qualitative research (Maxwell, 1992). Not all possible accounts of some individual, situation, event, or institution are equally useful, credible, or legitimate. Making a claim about causal relationships implies the possibility of being *wrong* about this and thus requires taking seriously the possibility of alternative accounts of these relationships and how these can be addressed. Validity, from a realist perspective, is not a matter of procedures but of the relationship between the claim and the phenomena that it is about. Although critical realism denies that we can have any objective perception of these phenomena to which we can compare our claims, it does not abandon the possibility of *testing* these claims against evidence about the nature of the phenomena.

I think that much of what qualitative researchers already do in developing and assessing evidence for their conclusions can be applied to the task of causal explanation, for two reasons. First, evidence for causality is not in principle different from evidence for any other sort of conclusion; the function of evidence, in general, is to enable the researcher to develop, modify, and test conclusions, and many of the qualitative procedures for doing this are applicable to causal investigation. Although some qualitative researchers hold, following Weber, that assessing the validity of interpretive claims is different in principle from assessing causal explanations,

Sayer argues that "in so far as reasons and beliefs can be causes of social events, the evaluation of interpretive understanding is not so different from that of causal explanations as is often supposed" (1992, p. 223). Second, many qualitative researchers are already making and assessing causal claims, but without couching these in explicitly causal language. Any claim that something "influences," "impacts," "shapes," "produces," or "transforms" something else is a causal claim and requires appropriate sorts of evidence to support that claim. Making the causal implication explicit allows a more rigorous evaluation of such claims.

Elsewhere, I have discussed (Maxwell, 2004c) some of the strategies that qualitative researchers can use for causal investigations and will not describe them in detail here. These strategies include standard qualitative methods such as intensive, long-term involvement, the collection of rich data, searching for discrepant evidence, member checks, and triangulation, as well as less commonly used ones such as intervention, comparison, the "modus operandi" strategy (Scriven, 1974), and the development of causal narratives and maps. My point is that qualitative researchers already have many of the tools for generating causal explanations and the evidence to support them. I believe that a realist understanding of causality can help qualitative researchers use these tools more effectively and develop new ways of assessing their conclusions.

Again, I am not claiming that a realist approach is the "correct" understanding of causality. I accept the possibility of multiple useful approaches to causality and see value in a dialog between these. Cartwright (2007) has provided a detailed argument for what she called "causal pluralism," the view that what causes are and what they do varies from case to case. She stated that current approaches "are not alternative, incompatible views about causation; they are rather views that fit different kinds of causal systems" and that "there is no single interesting characterizing feature of causation; hence, no off-the-shelf or one-size-fits-all method for finding out about it, no 'gold standard' for judging causal relations" (p. 2). I believe, however, that the realist approach I describe here is particularly compatible with qualitative methods and premises and can perform some useful work for qualitative researchers.

References

Archer, M., R. Bhaskar, A. Collier, T. Lawson, & A. Norrie. 1998. *Critical realism: Essential readings*. London: Routledge.

Baert, P. 1998. *Social theory in the twentieth century*. New York: New York University Press.

Becker, H. S. 1986. *Writing for social scientists: How to start and finish your thesis, book, or article*. Chicago: University of Chicago Press.

Bernstein, R. 1992. *The new constellation: The ethical-political horizons of modernity-postmodernity*. Cambridge, MA: MIT Press.

Bhaskar, R. 1978. *A realist theory of science*, 2nd ed. Brighton, UK: Harvester.

Bhaskar, R. 1989. *Reclaiming reality: A critical introduction to contemporary philosophy*. London: Verso.

Blumer, H. 1956. Sociological analysis and the "variable." *American Sociological Review* 22(1):683–90. Reprinted in H. Blumer, *Symbolic interactionism: Perspective and method*, pp. 127–39. Berkeley: University of California Press, 1969.

Britan, G. M. 1978. Experimental and contextual models of program evaluation. *Evaluation and Program Planning* 1(3):229–34.

Callinicos, Alex 1995. *Theories and narratives: Reflections on the philosophy of history*. Durham, NC: Duke University Press.

Cartwright, N. 1999. *The dappled world: A study of the boundaries of science*. Cambridge: Cambridge University Press.

Cartwright, N. 2000. An empiricist defence of singular causes. In R. Teichmann (Ed.), *Logic, cause, and action: Essays in honour of Elizabeth Anscombe*, pp. 47–58. Cambridge: Cambridge University Press.

Cartwright, N. 2007. *Hunting causes and using them: Approaches in philosophy and economics*. Cambridge: Cambridge University Press.

Cook, T., & D. T. Campbell. 1979. *Quasi-experimentation: Design and analysis issues for field settings*. Boston: Houghton Mifflin.

Davidson, D. 1980. *Essays on actions and events*. Oxford: Oxford University Press

Davidson, D. 1993. Thinking causes. In J. Heil & A. Mele (Eds.), *Mental causation*, pp. 3–17. Oxford: Clarendon Press.

Davidson, D. 1997. Indeterminism and antirealism. In C. B. Kulp (Ed.), *Realism/antirealism and epistemology*, pp. 109–22. Lanham MD: Rowman and Littlefield.

Denzin, N. K., & Y. S. Lincoln, Eds. 2000a. *Handbook of qualitative research*, 2nd ed. Thousand Oaks, CA: Sage.

Denzin, N. K., & Y. S. Lincoln. 2000b. Introduction: The discipline and practice of qualitative research . In N. K. Denzin & Y. S. Lincoln (Eds.), *Handbook of qualitative research*, 2nd ed., pp. 1–28. Thousand Oaks, CA: Sage.

Denzin, N. K., & Y. S. Lincoln. 2005. Introduction: The discipline and practice of qualitative research. In N. K. Denzin & Y. S. Lincoln (Eds.), *Handbook of qualitative research*, 3rd ed., pp. 1–42. Thousand Oaks, CA: Sage.

Dickinson, A., & D. Shanks. 1995. Instrumental action and causal representation. In D. Sperber, D. Premack, & A. J. Premack (Eds.), *Causal cognition: A multidisciplinary debate*, pp. 5–25. Oxford: Clarendon Press.

Erickson, F. 1986. Qualitative methods. In M. Wittrock (Ed.), *Handbook of research on teaching*, pp. 119–61. New York: Macmillan.

Ezzy, D. 2002. *Qualitative analysis: Practice and innovation.* London: Routledge.

Fielding, N. G., & J. L. Fielding. 1986. *Linking data.* Thousand Oaks, CA: Sage.

Greene, J. 2007. *Mixed methods in social inquiry.* New York: Wiley.

Guba, E. G., & Y. S. Lincoln. 1989. *Fourth generation evaluation.* Newbury Park, CA: Sage.

Haack, S. 1998. *Manifesto of a passionate moderate.* Chicago: University of Chicago Press.

Haack, S. 2003. *Defending science—within reason.* Amherst, NY: Prometheus Press.

Hammersley, M. 1992. Ethnography and realism. In M. Hammersley, *What's wrong with ethnography? Methodological explorations*, pp. 43–56. London: Routledge.

Harre, R. 1975. *Causal powers: A theory of natural necessity.* Oxford: Basil Blackwell.

Hempel, C. G., & P. Oppenheim. 1948. Studies in the logic of explanation. *Philosophy of Science* 15(1):135–75.

Henry, G., J. Julnes, & M. Mark. 1998. *Realist evaluation: An emerging theory in support of practice.* New Directions for Evaluation 78. San Francisco: Jossey-Bass.

Huberman, A. M., & M. B. Miles. 1985. Assessing local causality in qualitative research. In D. N. Berg & K. K. Smith (Eds.), *Exploring clinical methods for social research*, pp. 351–82. Beverly Hills, CA: Sage.

Kitcher, P., & W. C. Salmon, Eds. 1989. *Scientific explanation.* Minneapolis: University of Minnesota Press.

Kulp, C. B., Ed. 1997. *Realism/antirealism and epistemology.* Lanham, MD: Rowman and Littlefield.

Kummer, H. 1995. Causal knowledge in animals. In D. Sperber, D. Premack, & A. J. Premack (Eds.), *Causal cognition: A multidisciplinary debate*, pp. 26–36. Oxford: Clarendon Press.

Kvale, S. 1995. The social construction of validity. *Qualitative Inquiry* 1(1):19–40.

Lakoff, G. 1987. *Women, fire, and dangerous things: What categories reveal about the mind*. Chicago: University of Chicago Press.

Lakoff, G., & M. Johnson. 1999. *Philosophy in the flesh: The embodied mind and its challenge to Western thought*. New York: Basic Books.

Layton, R. 1997. *An introduction to theory in anthropology*. Cambridge: Cambridge University Press.

Leplin, J. 1984. Introduction. In Leplin, J. (Ed.), *Scientific realism*, pp. 1–15. Berkeley: University of California Press.

Lincoln, Y. S., & E. G. Guba. 1985. *Naturalistic inquiry*. Newbury Park, CA: Sage.

Lofland, J., & L. Lofland. 1984. *Analyzing social settings: A guide to qualitative observation and analysis*, 2nd ed. Belmont, CA: Wadsworth.

MacIntyre, A. 1967. The idea of a social science. *Aristotelian Society Supplement* 41(1):93–114.

Manicas, P. T. 1987. *A history and philosophy of the social sciences*. Oxford: Basil Blackwell.

Manicas, P. T. 2006. *A realist philosophy of social science: Explanation and understanding*. Cambridge: Cambridge University Press.

Mark, M. M., G. T. Henry, & G. Julnes. 2000. *Evaluation: An integrated framework for understanding, guiding, and improving policies and programs*. San Francisco: Jossey-Bass.

Maxwell, J. 1978. The evolution of Plains Indian kin terminologies: A non-reflectionist account. *Plains Anthropologist* 23(79):13–29.

Maxwell, J. 1990a. Up from positivism. *Harvard Educational Review* 60:497–501.

Maxwell, J. 1990b. Response to "Campbell's Retrospective and a Constructivist's Perspective." *Harvard Educational Review* 60:504–8.

Maxwell, J. 1992. Understanding and validity in qualitative research. *Harvard Educational Review* 62(3):279–300.

Maxwell, J. 2004a. Causal explanation, qualitative research, and scientific inquiry in education. *Educational Researcher* 33(2):3–11.

Maxwell, J. 2004b. Re-emergent scientism, postmodernism, and dialogue across differences. *Qualitative Inquiry* 10(1):35–41.

Maxwell, J. 2004c. Using qualitative methods for causal explanation. *Field Methods* 16(3):243–64.

McGinn, C. 1991. Conceptual causation: Some elementary reflections. *Mind* 100(4):573–86.

McGinn, C. 1999. *Knowledge and reality.* Oxford: Clarendon Press.

McKinley, R. 1971a. A critique of the reflectionist theory of kinship terminology: The Crow/Omaha case. *Man* 6(2):228–47.

McKinley, R. 1971b. Why do Crow and Omaha terminologies exist? A sociology of knowledge interpretation. *Man* 6(3):408–26.

Menzel, H. 1978. Meaning–who needs it? In M. Brenner, P. Marsh, & M. Brenner (Eds.), *The social contexts of method*, pp. 140–71. New York: St. Martin's Press.

Miles, M. B., & A. M. Huberman. 1984. *Qualitative data analysis: A sourcebook of new methods.* Thousand Oaks, CA: Sage.

Miles, M. B., & A. M. Huberman. 1994. *Qualitative data analysis: An expanded sourcebook.* Thousand Oaks, CA: Sage.

Mohr, L. B. 1982. *Explaining organizational behavior.* San Francisco: Jossey-Bass.

Murphy, R. 1967. Tuareg kinship. *American Anthropologist* 69(2):163–70.

Patton, M. Q. 1990. *Qualitative evaluation and research methods*, 2nd ed. Thousand Oaks, CA: Sage.

Pawson, R., & N. Tilley. 1997. *Realistic evaluation.* London: Sage.

Phillips, D. C. 1987. *Philosophy, science, and social inquiry: Contemporary methodological controversies in social science and related applied fields of research.* Oxford: Pergamon Press.

Premack, D., & A. J. Premack. 1995. Afterword. In D. Sperber, D. Premack, & A. J. Premack (Eds.), *Causal cognition: A multidisciplinary debate*, pp. 650–54. Oxford: Clarendon Press.

Putnam, H. 1990. *Realism with a human face*, edited by J. Conant. Cambridge, MA: Harvard University Press.

Putnam, H. 1999. *The threefold cord: Mind, body, and world.* New York: Columbia University Press.

Ragin, C. C. 1987. *The comparative method: Moving beyond qualitative and quantitative strategies.* Berkeley: University of California Press.

Robb, D., & J. Heil. 2003. Mental causation. *Stanford encyclopedia of philosophy.* http://plato.stanford.edu/entries/mental-causation/ (accessed December 28, 2007).

Salmon, W. C. 1984. *Scientific explanation and the causal structure of the world.* Princeton, NJ: Princeton University Press.

Salmon, W. C. 1989. Four decades of scientific explanation. In P. Kitcher & W. C. Salmon (Eds.), *Scientific explanation*, pp. 3–219. Minneapolis: University of Minnesota Press.

Salmon, W. C. 1998. *Causality and explanation*. New York: Oxford University Press.

Sayer, A. 1992. *Method in social science: A realist approach*, 2nd ed. London: Routledge.

Sayer, A. 2000. *Realism and social science*. London: Sage.

Schwandt, T. A. 1997. *Qualitative inquiry: A dictionary of terms*. Thousand Oaks, CA: Sage.

Scriven, M. 1974. Evaluation perspectives and procedures. In W. J. Popham (Ed.), *Evaluation in education—Current perspectives*, pp. 68–84. Berkeley, CA: McCutchan.

Shadish, W. R., T. D. Cook, & D. T. Campbell 2002. *Experimental and quasi-experimental designs for generalized causal inference*. Boston: Houghton Mifflin.

Smith, J. K., & D. K. Deemer. 2002. The problem of criteria in the age of relativism. In N. K. Denzin & Y. S. Lincoln (Eds.), *Handbook of qualitative research*, 2nd ed., pp. 877–96. Thousand Oaks, CA: Sage.

Suppe, F. 1977. Afterword. In F. Suppe (Ed.), *The structure of scientific theories*, 2nd ed. Urbana: University of Illinois Press.

Vidich, A. J., & S. M. Lyman. 2000. Qualitative methods: Their history in sociology and anthropology. In N. K. Denzin and Y. S. Lincoln (Eds.), *Handbook of qualitative research*, 2nd ed., pp. 37–84. Thousand Oaks, CA: Sage.

Weber, M. 1905. Critical studies in the logic of the social sciences. *Archiv für Sozialwissenschaft und Sozialpolitik*. Reprinted in M. Weber, *The methodology of the social sciences*. New York, The Free Press, 1949.

Weiss, R. S. 1994. *Learning from strangers: The art and method of qualitative interviewing*. New York: The Free Press.

Yin, R. 1993. *Applications of case study research*. Thousand Oaks, CA: Sage.

🗲 (Post)Feminist Methodology

Getting Lost, OR a Scientificity We Can Bear to Learn from[1]

Patti Lather
The Ohio State University

*This other thinking of knowledge if I can put it that way,
does not exclude science. But it overturns and overflows its
received idea.*
—Derrida, 1994, p. 34

This chapter focuses on recent feminist reinscriptions of practices of critique and analysis in qualitative research in order to begin to grasp what is on the horizon in terms of new analytics and practices of inquiry. As Wilson (1998) argues, after Sedgwick and Frank (1995), if feminist work is not to become routinized, static, and predictable, it must interrogate the enabling limits of its own practices, not to junk them but to shake them up. This is a sort of "faithful transgression" that is not so much self-correction as negotiation with complexity where feminist practice is "always already rewriting itself" (Wilson, 1998, p. 65). The goal is a generative undoing of a certain orthodoxy that is a necessary part of feminism making itself coherent and authoritative. Displacing fixed critical spaces enacted in earlier practices to which we are indebted, we move toward an "iterative productivity" (Wilson, 1998, p. 207) that is open to permanent dynamism.

In what follows, I unpack a variety of analytics and practices that I am gathering in the effort to put the nature of scientificity on the feminist agenda. This includes Eve Sedgwick's (1997) reparative reading, Gayatri Spivak's (1993) dislocating negotiation, and Elizabeth Wilson's (1998) analytics of breaching in terms of their usefulness toward what I call "philosophical ethnography."

Against positivist dreams of authentic, undistorted knowing on the part of the sovereign knower, such practices recommend analytic deferral and open up the unthinkable. At the heart of such efforts is a reinscription of scientificity where the question of what makes a science a science is positioned against the Popperian and even Kuhnian sorts of demarcation projects that have historically dominated in framing such questions. This chapter expands on my earlier work by exploring practices toward a counter-science that is constituted by the interplay between scientificity and the necessary interpretation that has historically been excluded from the received understanding of science.

Sedgwick's Reparative Reading: Toward Undoing Simplicity

In "Complicating Cheerleading," a review of Natalie Adams and Pam Bettis's (2003) book, *Cheerleader! An American Icon*, Lu Bailey and I (2006) work to foreground layered meanings, honor investments, infuse with productive theoretical weight, and foreground the messiness of shifting and competing meanings, all toward complicating a practice "alternatively honored and ridiculed" in American cultural critique.

In this, we rely heavily on queer theorist Eve Sedgwick, who, in the introduction to *Novel Gazing* (1997), writes of "reparative reading." She distinguishes this from what she terms the more typical "paranoid model" of critical theory, which is about exposing and demystifying. Termed "a hermeneutics of suspicion" by Paul Ricoeur in writing of Marx, Nietzsche, and Freud, such a practice situates the theorist as "the one who knows," a master of revealing the false consciousness of others. In contrast, Sedgwick calls for a more generous critical practice, one that is more about love than suspicion and draws on rich phenomenological accounts of embodied experiences, feeling, and intimacy. This is about difference without opposition, differences that are expanded rather than policed or repressed or judged. Sedgwick associates such a critical practice with the work of consolation and making whole, of love and political hope, an ethic of giving up authority to the otherness of the wholly Other, a more "slip-slidy" sort of effect than the confident mastery of the more typical paranoid model of critique.

This slip-slidy effect has grown out of Sedgwick's encounters with queer culture, Buddhism, and mortality via her recurrent breast cancer. It is offered as a persistent effortfulness that makes a present by generating fresh, "deroutinizing methodologies" (Sedgwick, 1997, p. 3). The move is toward recognitions, pleasures, and discoveries that are more reparative than suspicious, a working of positive affect instead of the banality of the merely de-idealized/disenchanted. The goal is to assemble and confer plenitude on an object that will then have resources to offer. It is not cure so much as undertaking a different range of affects, ambitions, and risks in terms of extracting sustenance from the objects of a culture, particularly objects that have received scorn from more typical critical practices. The hope is an escape from the exhaustions of the hermeneutics of suspicion and, instead, "twisting, citing, queering" the objects of a culture, even if that culture has historically functioned to not sustain the very queerness that might generate some way out of the present exhaustions. This is using "the violating yet perversely enabling epistemic configuration" (Barber, 1997, p. 403) that is the ground of queer theory toward different practices of knowing and doing.

This critical practice is generous and pleasurable in the risks it takes and provides a different sort of reading of what Adams and Bettis have done in this book. Yes, the book is a bit of a surprise in terms of feminist analysis of cheerleading, a surprise to the authors themselves who became "cheerleading converts" (Adams & Bettis, 2003, p. 142) in the process of their four years of ethnographic and archival work for the book. Yes, the book interrupts a more typical relentlessly sober critical practice of delineating the ways cheerleading reproduces patriarchal, capitalist culture. But there is something to be said for the sort of doubled analysis at work here, an analysis that both brings a feminist reading of cheerleading to a broad audience and pushes feminist analysis in directions that take "joy, pleasure, and fun" into account in imagining not the end of cheerleading, but a way to use the multiple meanings of cheerleading as a sort of cultural praxis. This is a sort of analysis that complicates what we might think cheerleading and, perhaps, feminist cultural analysis are all about.

Spivak's Dislocating Negotiation: Developing "Thinking Technologies"

Gayatri Spivak urges that we not be dismissive of empirical work, that we wrestle with data and value how they help us not homogenize or marginalize "the actual." We need to learn how to rescue empirical work, "honor" it (Spivak, 1993, p. 17) via a double movement between theory and data. About being "thoroughly empirical" without being blindly or complacently empiricist, she writes: "It seems to me that to be empirical in this way would be a much greater challenge, require much harder work, and would make people read different things, primarily texts of active social work" (Spivak, 1993, p. 16). This is part of Spivak's commitment to "undermining the vanguardism of theory" (1993, p. 15) that uses the rigor of the negative, the detour through the sign, to shake up theory as well as practice.

An example of such work is that of Dorothy Staunaes and Dorte Marie Sondergaard's (Forthcoming) reception study of a research-based intervention into gender equity in a Danish corporation. The authors were contracted to bring forward a new language toward more complex understandings of gender equity and the blockages of women moving up the corporate ladder. Putting a sort of poststructural praxis in motion, their goals were to develop "thinking technologies," retool concepts, interrupt deficit discourses, and disturb hegemonic constructions that feed habit, common sense understandings, and processes of inclusion/exclusion. Using research findings to organize workshops toward speeding up organizational reflexivity via new words and storylines, they ask what action and policies are possible if we break out of embedded discursive practices and destabilize established frameworks of thinking.

Foregrounding a generous reading of the complexity of stakeholder subjectivity, their analysis of "epistemological mismatches" supplants a more typical focus on an undertheorized and overly rationalized "resistance" by looking at the thinking repertoires of stakeholders, especially the "messy crossings" that characterize complex organizations and subjectivities. What is the "distributed meaning making" in terms of reception? How does research interfere with rationalities, identities, and hierarchies?

As a text of active social work, Staunaes and Sondergaard put empirical flesh on the more typical abstract efforts to put post-structuralism to work in contract/evaluation and policy contexts of neoliberal regimes of usefulness, where research is situated as a commodity that "pays off" in terms of greater efficiency and profit. Their counsel is, instead, to learn how to read out the constellations that research findings collide with and ask how new narratives are differentially livable across varied stakeholders in situating research as an engagement with the "'otherness' that is usually not spoken about in the more authoritative stories about research" (Markussen, 2005, p. 331), the "realities that do not share in the privileges of the hegemonic" (Markussen, 2006, p. 291).

Wilson's Analytics of Breaching: Toward Generative Undoing

In her book on neural geography, Elisabeth Wilson attempts such a dislocating negotiation with feminist psychology and cognitive science. Wilson urges that we think of scientificity as other than "an oppressive empiricism in rigid opposition to interpretation" (1998, p. 94). Her interest is a sort of disorderly pursuit of the scientific that is a constitutive play between equivocation and conventionalization, a sort of "generative undoing" (1998, p. 101) via SMALL moves that acknowledge enclosure of the very thing we are attempting to undo.

This entails rethinking the relation between empiricism and philosophy and involves Derrida's idea of breaching as a force that forges a path and the space thus opened up (Wilson, 1998, p. 167). Such an economics of force attends to how the empirically elusive confounds demands for presence. This is a negotiation that structures the empirically graspable as not not philosophy by functioning as a careful displacement of a philosophy of presence, exploiting these tensions in order to think mobility.

Such a move situates the critical and the traditional in debt to one another, not in opposition but not complementary either. Perhaps "treasured incommensurabilities as well as correspondences" (Wilson, 1998, p. 198) is better said, a sort of doubled move that works the ambiguity of constancy and variation as a sustainable orientation in our practices toward a different way of knowing. The effort becomes one of focusing on rethinking the object in a way that captures the force of the power, subtlety, and productivity of science by opening up our critical habits.

This "analytics of breaching" (Wilson, 1998, p. 204) is an infraction of immobile boundaries and a displacement of fixed political-critical spaces. In the case of feminist work, breaching the boundaries asks how it makes itself coherent and authoritative, how it consolidates itself at the cost of staying fresh, deroutinized. A breach is both a refusal of static boundaries and the space this refusal opens up (p. 207). Here, a sort of "iterative productivity" might result, more than the contained and the repetitive, open to its own mobile disposition.

An example of this is Turid Markussen's (2006) theorizing of research methods as performative practice in the case of a 2002 preliminary study of "prostitution" in a multiethnic context in north Norway by Britt Kramvig and Kirsten Stien.[2] Markussen's "narration of methodology" (2006, p. 305) is located in queer feminist studies, science studies, and renewed concern with bodies and matter and works as a sort of secondary analysis of a project that it amplifies, interferes with and adds to, attending to its aporias. Focusing on an enormously evocative—even haunting— "body work" (p. 293) methodology capable of capturing more nuanced layers of experience, both Markussen's "deconstructive cultural analysis" (p. 282) and the research project she analyzes enflesh a "deconstructive methodology."

Foregrounding "'a more generous sense of method'" (Markussen, 2006, p. 293, quoting John Law) capable of capturing the elusive via an embodied knowing, Markussen looks particularly at how researcher fear shaped this study of male relations with Russian women on the northern borders. Kramvig and Stien read their own dream data as an indicator of how they were inscribed in hegemonic fears of different sexualities and Saami ethnicities to reshape their research so that it might "'take the perspective of the men'" (p. 295) so as to work against their feminist commitments. They transformed that fear into an effort to undo the hold of that discourse on themselves in ways that included a body-wise vulnerability that worked to put them at the same level as the men. Such "access" let them apprehend more subtle and inarticulated sexual and ethnic dimensions to trouble easy ideas of "we" and "they" in the problematic of prostitution and how these boundaries play a part in enabling a trafficking in bodies for sexual purposes. Kramvig and Stien also explore their own affective presence to hint at a different intimate and sexual dynamic than that assumed between Norwegian bachelors and Russian prostitutes in houses of hurt and comfort where "'more tea-drinking than sex'" appeared to be going on (Markussen, 2006, p. 305, quoting Kramvig and Stien).

Attuned to contemporary concerns with doing difference differently, Markussen's analysis of Kramvig and Stien's research that is powerful in terms of ethnic specificity as well as a very nuanced sexuality gives life to Spivak's definition of deconstruction as that which helps us think against ourselves. What gets "undone" in both the empirical work and Markussen's analysis of it are "prostitution" and "sale of sex," "the very terms within which their research is framed" (Markussen, 2005, p. 331). In such "ontological encounters ... the terms of the real are allowed to shift," enacting new possibilities of living "in whatever small ways" (p. 341) in a demonstration of "performativity as emergent methodology."

Getting Lost: Philosophical Ethnography as a Move toward a Reinscribed Scientificity

> *The proposal here is not that of giving up on knowing. To the contrary, what is at stake is the political objective to confront the postcolonial condition of love and knowledge simultaneously by cultivating a feminist ability of engaging with (not knowing) that which is constituted in part by its own effacement and limits.*
> —Davis, 2002, p. 157

My recent *Getting Lost: Feminist Efforts toward a Double(d) Science* (Lather, 2007) is a book about a book about an experience of the very limits of knowing in the context of a study of women living with HIV/AIDS (Lather & Smithies, 1997). Its interest is a science based less on knowledge than on an awareness of epistemic limits where ethics begins with an embrace of such limits as constitutive of ethical knowing: decolonizing, postimperial. Here, constitutive unknowingness becomes an ethical resource, and aporetic suspension becomes an ethical practice of undecidability. In what follows, I attempt to situate this book within recent moves in feminist methodology.

Judith Butler writes that "feminism is a mess" (2004, p. 175), given the melt-down of its central terms, now situated, in best practice, as historical and performative in their continued rearticulation out of engaged political practices. As such, the feminism to which I am committed demonstrates how putting one's necessary categories in crisis can help us see how such categories work across time and what they exclude. This is a kind of double(d) movement that uses and troubles a category simultaneously, operationalizing the classic move of deconstruction: under erasure. This is a sort of loss, a disorientation where openness and unknowingness are part of the process, a self-reflexive, nondogmatic feminism that relishes conflicting interpretations without domesticating them, a permanent unsettlement in what might be termed a postfoundational feminism. Here feminism is both freed from the demand to be one thing in its task of challenging how knowledge is constrained by a "patriarchal symbolic" (Butler, 2004, p. 208) and lost, "ruined by the improper use of its proper name" (p. 233, speaking of philosophy), a self-loss that is the beginning of a post-idealist community. To turn, then, to scientism and scientificity in the context of a feminist effort toward a double(d) science is to address the science possible outside of the constraints of the patriarchal symbolic that Butler speaks to and against so powerfully.

Fonow and Cook's recent survey of "newer trends and debates" (2005, p. 2215) in feminist methodology includes the deepening of the crisis of representation where we can't "'get the real right'" (p. 2222). In this, recent turns in feminist analysis are concerned with "respect[ing] the demand for complexity" (McCall, 2005, p. 1786). This latter particularly refers to a stance toward "categorical complexity" (p. 1774) spurred by both the critique of feminism by women of color and the varied "post" movements that have so troubled Western philosophy, history, and language.

Although feminist theory has always had a metatheoretical moment in thinking about how we think (Hanssen, 2001, p. 73), more recent articulations raise troubling questions about such meta issues and learning to learn differently where "giving voice," "dialog," "telling and testifying," and "empowerment" have lost their innocence. At least since Wendy Brown's 1995 "Wounded Attachments," resentment politics and the exclusionary work that identity categories do in feminist work are much critiqued. Rosi Braidotti (2005) notes how the theoretical agenda has been reset in what she refers to as "post-post" times toward embodied materialisms, situated epistemologies, scattered hegemonies, and disseminated hybridities. The task is to do justice to the complexity and instability of all of this in addition to the dislocated identities of posthumanism that challenge oppositions of language/material and culture/nature.

The result is what Braidotti terms a sort of "postsecular" ethics (2005, p. 178) at "the end of postmodernity" (p. 171) or "late postmodernity" (p. 175), where feminist post-postmodernism faces a resurgently conservative, neoliberal timespace. Here, dialectics are inadequate in coming to grips with our time and what it might mean to try to make a difference in it. In a Deleuzean vein, her advice for strategy and hope is the "becoming minoritarian of Europe," where "the centre has to deconstruct its powers and let them lie, while the margins are the motor of active processes of becoming" (p. 174).

In addition to the exemplars already discussed, what this might look like begins to take shape in the displacements that abound across a broad array of trends and movements in the field of feminist methodology: "the ability of not knowing" (Davis, 2002); holding open a space for treating the "*not known*" creatively (Martin, 2001, p. 378); "a challenge to *learn*, and not to *know*" (Probyn, 2000, p. 54); the limits of empathy, voice, and authenticity (Lather, 2002); and "to persistently not know something important" (Kostkowska, 2004). Much of this echoes what Gayatri Spivak has been saying for years in terms of learning to learn from below. Alongside unlearning our privilege as a loss, more recently, Spivak (2000) urges that we move toward "claiming transformation" and standing together as subjects of globalization as we acknowledge complicity to act in less dangerous ways in a "non-Euro-US world." Justyna Kostkowska (2004) captures such moves well in her essay on the work of Nobel Prize–winning poet, Wislawa Szmborska's privileging of uncertainty and doubt where we are fortunate to not know precisely: "This is not a will *not* to know, as the condition of ignorance, but an ability to engage with what escapes propositions and representation" (p. 199).

Up against the limits of deconstruction, the task becomes to "live with its not knowing in the face of the Other" (Butler, 2001, p. 17). To not want to not know is a violence to the Other, a violence that obliterates how categories and norms both constrain AND enable. "We must follow a double path in politics," Butler (p. 23) urges, using familiar terms and categories but also "yielding our most fundamental categories" to what they rend unknown. This is the double(d) science I am calling for, a double task that works the necessary tensions that structure feminist methodology as fertile ground for the production of new practices.

Conclusion

Something you don't understand anything about allows for hope; it is the sign that you are affected by it. So it's a good thing you didn't understand anything because you can never understand anything other than what you of course already have in your head.
    —Lacan, 1971, quoted in Fink, 2004, p. 176, n. 2

The stakes of continuity and futurity, inheritance, and transformation are at work in such practices. Given the impossibilities attendant on complex systems, the 20th-century crisis of word and meaning defines modernity. The postmodern, then, from Nietzsche on, constructs a different relation to the exhaustion of science as certain knowledge, a subsided shock, a negativity that is outside Hegelian logic, a more heterogeneous logic, both culmination and negation of the completion of the crisis of modernism. Here the death of God or any master signifier and the end of "the West and the rest" sort of thinking are re-valenced as hardly news. The task is to reanimate via that which is still alive in a minimally normative way that does not reinscribe mastery. By creating new spaces on the edge of the intelligible, projects are put at risk rather than set up for accommodational inclusion or positioned to claim a better vantage point. Work is situated as ruined from the start, a symptomatic site of the limits of our knowing.

Here feminist methodology begins to elude its capture in Hegelian terms of the dialectic and the universal, "the 'pompous march of historical necessity'" (Benhabib, quoted in Alcoff, 2000, p. 849), where big bang theories of social change have not served women well. Here something begins to take shape, perhaps some new "line of flight" (Deleuze and Guattari, 1987), where we are not so sure of ourselves and where we see this not knowing as our best chance for a different sort of doing in the name of feminist methodology.

Notes

1. From *Adjusting Reality*, Jette Kofoed and Dorthe Staunaes, eds. Copenhagen: Danish Pedagogical University, pp. 269–78, 2007. Originally presented at the 2nd International Congress of Qualitative Inquiry, May 4, 2006. Accepted for reprint publication in *International Review of Qualitative Research*.

2. A variety of materials have come out of this governmentally commissioned study, mostly in Norwegian and many unpublished. See Markussen (2005, 2006) for citations as well as background on how a "pragmatic document written for a funding body" (2005, p. 336) was picked up by media outlets in a way that Kramvig and Stien were able to use in (re)shaping the study itself in more discursive directions. Markussen writes of this as a "bold strategy" in a preliminary report to a government in its "interweavings of sexuality, gender, ethnicity, migration, economic inequality, research, politics and public policy" (2005, p. 338).

References

Adams, N., & P. Bettis. 2003. *Cheerleader! An American icon*. New York: Palgrave.

Alcoff, L. 2000 Review essay: Philosophy matters: A review of recent work in feminist philosophy. *Signs* 25(3):841–82.

Alvesson, M. 2002. *Postmodernism and social research*. Buckingham, UK: Open University Press.

Bailey, L., & P. Lather. 2006. Complicating cheerleading [Review of *Cheerleader! An American icon*, by N. Adams and P. Bettis]. *Qualitative Studies in Education* 19(2):253–60.

Barber, S. 1997. Lip-reading: Woolf's secret encounters. In E. Sedgwick (Ed.), *Novel gazing: Queer readings in fiction*, pp. 401–43. Durham NC: Duke University Press.

Braiddoti, R. 2005. A critical cartography of feminist post-postmodernism. *Australian Feminist Studies* 20(47):169–80.

Brown, W. 1995. Wounded attachments: Late modern oppositional political formations. In J. Rajchman (Ed.), *The identity in question*, pp. 99–228. New York: Routledge.

Butler, J. 2001. The question of social transformation. In E. Beck-Gernsheim, J. Butler & L. Pulgvert (Eds.), *Women and social transformation*, translated by J. Vaida, pp. 1–28. New York: Peter Lang.

Butler, J. 2004. *Undoing gender*. New York: Routledge.

Davis, D. R. 2002. (Love is) The ability of not knowing: Feminist experience of the impossible in ethical singularity. *Hypatia* 17(1):145–61.

Deleuze, G., & F. Guattari. 1987. *A thousand plateaus: Capitalism and schizophrenia*. Translated by B. Massumi. Minneapolis: University of Minnesota Press.

Derrida, J. 1994. *Specters of Marx*. Translated by P. Kamuf. New York: Routledge.

Fink, B. 2004. *Lacan to the letter: Reading Ecrits closely*. Minneapolis: University of Minnesota Press.

Fonow, M., & J. Cook. 2005. Feminist methodology: New applications in the academy and public policy. *Signs* 30(4):2211–36.

Hanssen, B. 2001. Whatever happened to feminist theory? In E. Bronfen & M. Kavka (Eds.), *Feminist consequences: Theory for the new century*, pp. 58–98. New York: Columbia University Press.

Kostkowska, J. 2004. "To persistently not know something important": Feminist science and the poetry of Wislawa Szmborska. *Feminist Theory* 5(2):185–203.

Lather, P. 2002. Postbook: Working the ruins of feminist ethnography. *Signs* 27(1):199–227.

Lather, P. 2007. *Getting lost: Feminist efforts toward a double(d) science*. Albany: SUNY Press.

Lather, P., & C. Smithies. 1997. *Troubling the angels: Women living with HIV/ AIDS*. Boulder, CO: Westview Press.

Markussen, T. 2005. Practising performativity: Transformative moments in research. *European Journal of Women's Studies* 12(3):329–44.

Markussen, T. 2006. Moving worlds: The performativity of affective engagement. *Feminist Theory* 7(3):291–308.

Martin, B. 2001. Success and its failures. In E. Bronfen & M. Kavka (Eds.), *Feminist consequences: Theory for the new century*, pp. 353–80. New York: Columbia University Press.

McCall, L. 2005. The complexity of intersectionality. *Signs* 30(3):1771–800.

Probyn, E. 2000. Shaming theory, thinking dis-connections. In S. Ahmed, J. Kilby, C. Lury, M. McNeil, & S. Skeggs (Eds.), *Transformations: Thinking through feminism*, pp. 48–60. London: Routledge.

Sedgwick, E. 1997. Paranoid reading and reparative reading, or, you're so paranoid, you probably think this essay is about you. In E. Sedgwick (Ed.), *Novel gazing: Queer readings in fiction*, pp. 1–37. Durham NC: Duke University Press.

Sedgwick, E., & A. Frank. 1995. *Shame and its sisters: A Silvan Tomkins reader*. Durham NC: Duke University Press.

Spivak, G. 1993. *Outside in the teaching machine*. New York: Routledge.

Spivak, G. 2000. Claiming transformation: Travel notes with pictures. In S. Ahmed, J. Kilby, C. Lury, M. McNeil, & B. Skeggs (Eds.), *Transformations: Thinking through feminism*, pp. 119–30. London: Routledge.

Staunaes, D., & D. M. Sondergaard. Forthcoming. Who is ready for the results? Reflections on the multivoicedness of useful research. *International Journal of Qualitative Studies in Education*.

Wilson, E. 1998. *Neural geographies: Feminism and the microstructure of cognition*. New York: Routledge.

8 | Qualitative Researchers' Conceptualizations of the Risks Inherent in Qualitative Interviews

Janice M. Morse
University of Utah

Linda Niehaus
University of Alberta

Stanley Varnhagen
University of Alberta

Wendy Austin
University of Alberta

Michele McIntosh
University of Alberta

Presently, qualitative research proposals are evaluated and approved by institutional review boards (IRBs) (or in Canada REBs [research ethics boards]) using criteria that were developed to guide biomedical research from the principles arising from the Belmont Report (National Commission for the Protection of Human Subjects of Biomedical and Behavioral Research, 1978). The intent of these guidelines has been the "protection of human subjects from harm" and hence to minimize risk in research. As these guidelines were intended for experimental biomedical research, it has been argued that they are inappropriate for the review of human science research (Gunsalus et al., 2007). Furthermore, although no hard data exist, the structure and mode of functioning of IRBs/REBs result in requirements for conducting qualitative research that are often inappropriate and remarkable for their lack of consistency between applications, committees, and institutions (Gunsalus et al., 2007). This chapter reports on an Internet survey of qualitative researchers that explored their experiences regarding their perceptions and nature of risk in qualitative research using unstructured interviews.

Assumptions in the Process of Reviewing

The primary purpose of an IRB review of proposals is to determine that the rights of human subjects are protected as well as preventing harm during the research process. Subjects' rights are ensured by examining the content and timing of consent (i.e., how will it be obtained and by whom, to ensure that coercion does not occur), and the content of the consent (what the subjects will be informed about the project to ensure that it is comprehensible and that they will have the opportunity to ask questions). Next, committees examine the research procedures—what is being asked of the subjects and what will be done to them. In addition to the risks, the review process also examines any benefits to the subjects themselves and to society at large. It is the judgment and "proper province of research ethics committees" (Johnson, 2007, p. 98) to request changes to the research protocol that will modify the risks, including *not approving* the research project if the risks are considered too high or the benefits do not appear to compensate for the risk involved. The onus is on the researcher to "plan specific, relevant measures to eliminate the risk, to minimize the impact of the risk, should it be realized, or to cope with (or compensate for) any harm that eventually accrues to the participant" (Long, 2007, p. 63).

Along with this review process, IRB committees also provide oversight for ongoing research, monitoring progress and receiving any complaints about the project. Projects are periodically re-reviewed, usually annually, and if changes occur in the protocol.

Misfit of Assumptions of Review and Qualitative Research

The IRB review process, developed for biomedical research, has been applied to social science research, including the review of qualitative research. The same biomedical committee frequently reviews disciplines in the health sciences and places the same requirements on qualitative research, including the use of a consent form developed for biomedical purposes and one listing inappropriate risks. Furthermore, the lack of standardization in qualitative research makes the process of review frustrating for both the committee and the researcher. In qualitative inquiry, the emergent nature of the research design means that the investigator usually does not know specifics; for instance, exactly how many people will eventually participate in the study, precisely what questions will be asked of the participants during unstructured interactive interviews, how long the interviews will last, or even how many times the researcher will contact participants. In short, qualitative researchers are unable to provide the level of detail these committees request and expect. This problem is further confounded by a committee membership unfamiliar with the assumptions and procedures of qualitative inquiry.

Consent procedures are often also problematic. Qualitative researchers argue that the institutional requirements of consent interferes with researcher-participant relationships; is not pertinent to models in which the participant has control; interferes with the public nature of observational research; and that consent is not a one-time event but is ongoing throughout the project (van den Hoonaard, 2002). Finally, conflict with IRB committees sometimes occurs over the roles and relationships between the researcher and participants in qualitative inquiry. IRB committees that insist on anonymity for participants, for instance, clash directly with participatory research in which the participants serve as co-investigators or even as coauthors, or with biographical research (in which anonymity is impossible), or feminist inquiry (which respects the person), and gives named attribution for participants' contributions to a project (Weinberg, 2002). Small purposeful samples also make it difficult to ensure anonymity within the community studied.

Whereas some have recommended that research in the social science and humanities be exempted from the IRB system, AAUP (2006b) believes "What it is deeply troublesome is the fact that research on human subjects must obtain IRB approval whether or not it imposes a serious risk of harm on its subjects," but that it would be a mistake "to exempt research in the social sciences and humanities, leaving the IRB system to govern all biomedical research and only biomedical research" (p. 3). A better change would be to address itself "not to the discipline of the researcher, but by the methods by which the projected research would be conducted." AAUP recommends "that research whose method-ology consists entirely of collecting data by surveys, conducting interviews, or observing behavior in public places be exempt from the requirement of IRB review" (2006b). The exception to this is research in which the "subjects can be directly and indirectly iden-tified, and that such disclosure could reasonably place the subject's at risk of criminal or civil liability or be damaging to the subjects' financial standing, employability, or reputation." (p. 3).

It is also important to note that regulations vary between countries: In the United States, regulations classify research that uses digitized recordings as data in the category of "expedited review," implying that it is considered to be low risk for partic-ipants. In 2004, oral history became exempt from IRB review (AAUP, 2006a; Carome, 2005; Richie & Shopes, 2007), and, making the case that his "research more closely resembles oral history than clinical drug trials," Denzin (n.d.) has successfully lobbied for this exemption to be extended to interpretive research in the College of Communication at the University of Illinois, Urbana-Champaign.

Although the bottom line is the protection of human sub-jects from *harm,* it is important to note that a survey of qualitative researchers or participants in qualitative research has not been undertaken, nor have IRBs/REBs been surveyed to determine if they have received complaints of harm extending from qualitative research. In other words, although medical research has docu-mented harm and IRBs proactively seek to prevent future inci-dents, in qualitative inquiry little is known about the risks from which these reviews are supposedly protecting human subjects, the incidence and nature of harm, or even if any harm results. This is particularly serious, as IRBs may not have a member with expertise in qualitative methods and often delay, alter, and even block the conduct of research (Gunsalus et al., 2007; Lincoln,

2005; Lincoln & Tierney, 2004).

This is not to claim that qualitative inquiry is without risks, merely that these risks are different and largely unknown. Qualitative health research, for instance, is frequently conducted with vulnerable populations—children, the mentally infirm, those hospitalized or imprisoned, or those in pain or dying. There is also evidence that during interviews participants often reveal signs of distress as they are describing emotionally distressing events (Morse, 2002). Therefore, the questions that this research addressed were:

1. What is the perceived nature of *risk* and *harm* in research using qualitative interviews?
2. What is the nature of participant distress observed during qualitative interviews?
3. Is this distress perceived by researchers as abnormal and harmful, or, within the context of the interview topic, a normal response?
4. What strategies do qualitative researchers use during their interviews to mitigate participant distress?

We conclude the chapter by suggesting appropriate principles assessing qualitative proposals during the IRB/REB review.

Methods

Researchers whose names appeared on a mailing list at the International Institute for Qualitative Methodology were invited to participate in an online survey. We made contact with them with an e-mailed letter, requesting that they access the English-language survey from the URL link. Once the consent form was completed, the respondents could then access, complete, and submit the questionnaire. The website was secure and all survey information was treated as confidential. To protect anonymity, respondents' names were not attached to survey responses.

The survey included twenty-five semistructured, open-ended questions in which the question stem was presented and the participants were free to respond in their own words. Semistructured questions are used when the investigators understand the domain of inquiry but cannot anticipate all of the possible answers necessary for the construction of a structured questionnaire. The questionnaire also contained structured questions, and the responses to these were reported elsewhere.

As questions in a semistructured questionnaire were asked of all participants, and asked in the same order, the responses were analyzed at the end of data collection rather than as an ongoing process throughout data collection. Content analysis was conducted within each question; the responses were grouped into categories; and all the responses in each category were synthesized.

Demographic characteristics of the 517 respondents are presented on Table 1. Of importance, 386 (74.7%) stated that they had experience with unstructured interviews, 449 (86.8%) with semistructured interviews, and 371 (71.8%) with focus groups; 188 (36.4%) rated themselves as gaining competence with interviewing; most rated their skills at interviewing as competent (see Table 2).

Results

Nature of Risk in Qualitative Research
Defining Levels of Risk

The first question asked respondents to define levels of no-, low-, medium-, or high-risk research. Such categorization resulted in much cross-over in responses, such that it was clear that such fine delineation of risk was not possible. The contextual nature of risk in qualitative inquiry is shown in the responses that our participants did attempt.

No risk. Most respondents reported that there was no such thing as a no-risk situation involving human beings or human experiences, and therefore human research, because risk was ubiquitous in everyday life. Other respondents reported that although no-risk research was possible, removing the risk also removed significant content, rendering the research superficial, mundane, and worthless: " Every interview comes with a risk. 'No risk' may mean avoiding the information that is likely to cause distress. This approach may, in actual fact, deplete the value of the interview."

Table 1: Demographic Characteristics of Respondents (N = 517)

Characteristic	N (%)
Gender	
Male	101 (19.5%)
Female	411 (79.5%)
Missing	5 (1.0%)
Highest level of education	
Masters	128 (24.8%)
Doctorate	344 (66.5%)
Other (or Missing)	45 (8.7%)
Primary employer	
University	354 (66.5%)
Non-university	136 (28.3%)
Missing	27 (5.2%)
Discipline	
Health Sciences	248 (48.0%)
Non-health Sciences	263 (50.8%)
None or missing	6 (1.2%)
Country of employment	
United States	146 (28.2%)
Canada	113 (21.9%)
United Kingdom	62 (12.0%)
Australasia	64 (12.4%)
Other or missing	132 (25.5%)

Thus, it was clear that if the interview topic was about a distressing subject (such as bereavement or loss), such distress was contextualized within the topic itself—as well as inherent in the everyday event under study. As such, the distress occurs as a normal part of everyday life, and to avoid it invalidates the research.

Low risk. Researchers described low-risk inquiry in terms of what it was not—a topic that was *not* emotionally charged, *not* sensitive, *not* personal, *not* controversial, and *not* requiring

Table 2: Self-Assessed Competency of Participants by Type of Interview Research Primarily Conducted

Self-assessed competency	Type of Interview			
	Unstructured (n = 268)	Semistructured (n = 159)	Group (n = 42)	Total (n = 469)
Novice	16 (6.0)	9 (5.7)	2 (4.8)	27 (5.8)
Gaining competence	79 (29.5)	48 (30.2)	12 (28.6)	139 (29.6)
Competent or very competent	173 (64.6)	102 (64.2)	28 (66.7)	303 (64.6)
Missing	131 (25.3)	68 (13.2)	156 (30.2)	Missing

confidential disclosure. Low-risk interviews were characterized as "safe" topics that focused on mundane, power-neutral, impersonal, factual, and nonthreatening topics such as those "commonly discussed with strangers in frequently occurring social situations." Interestingly, low risk was described in terms of "public" topics that were *not* intimate, secret, nor offensive to others, and did not make the participant feel vulnerable. Respondents also characterized low-risk qualitative interviews as those during which interviewers are experienced and well prepared.

Medium risk. Participants had the most difficulty identifying the particular characteristics of medium risk. "There is a scale along which all studies lie, and the moderate risk situations have some characteristics of both low- and high-risk situations but are not exclusively either."

High risk. High-risk research is that which may cause harm; that is, long-lasting psychological or physical harm (such as working in a "dangerous part of town"). High-risk qualitative inquiry also involves individuals from vulnerable populations and inexperienced, unprepared interviewers, "fly-in, fly-out interview approach" (Love 'em and leave 'em), or highly emotional topics that elicit shame, anger, deep sorrow, or other "mental health crises."

The interviewers may have "poor listening skills, lack of empathy, and understanding," and the interviewees may have suicidal tendencies. The high-risk interviewee lacks support services. Some researchers may cause harm by continuing when the participant does not want to continue or is fatigued, as in the frail elderly.

If the topic is highly sensational or controversial, and the field "so unique or limited that confidentiality and anonymity may be breached by some self-interested participants" and "may disclose highly illicit or illegal behaviors," these participants may not understand the mandatory reporting requirements, yet may disclose self-incriminating information and therefore risk criminal "prosecution, deportation, loss of livelihood, family disruption or other major life change if the content (of the interview) were to be revealed."

High-risk research also violates ethical standards, such as "forced participation" or the "use of money as a coercive tool" for instance, homeless groups:

> Discussions of traumatic events that participants have experienced, illegal behaviors, painful losses, illnesses, disabilities. Discussion of inappropriate services, being blamed for problems, especially where there is a risk that the information could be shared with people who have power over the participants.

> I think that the worst danger comes from an authoritarian and disrespectful attitude from the researcher. ... I don't even want to imagine this kind of research in the hands of a "political enemy" of the people studied.

Defining Harm in Qualitative Inquiry

To place harm in the context of research as a whole, qualitative inquiry does not cause physical harm, and the avoidance of psychological harm, within context, is under the control of the participant (Cassell, 1980). One researcher stated: "We are not doing police interrogations and any experienced, competent, or properly trained interviewer is going to stop at this point (of doing harm). ... The ethical trade-off may be the need to collect information for scientific purposes (considering) the comfort of the informant."

This does not deny that harm may result within malignant

or inappropriate intimate questioning, but that is unlikely to occur within a ninety-minute interview. Qualitative researchers are neither police nor therapists. However, when the researcher's relationship with the participant is combined with other roles, such as caregiver, and the "interviewer and participant have other relations, the participant may fear they would be treated otherwise if they do not participate." In other words, conducting research in one's own work setting may be considered, from the participant's perspective, as coercive.

Perceived Benefits

Researchers stated that the benefits of the interview process outweighed the risks for participants. The opportunities afforded participants to talk about their experiences was beneficial, as they may be the first times they have spoken freely to anyone about the experiences. Thus, it may help them to do so in other safe circumstances, such as counseling. The interview also may help participants integrate some unpleasant experience into their lives. In addition, secondary benefits may be derived apart from the actual topic of the research, such as contributing to the improvement of care or of health services.

Risk Is the Cardinal Sign of Good Qualitative Inquiry

Qualitative researchers pointed out that because of the emergent nature of qualitative inquiry, the inductive stance of the researcher, and the control of the research interview being largely in the hands of the participant (rather than the researcher), the possible risks of qualitative interviews could not be predicted or foreseen at the beginning of the interview. ("There are always risks that are not evident until the research has begun or even is over.") This insight reveals that the a priori review of qualitative inquiry for the "protection of the subject" is of limited value. Rather, researcher preparation for how to respond appropriately, to comfort or console those participants who appear distressed, should be prioritized.

Components of Risk

Participants described qualitative risk in several dimensions: as that pertaining to the participant, the researcher, the topic, the context, and the research relationship. Some of the participants' descriptions reiterated published guidelines; others were more reflective.

Importantly, the most outstanding distinction of qualitative interviews was that qualitative interviews involved human experiences in their totality. Unlike quantitative research, qualitative interviews are not dispassionate, disembodied, or removed from the context; nor is the content rated or substituted with score(s). Experiential subjectivity and emotion are the hallmarks of qualitative inquiry, and it is from this that the researcher's assessment of risk evolves. It is this emotion that is the cardinal factor in shaping risk, is risk itself, and enables risk assessment. Emotion makes the process of telling or the relating of the event "real" for the person, as he or she reconnects with the event. This reconnection contributes to the "psychological vulnerability" of the participant, especially when the topic is traumatic, such as topics pertaining to dying, suffering, and profound loss. Thus, the emotional tone of the interview is pertinent to the discussion of all aspects of risk discussed below.

Risk related to the participant. Many of the risks relating to the participant are addressed in IRB review: factors that undermine voluntary participation such as financial incentives ("use of money as a coercive tool") that coerce and remove the freedom to participate. Risks that were reported as not considered within IRB review included some forms of coercion (e.g., when "participants were invited to participate by their physicians"). Normally, in qualitative inquiry, sample selection involves voluntary participation. This freedom to agree or to refuse to be interviewed is key to the participant's choice to speak or not to speak about the topic and to decide to what depth to engage. When interviews are unstructured, the participant has freedom to determine the topic, the scope, and what is said in the interview. The participants themselves have the means to control or to influence the emotional tone and content of the interview. As one researcher noted, "The participant is describing what is currently an unresolved/

difficult/transitional experience. The phenomenon is described as currently being lived." However, with the nature of this type of research, the directions and types of information cannot be fully anticipated.

At the same time, characteristics of the participant and the experiences that they represent may also make the participant vulnerable. Research participants identified vulnerable persons as: prisoners of war, those who are psychotic or emotionally traumatized, those who are asked to speak about illicit activities (that they would not otherwise disclose), those who are in stressful situations, those who have done harm to others, or victims of interpersonal or other types of violence. Other participants identified difficult experiences, such as "loss of health, death or grieving processes, critical decision-making processes, or unpleasant family relationships." Research participants noted that people in acute crisis, or in the midst of a difficult experience, are vulnerable, and those who have not had the time to "process" or resolve a crisis may be highly emotional. The unpredictablity of the participants' emotional state increases the potential complexity of the qualitative interview. The researcher may be "unaware of potential problems or issues that the participant has brought to the interview." Participants who are given "latitude in setting the [interview] agenda means that they may not bring up things that may be disturbing to them." Furthermore, some participants may be unaware of "what is upsetting to them until they start to talk about it."

Risks related to the researcher. The qualitative interview is one of emotional or embodied engagement with a participant, so the interviewer, in some sense, must be affected by the participant's feelings and story. The participant's distress may trigger emotional responses and memories in the researcher and even disturb the researcher's sleep, causing fatigue. The interview may be so intense as to overwhelm the researcher, who is then not able to conduct further interviews or conduct analysis. The interview may trigger memories within the researcher, so that the researcher becomes emotionally involved with the participant. This "lack of self-awareness or reflexivity," not realizing the potential of research on the researcher, may take its toll. Respondents noted that "the researcher needs debriefing after 'heavy' interviews. The personal effects [of the interview] can be long-lasting." Participants recommended debriefing after the interview, and "to take care of yourself—to recreate yourself and your energy, and share [the interview] with trusted team member or supervisor/colleague."

The emotional intensity of an interview may possibly overwhelm the interviewer. There is risk of "not being able to hear what is being said by being personally overwhelmed." Should this occur, the researcher might be unable to console the distraught participant. Researchers must consider the emotional risks to other team members and also consider the emotional risks of those who work with the data, including other members of the research team and the transcriptionist. Participants referred to this as "safeguarding emotional safety." Interviewing is not without physical risks. Interviewers must carry a cell phone, notify others about their whereabouts, and NOT go into a participant's home alone.

The Risks of Being Manipulated

Researchers are human, and we sometimes forget that, especially if one is a part of a "helping" profession so that the urge to intervene is very strong. Participants noted that one could "get angry or upset at the participant's experiences," yet intervention is not an option in the research role as the project was proposed, and the best the researcher can do in the circumstances is to consider the injustices and formulate a research question around that topic. Participants advised researchers to "know your boundaries."

Purposeful sampling was considered possibly hazardous to the research design as a whole by some participants. If participants had an agenda, it was possible for them to skew the study: "The risk of being manipulated and strategically maneuvered are high."

The "dangerous participant." At the same time, researchers may be exposed to the dangerous participant. Researchers reported feeling vulnerable to both physical and verbal assaults by participants. For instance, there is a potential threat by those who are physically able to assault the interviewer—"those who have a history of crime or violence and drug or substance abuse." In addition, participants who experience adverse outcomes such as destabilization secondary to their participation may become a risk to the investigator (e.g., the "Vietnam vet with PTSD [posttraumatic stress disorder] who may experience triggered flashbacks"). The researcher may also be verbally threatened or attacked by a participant who is "disrespectful, arrogant, or belligerent" or "hostile, angry, or deeply saddened."

Participants who have another agenda or expectations involving their participation also constitute risk, for example, those who participate to "set the researcher straight" or to get some professional help or to access services. Such participants "cannot be managed, it [their behavior] is a result of their personality/issues." Thus, it is not always possible to anticipate undesirable behavior by participants, so this behavior cannot be predicted and the researcher cannot be prepared. If the researcher has knowledge or experience, or, as one participant in our study wrote, if the knowledge or experience is "one in which a researcher is as aware as possible of the emotional terrain likely to be involved in the subject matter and the participants," then the researcher can carefully monitor the participant's emotional state during the interview and assist in pacing the interview by providing breaks and so forth, so that the participant can better control his or her emotional level.

One of the difficulties for the IRB is knowing the level of competency of the researcher to respond to distress manifested by the participant during the interview. If the researcher is a counselor, nurse, or pastor, for instance, accustomed to responding professionally to clients or patients in distress, then the IRB committee may be confident of the researcher's competence, and if a study is perceived to be about a topic that may reveal participants' angst, the committee may be confident that the situation will be "managed" in the most responsible way. However, none of the researcher participants noted such an evaluation in the review process; rather, the IRB required a counseling referral network to be established before the commencement of the study.

Such an a priori support network may be problematic for two reasons: (1) If distress becomes evident during the interview, a referral sometime after the interview ends would not cover the immediate situation; and (2) it assumes that distress manifest during and after the interview is an abnormal manifestation, caused by the research interview (and therefore must be rectified by the researcher), rather than such distress being a part of the participants' normal response to the events about which the interview is being conducted. In fact, if the interview is about a topic such as the illness and death of a loved one, the absence (rather than presence) of distress may be indicative of a need for counseling. Alternatively, it may be indicative of problems, such as the invalidity of the interview situation or a lack of trust in the researcher-participant relationship resulting in the blocking of such normal responses.

Risks related to the topic. As noted above when discussing low-risk research, the topic is an important component to consider when assessing risk. It is the topic that may lead the participant to *feel* vulnerable or threatened when asked to divulge personal, emotional, illegal, or sensitive information. Personal topics or situations can cause emotional arousal—sorrow, grief, frustration and anger, anxiety and shame. These topics can be about money, sexuality, one's body, personal safety (e.g., violence, deportation, or illegal behavior), sickness or dying (e.g., pain, death of a loved one, or a mental health crisis), sense of identity or shame (e.g. topics that are culturally taboo or loss of job, or failed marriage), or about ways in which they experienced disappointment (e.g., financial loss, loss of a home). Sometimes the arousal of emotions may be extremely risky, such as the triggering of posttraumatic stress, those associated with repressed memories or with a psychotic episode, or fury that may be self-directed or directed at the researcher. Surprisingly, participant threats of suicide were not mentioned in the data, perhaps indicating the very low incidence of such threats.

Risks related to the relationship. The researcher has some control over the relationship, and the power imbalance favors the researcher. Risk may be increased if the researcher fails to gain the participant's trust; or decreased if trust is obtained. In a low-risk situation, the researcher establishes trust and rapport and is respectful and sensitive but not too emotionally close to the participant. The researcher may become "touched" by the interviewee's plight and feel a need to personally assist, rather than refer the interviewee, thus becoming involved with the interviewee.

Risks related to the environment. Respondents identified that the places in which the interviews were conducted were sometimes physically dangerous (such as interviewing drug dealers in the dealers' homes). Environments that are emotionally risky were those that held an unpleasant association for the participant (for instance, a hospital environment may trigger memories or an overpersonalized office environment with family photos may remind participants of their own losses). Cultural spaces were also considered as constituting risk (e.g., "doing research in countries engaged in civil or national disturbance"). Risk was further brought into play by lack of researcher preparation (such as "going into situations where no one knows their whereabouts and there is a risk of physical harm or danger") or by going to "high-risk environments such as a troubled home, a dangerous part of town and the like."

Risks related to the outcomes of the research. Participants in our study noted that the risks of research may not come from the data collection, but from the findings. One wrote:

> The risk to the participant came not from the interview itself, but from the written findings that was the result of the interview. One participant experienced distress related to the narrative. I think she felt that she did not come across well in the narrative, and it seemed to disrupt her sense of self.

Agencies may not be comfortable with the researcher's findings, even if the study has been requested or contracted by them. Researchers felt that agencies were "bullying (them) to change findings."

Mitigation of Risk

Researchers noted several strategies for mitigating the risk in interviews. First, excellent interviewing skills, including offering to stop the interview, was noted by many, as was developing trust with the participant at the beginning of the interview. Researchers must "create empathy, and a good relationship before starting the interviews. Explain clearly before starting: purpose of the research, procedures, possible discomforts, confidentiality, and their right to refuse."

With high-risk research, the "interviewers must be skilled and the interview team must be well-prepared and briefed with a protocol to follow if difficult situations arise." "Researchers must have knowledge of community resources available for assistance."

Junior researchers must have back-up from their advisor/principal investigator.

However, the participant's emotion in itself was not a cue to actually stop an interview, but to *offer* to stop the interview. To stop an interview based on the expression of emotion could possibly be harmful as it could be perceived as a rejection of the participant and his or her feelings. The decision to stop the interview should be made jointly by the researcher and the participant.

Discussion

The results of this study endorsing the emergent and unpredictable nature of qualitative inquiry reveal the inadequacy of the present system of IRB review for qualitative research. As many authors have noted, consent in qualitative inquiry is not a one-time legality obtained at the beginning of the study but a contract that is renegotiated and reobtained throughout the data-collection process. Further, the unknown nature of qualitative inquiry and the uncertainty of the progress of the study reveal the incongruence of using biomedical criteria for review. Rather than transposing their gaze from research that removes or transcends emotion, IRBs are faced with a method that places a fundamental challenge to risk assessment. For instance, does emotive expression such as crying/distress during the telling of one's story constitute harm or benefit? Does the telling result in relief? Is the manifest distress healthy or unhealthy? The limitations of the rule-bound nature of IRB regulations and recommendations become evident, and the onus for ethical conduct of interview, therefore, rests heavily on the shoulders of the qualitative researcher and makes ethical behavior of the qualitative researcher reflexive and context dependent, rather than prescribed. In addition, IRBs must augment their approach to risk assessment with a consideration of this subjectivity/emotion inherent in qualitative inquiry.

Further, risk in qualitative inquiry is not something that can be predetermined within a risk/benefit ratio. Rather, the level of risk may be "realized only in the process of conducting an interview"; thus, risk assessment is processual, emergent, and ongoing, and it is the responsibility of the researcher to be constantly vigilant to "deal with the unexpected." Long's (2007) recommendation that risks be identified and prepared for, although ideal and sometimes attempted, is also linear and, in qualitative practice, unrealistic. In light of this, researchers who think that by having "the procedures in place, [IRB] ensures a low-risk situation" fail to appreciate this emergent nature of risk. Researchers should also be aware of the participant's right to withdraw data from the study following the completion of the interview; in the United States it is possible to obtain a National Institutes of Health certificates of confidentiality to prevent forced disclosure of data (as in a subpoena of data from a drug-related study; see http://grants.nih.gov/grants/policy/coc/index.htm).

Previously, the American Association of University Professors (AAUP, 2001) raised questions about the appropriateness of committee review and approval as a mechanism for protection for human subjects for interview research. Given the findings of this study—that is, the large component of risk emerging unexpectedly and the onus being on the researcher for its mediation—we recommend that other models of oversight be explored for qualitative interview research. Programs that teach qualitative inquiry, for instance, must include research ethics education, information about the potential responses of participants and researchers, and strategies for mitigation. Given the professional license for researchers to regulate and monitor themselves, placing the burden on educational programs appears more appropriate and useful than the present system of a priori review. If qualitative researchers who use surveys and conduct interviews or observations in public places (or other contexts with appropriate permissions) attended appropriate programs, they could then apply for exceptions from IRB approval.

Principles of Assessment for Review of Qualitative Proposals

Although we have a system of IRB approval for qualitative inquiry, we recommend the following principles for qualitative researchers and for IRB committees' review of proposed research and oversight of the research project:

1. Risk in qualitative inquiry is not a commodity that can be exclusively evaluated at the proposal stage. Risk may occur throughout the research process, is emergent, and ongoing; so, too, must be risk assessment be reflexive and ongoing.

Given the subjective nature of the research process and the dynamics within qualitative inquiry, a priori estimates of risk/benefit ratios are largely inappropriate. Risk in qualitative inquiry cannot be calculated as a probability statistic. To ensure the researchers' capacity to assume the ongoing responsibility for risk assessment and amelioration that is uniquely the researchers', IRBs need to review the discipline, preparation, and qualifications of qualitative researchers as well as assess the risk inherent within the topic per se and the vulnerability of the population.

The ethical education of the researchers presently focuses on the federal guidelines (such as Tri-Council Policy Statement, 1998) and attend to participants' rights, issues of consent, and processes of referral should an untoward event occur. But these programs lose relevance when one considers that harm in qualitative inquiry cannot easily be anticipated. There is a need to include content on strategies for understanding the research experience within the context of the participants' lives. The Tri-Council Policy Statement (1998) is unique in its definition of minimal risk:

> If potential subjects can reasonably be expected to regard the probability and magnitude of possible harm implied by participation in the research to be no greater than those encountered by the subject in those aspects of his or her everyday life that relate to the research, then the research can be regarded as within the range of minimal risk. (p. 15)

However, this standard of "everyday life" remains open to interpretation. The responsibility for identifying potential harm relies on the moral integrity of the researcher, events that occur in the process of data collection, or what may result from the publication process. The possible ramifications of the interview process on the interviewer, and events triggered, such as violence, should also be included.

2. The qualitative researcher's preparation for the interview must include the familiarity with existing knowledge of the topic that allows for anticipation of its "emotional terrain."

Preparation of qualitative researchers is critical; not only must interviewers be knowledgeable about formal ethical responsibilities, for example, the rights of the participants (e.g., the right to be informed about the content of the interview and to refuse to participate; the right to stop the interview; and so forth) and relational ethical responsibilities (e.g., sensitivity, respect, authenticity), they must be adept at attending to and responding to participants' emotional manifestations during the interview, while maintaining appropriate boundaries within the methodological goals of the project. It is important that the researcher be aware of the changing emotional responses of the participant during the interview and assess and observe the participant at the end of it. The researcher should be ready to debrief the participant if necessary and not leave the participant, but spend time, possibly offering tea or coffee, until the participant's conversation (and ability to make "small talk") has returned to normal. This preparation and ongoing mentoring of the research team is the responsibility of the principal investigator.

3. Risk assessment, avoidance, and alleviation are the ongoing responsibilities of the researcher.

A "risk safety net" should be constructed prior to the beginning of the project that will enable the researcher to anticipate how he or she may ethically, respectfully, and sensitively respond to all events that may be anticipated. These should be discussed between the student and his or her supervisory committee, referring to the increasing literature that is now being established on this topic and should become essential content in qualitative methods courses. The onus is also on the researcher to respond to any unanticipated events and establish a consulting and reporting pathway, should any untoward events actually occur.

4. Researchers must be cognizant of their own vulnerability and that of the research team.

This vulnerability is physical, emotional, and/or social. Researchers must protect themselves from physical harm, by carrying cell phones, for example, and being aware of and avoiding placing themselves in a jeopardous position. Emotional harm for the researcher extends from overidentifying with participants' stories or attending to the cumulative effect of the interviews as a whole during interviewing and analysis to the lack of a mechanism for debriefing.

5. In protecting anonymity and confidentiality, the qualitative researcher's responsibility is first to the participant and the setting, and second to the research goals.

Qualitative researchers commonly protect the anonymity of participants by providing a pseudonym, although participants are increasingly requesting to be named in research. In addition, researchers do not provide demographic information that may be linked to the individual—because of small samples, the use of several demographic tags may aid in the identification of participants. However, such practices may also compromise the validity of the research (Davis, 1991).

6. Researchers must be aware that risk of harm to participants can lie in the participant's response to the results of the research. Some times writing is a balance between accuracy and tact, and if certain facts are not essential, it may be kinder to omit these details (Ellis, 1995).

This principle implies the need for a dissemination plan. Sometimes participants may read the reports and react unfavorably to what is read. If the findings are going to be available in an environment where anonymity is unlikely, the researcher must be aware that the findings have the potential to affect relationships in that environment. Thus, how results are disseminated needs to be carefully considered, and it may be important to discuss the results with a participant before presentation or publication.

Conclusion

In this chapter we reported on research that asked qualitative researchers to identify the risks inherent in qualitative research using unstructured interviews. Although participants' emotional responses are often "normal" responses to serious losses, the onus is on the researchers to respond appropriately and to mitigate the emotional response. This includes attending to the responses of the research team, including the transcriptionist. Serious risks rarely extend to physical harm, but researchers should be prepared for such problems. We have suggested six principles that can be used to guide researchers in such preparation.

Acknowledgments

Funding for this study was provided by the CIHR (Canadian Institutes for Health Research), Grant # 11669. This work was completed at the International Institute for Qualitative Methodology, University of Alberta, Canada.

References

American Association of University Professors (AAUP). 2001. Protecting human beings: Institutional review boards and social science research. *Academe* 87(3):55–67.

American Association of University Professors (AAUP). 2006a. Oral history exempt from Federal oversight. *Academe Online.* http://www.aaup.org/AAUP/pubsres/academe/2004/JF/NB/OralHist.htm (accessed November 28, 2007).

American Association of University Professors (AAUP). 2006b. *Research and human subjects: Academic freedom and the institutional review boards (2006).* http://www.aaup.org/AAUP/comm/rep/A/humansubs.htm (accessed October 3, 2007).

Carome, M. A. 2005. Clarification of OHRP's position on oral history information (e-mail). http://www.UTexas.edu/research/RSC/humanresearch/specialtopics/documents/michaelcaromeUpdated.pdf (accessed November 22, 2005).

Cassell, J. 1980. Ethical principles for conducting fieldwork. *American Anthropologist* 82(1):28–41.

Davis, D. S. 1991. Rich cases: Ethics of thick description. *Hastings Center Report* 21(4):12–17.

Denzin, N. K. n.d. IRBs and the turn to indigenous research ethics. Unpublished paper, College of Communication, University of Illinois, Urbana-Champaign.

Ellis, C. 1995. Emotional and ethical quagmires in returning to the field. *Journal of Contemporary Ethnography* 24(1):68–98.

Gunsalus, C. K., E. M. Bruner, N. C. Burbles, L. Dash, M. Finkin, J. P. Goldberg, W. T. Greenough, G. A. Miller, M. G. Pratt, M. Iriye, & D. Aronson. 2007. The Illinois white paper: Improving the system for protecting human subjects: Counteracting IRM "mission creep." *Qualitative Inquiry* 13(5):617–49.

Johnson, M. 2007. Criticizing research from an ethical point of view. In T. Long & M. Johnson (Eds.), *Research ethics in the real world: Issues and solutions for health and social care*, pp. 85–102. Edinburgh: Churchill Livingston.

Lincoln, Y. S. 2005. Institutional review boards and methodological conservatism: The challenge to and from phenomenological paradigms. In N. K. Denzon & Y. S. Lincoln (Eds.), *Handbook of qualitative research*, 3rd ed., pp. 165–82. Thousand Oaks, CA: Sage.

Lincoln, Y. S. & W. Tierney. 2004. Qualitative research and institutional review boards. *Qualitative Inquiry* 10(2):219–34.

Long, T. 2007. How are these ethical issues to be resolved? In T. Long & M. Johnson (Eds.), *Research ethics in the real world: Issues and solutions for health and social care*, pp. 85–102. Edinburgh: Churchill Livingston.

Morse, J. M. 2002. Emotional re-enactment (Editorial). *Qualitative Health Research* 12(2):147.

National Commission for the Protection of Human Subjects of Biomedical and Behavioral Research. 1978. *The Belmont Report: Ethical principles and guidelines for the protection of human subjects of research* (DHEW Pub. No. (OS) 78-0008). Washington, DC: US Government Printing Office.

Richie, D. A., & L. Shopes. 2007. Oral history excluded from IRB approval. http://alpha.dickinson.edu/oha/org_irb.html (accessed May 18, 2007).

Tri-Council Policy Statement, 1998. Ethical conduct for research involving humans should be cited thus: Canadian Institutes of Health Research, Natural Sciences and Engineering Research Council of Canada, Social Sciences and Humanities Research Council of Canada, *Tri-council policy statement: Ethical conduct for research involving humans* (with 2000, 2002 and 2005 amendments). www.pre.ethics.gc.ca (accessed November 28, 2007).

van den Hoonaard, W. C. 2002. *Walking the tightrope.* Toronto: University of Toronto Press.

Weinberg, M. 2002. Biting the hand that feeds you, and other feminist dilemmas in fieldwork. In W. Van den Hoonaard (Ed.), *Walking the tightrope*, pp. 79–94. Toronto: University of Toronto Press.

Section III

Performative Interventions

9 | Narrative Poetics and Performative Interventions[1]

D. Soyini Madison
Northwestern University

Practice without thought is blind;
thought without practice is empty.

—Nkrumah, 1964, a popular expression

One day in my performance ethnography graduate seminar, a student who was frequently absent and not keeping up with the course readings was becoming more and more frustrated with the critical and theoretical aspects of the course. He did not approve of my approach that included critical and political theory in a course he felt should focus exclusively on performance "methods." Toward the end of one session, he looked around at all of us sitting in the seminar circle and said: "With all this emphasis on theory and politics, you are not really interested in what people are actually doing in your fieldwork; but, instead, you are telling people what to do!" My blood was boiling at the accusation that all that was said, read, done, and discussed in the seminar up to this point was so blatantly diminished to "telling people what to do!" Although the young man was often absent and not keeping up with the rest of the class, I took his complaint seriously. Perhaps he was not doing well in the class because there was some truth to his accusation and I was overemphasizing theory and politics at the expense of sound methodological practice. The student's comment was also difficult to understand, because it has always been impossible for me to separate theory from method. How can there be such a thing as *critical methods* without critical theory or politics and political theory? Can't we embrace theory and politics in the field and work for social justice—out of which our methods are generated—without being accused of "telling people what to do"?

A few weeks before the unhappy student's remark, I attended a presentation on campus by two Afro Peruvian women who were human rights activists in Peru. Their talk was inspiring and informative. One of the points they made that will always stay with me concerned the motives of fieldwork research. They said it is a problem and waste of time when academics come to Peru to engage in what they called "folklore" encounters. The women explained that rights violations and structures of racial oppression and poverty have affected their communities for generations, but academics come and want to know about "beads, songs, myths, and weaving without associating them to the material conditions of our lives." According to these activists, some of us seem to care more about "crafts and customs while ignoring the injustices that pervades the day to day." The women were concerned that the apolitical approach that extricates the dirty details of political life for "weaving and myths" was another form of "romanticizing the native" while white-washing the urgent realities of oppressive forces. I left the presentation of the Peruvian activists even more determined to teach and write in ways that recognize the importance of theories that inform a critical approach to methodology—a critical approach guided by political theory that matters on the ground, but at the same time believing in the power and beauty of cultural expression.

After the student made the comment, I thought about the Peruvian activists. The student equated a critical theory approach to methodology as "telling people what to do"; the Peruvian activists equated a lack of political and critical consciousness in the field as "folklore encounters" that ignored material suffering. What critical performance ethnography hopes to bridge is the frustration and feelings of lack in both these positions: the poetics of a space *and* its politics as well as its politics and its poetics. Haven't we learned by now those expressive and cultural traditions always occur within the machinations of power that encompass them?

• • •

Critical performance ethnography is animated by the dynamics interacting between power, politics, and poetics (Alexander, 2006; Conquergood, 2002; Denzin, 2001, 2003; Hamera, 2006; Langellier & Petterson, 2004; Pollock, 1999). In this chapter, I examine these dynamics within the oral narrative performances of local human rights activists in Ghana, West Africa, who are working for the rights of women and girls against traditional cultural practices that impede their freedom and well-being.

For several years, I have been conducting field research with Ghanaian activists working in rural areas. They are involved in remarkable and courageous initiatives for the defense of human rights, particularly as they relate to women and girls. The activists discussed here are concerned with a specific cultural practice known as Trokosi by most rights activists and Troxovi by most adherents of traditional African religion. The Troxovi/Trokosi practice involves a young girl usually between the ages of six to twelve, depending on the location, who is assigned to a village shrine. This can be for a certain period of years or for the duration of her life; again, this depends on the area where the shrine is located. In some areas, the Troxovi/Trokosi (the name given the females as well as the name of the practice) are sent to the shrine in atonement for a crime or transgression that is said to be against God and the community. The crime is committed by a family relation, usually a male, and can range from a variety of transgressions such as an insult, stealing, or an act of violence. To appease the wrath and punishment of God against the family or village for the moral transgression, the virgin girl of the family is sent as reparation for the crime.

In certain shrines, the girls are forced into slave labor and often become concubines for the shrines priests. According to many traditionalists, these shrines are not genuine Troxovi/Trokosi shrines. It is said that these shrines are actually violating the principles of the religion and are considered "breakaway or outlaw" shrines. In other areas, in what traditionalists regard as genuine Troxovi/Trokosi shrines, the women and girls attend the shrines for "moral and cultural training," serving as "protection" or "proper moral teaching" from a family that has violated the moral codes of the community and religion. In these shrines, the traditionalists say that the girls have freedom of movement and may live at home; moreover, it is against the laws of the religion for the priests to sexually abuse them. Instead, they must to be treated respectfully.

Since I began my research, the Troxovi/Trokosi institution[2] has undergone many changes. Some traditionalists and rights activists have joined together in a campaign to reform the institution and eradicate shrines and expel shrine priests in areas where human rights violations were being committed. Some of these shrines remain for religious worship, but in several cases the girls and women are no longer being sequestered or abused. However, there are some areas where Troxovi/Trokosi girls and women are still being violated and "breakaway" shrines are practicing "underground."

This chapter presents the oral narratives of rights activists who are working against these breakaway or "outlaw" shrines. I hope the chapter serves as a bridge and opportunity for readers to listen to indigenous activists telling us (and each other) what *they do*. The chapter operates from a polemic of social justice relative to human rights, but my intention is to use it as a platform and a means to forefront the polemic of those Ghanaians *themselves* who are fighting for the future of their own country, critiquing their own traditions, defending human rights from their own tactics and strategies, and desiring that others hear what they say and be exposed to what they do. I am claiming the "native point of view," but I would be committing the same crime of false objectivity as researchers who do not take responsibility for their biases, who refuse to recognize their inherent subjectivity and their ingrained power over the data (a power that always trails the ethnographic project) if I did not state in the beginning my admiration, support, and bias toward these activists and their work.

These narratives are examples of critical performance ethnography because each narrator poetically narrates his or her own indigenous and critical methodologies based on the politics of their performative interventions in defending the human rights of Others. As a critical performance ethnographer, I am "being there" within the time and space of others who guide, advise, and inspire me to further embrace performance (in different and contextually specific ways) as a means to interpret, illuminate, and advocate a politics of change. I interpret the in-depth interview with each rights activists through a performance lens to capture the complexity and multilayered dimensions reflected in the expressiveness of the human voice and body in the act of telling as well as the immediate environment or scene—ripe with influence and meaning— of the telling. In this sense, poetic transcription aims to capture the signification of what Richard Bauman (1977) calls the narrative event and the narrated event, or what Della Pollock (1999) calls the telling and the told. Poetic transcription aims to capture the content of *what* is said and the form of *how* it is said in gesture, movement, vocal affect, and the symbolic surrounding reported and expressed.

The chapter will present two oral narratives by members of International Need Network, Ghana. International Needs Ghana (ING)[3] is a human rights organization that has been at the forefront of reforming the Troxovi/Trokosi institution and releasing or liberating girls and women from certain shrines. The first narrative by Patience Vormawor describes the tactics employed by ING in the liberation of Troxovis/Trokosis from the religious shrines that inhibit their freedom. The second narrative by Agnes Okudzeto describes the ING school for liberated Toxovi/Trokosi that was prompted by a response to a charge made by a particular traditionalist who opposes the work of ING.

Throughout the narratives, I weave my own commentary and observations to illuminate the *implications* of their words and experience. There has been general and legitimate criticism far and wide of this "weaving" approach of researcher and Other by numerous observers and practitioners of qualitative research (including myself on occasion). In summary, the criticisms argue:

- The researcher's analysis is an intrusion where the subject's narrative is often *silenced*. The authoritative voice and heavy hand of the researcher overshadows the voice and presence of the narrator. The researcher's analysis "upstages" the narrative, leaving the narrator's actual words almost forgotten and their meanings but whispers in the booming volume of the researcher's interpretation.

- The researcher's analysis is his or her own idiosyncratic interpretation and *distorts* the interpretative report and expressions of the narrator. The researcher does not necessarily silence the narrative but rather imposes a reversal or counter-directional meaning to the directions and implications of meanings that constitute the narrative. Keep in mind that the researcher's interpretation does not deepen narrative analysis here or open possibilities of meanings but actually closes them by "twisting" and "distorting" the paths of truths that define the narrative and bring it into existence. The "falseness" of the researcher's interpretation betrays the promise of illumination and self-reflexive engagement.

- The researcher's analysis promotes theoretical jargon that renders the narrative analysis itself *ineffectual* at best and silly at worst. The researcher becomes so enamored with "theoretical speak" and impressing colleagues that honoring the narrative becomes less important than acrobatics of abstraction and theoretical word play. The researcher's analysis does not necessarily silence or distort the narrative, it just becomes undesirable to it. It becomes an alien indecipherable object alongside the vitality of a narrative still open for honest interpretation.

- The researcher's analysis is descriptive analysis that is only a simple restatement, a *redundant* summary that becomes an obtuse repetition of what is already apparent and more powerfully articulated in the words of the narrator. Here, the narrative is narrated again, but only second hand, by the researcher in the absence of new insights and possibilities of meaning. Analysis becomes useless repetition.

Although I often agree with these criticisms, I also believe that a delicate balance of analysis can open deeper engagement with the narrative text and unravel contexts and connections within the undercurrents of the narrative universe without the researcher acting as a psychoanalyst, clairvoyant, or prophet. By including commentary, I hope to attend to the narration—as one is compelled to attend to or interpret the significance of any object or text rich with meanings, history, value, and possibility—by entering selected moments of subtext and implicit moments of signification to engage the depth of inferences, the overreaching consequences, and the politically valuable import so that we as readers may be offered an *additional realization of the narrative and the narrator*. In summary the aim is:

- The researcher's analysis serves as a *magnifying lens* to enlarge and amplify the small details and the taken-for-granted. Too often hidden in plain sight of words spoken and written are meanings and implications below the surface that need to be excavated, contemplated, and engaged. We may listen to a story or point of view and on first impression it may come across as nothing special or uneventful. The researcher points to those moments or small details that we might take for granted as "ordinary talk" or prosaic and opens us to layers of complexity and associations that we may otherwise not come to realize.

- The researcher's analysis serves to *clarify and honor the significance* of the "telling and the told" (Pollock, 1990).

- This point is particularly important for performance ethnography. The interview is more than just questions and answers that simply happen to occur in an innocuous location. It is a substantive event—a surrounding scene of signification and its objects—a gestalt where the immediate telling becomes a richly descriptive environment of symbolic worth. And, it is one where the immediacy of the telling environment frames and relates to its content or told. Now, the interview becomes an eventful enactment of witnessing, testimony, and dialog constituted by a form (i.e., engaged, meaningful bodies and a scenic space that is no longer ignored by *what* is said as content or prior information). The researcher's analysis serves to employ theory to *unlock the multiple truths* embedded below the surface. Theory acts as a bright light out of which we can now see with fullness and precision what has always been present and in our midst but before was obscure and more difficult to name and reach. Theory must be quintessentially revelatory. It should not block our access to the narrative but lead us deeper into its paths or truths. Instead of theory becoming its own narrative (in interpreting the narratives of Others), theory reveals how we may encounter, describe, and name the narrative's essential insights. Without theoretical analysis, the power, complexity, and expanse of narrative knowledge become unengaged.

• The researcher's analysis serves to emphasize, reiterate, and *make apparent the beauty and poignancy* of description. As narrators describe certain persons, places, things, and ideas, the researcher may feel compelled to then describe the description. Instead of relying entirely on theory or more cognitive analysis, the researcher now embraces the emotions and sensuality of *what* is being described and *how* it is being described—the telling and the told—to illuminate the textures, smells, sounds, tastes, and sights being rendered within the content of the told and within the form of the telling. Performance ethnography demands a felt-sensing experience—emotions and sensuality—that uses lyrical, poetic, or performative language to wisely embellish the existential gestalt of the interview event, making it more present before us, with heart and beauty.

I bullet point what I believing to be the labor of analysis not to claim a kind of authority for the researcher but to acknowledge the great importance of narrators and their narratives in our fieldwork.

The subaltern does speak, always, and, we must listen with more radical intent (Aubrey 1997). These subaltern knowledges are sometimes hidden away in locations that are at times hard for us to reach as they speak the philosophies, logics, and approaches of their life worlds and in their own languages. How indigenous people in this global/local dance and struggle often making a way out of no way—creating tactics for survival and victories out of the vestiges of extremely unjust state of affairs—is what we call on our local advisors in the field to help us try to comprehend. We listen so we can be of use to them—a messenger and an interpreter to make what they say and do known to other Others.

Juliana Makuchi Nfah-Abbenyi states that within the

narratives of African women writers, "theory is embedded in the polysemous and polymorphous" nature of the narration. I contend that this is also true of the oral narratives that inform and enrich our fieldwork. Nfah-Abbenyi goes on to state that narratives "reinscribe and foreground teleological, ontological, and epistemological insights and praxis relevant to the specific histories and politics that preceded" them (1997, p. 20). For Nfah-Abbenyi, these narratives as theory (or theories as narratives) are not only preceded by history and politics but show us that "indigenous theory is autonomous, self-defining, and exists in unconventional places ... such theory can qualify as a kind of performance in print" (p. 20).

"We Are Not Outsiders:" Local Narrations of Rights and Critical Methodologies

It is a September morning in 1999 during the early stages of my fieldwork, and I am at the office of ING, the NGO that has taken the lead in reforming the institution of Troxovi/Trokosi. ING is located in The Scripture Union office building in Accra. As I come to the second floor of the building, I meet the director, Reverend Walter Pimpong. He greets me with a big smile; he has a calming and warm presence. I tell Walter I have come to interview Patience. He is pleased and suggests we conduct the interview in his private office where we will have more privacy. I am looking forward to this time with Patience, because when we are together in the field she has no time to talk about herself or discuss personal reflections of her work. She is too busy focusing her attention on the people who need her help—listening, talking, and doing what needs to be done. I have watched her time and again in various villages of the Volta region interact with people with respect and affectionate attention, as if nothing in the world was more important to her than them and what they say to her. Patience has been one of the activists working very closely with the community as well as the shrine owners and priests in liberating several Trokosi women and girls from the shrines.

The room is air-conditioned and a nice relief from the suffocating December heat in Ghana. There is a large desk in the front of the room. On the wall is a poster with the picture of a young Trokosi girl wearing brightly colored African fabric; both her hands are placed on the top of her head to signify mourning or suffering. Written across the poster in red and white letters are: "Stop Trokosi Now!" and, beneath it, "… respect the rights of girls and women." Patience takes a seat on the couch across from the desk; I sit in the chair next to her. Patience is soft-spoken with a gentle manner. She is a striking woman, tall with a round face and high cheekbones. She sits with both hands resting in her lap. I ask about the campaign ING has waged to liberate the Troxovi/ Trokosi against a religious tradition that is ancient and where the belief is so strongly held and defended. I ask her to talk about the strategy of persuading the priests and shrine owners to free the women and girls. Patience confidently speaks into the tape recorder sitting on the table next to the couch:

> *Before a release, we go to visit the shrine priest.*
>
> *We find out from him how he feels about the Trokosi system.*
>
> *We find out why he feels he can or can not release the women and girls.*
>
> *We try to find out what he can do to help them.*
>
> *We counsel him in adjusting to things he does not understand.*
>
> (Patience moves closer in toward me—her voice softens.)
>
> *Those who don't know our work fear that we are coming to break the whole shrine.*
>
> *But we come to help make the shrine more progressive, more humane.*
>
> *After we come to an understanding* (pause) *we ask the priest to release the women and girls.*
>
> *If he understands and we come to an agreement* (speaking tenderly) *he will let us speak to the Trokosi.*
>
> *We meet the girls and we counsel them one by one.*
>
> *We help them psychologically about being separated from their parents,*
> *about being sent into the shrine,*
> *about going back into the village,*
> *about what kind of work they will do,*
> *about who they will live with.*

(She clasps her hands and places them gently on her lap. She tilts her head toward me.)

about how they will take care of their children

The "power of persuasion" is given profound force and meaning because persuasion here is dependent not only on human lives and freedom but on the disruption of a sacred world-view. How do you persuade one human being not to deny the humanity of another? How do you make them listen to you? How do you make them stop believing in what they believe is God's will, when God's will means devaluing the lives of others? The urgency of the kind of "persuasion" being crafted here begins with empathy and respect that is explicitly concerned with how the other feels and understands. This is a magnanimous gesture because it is ultimately a confrontation with "wrongness." To sit across from someone you know is not only wrong but also acting wrongfully and to *genuinely listen* to them is not only a good tactic of persuasion but also an act of compassionate engagement. The structures of feeling that encompass the Troxovi/Trokosi practice must be replaced by another discursive practice and another structure of feeling that must begin with trust. Feelings of wrongness are eclipsed by the importance of being trusted. Trust is the foundation on which persuasion begins—compassionate engagement and empathetic listening become its method.

In *The Teachings of Ptahhotep* (*ca.* 2400 BCE), one of the earliest ancient Kemetian (Egyptian) "books of instruction" (Hord & Lee, 1995, p. 17), the mayor of the city, Vizier Ptahhotep, presents an elaborate list of approximately thirty-seven codes of conduct. These codes are "life instructions" that assures each individual a place in the eternal network of the universe after his or her death. This is one of the codes in the ancient writing that speaks to the notion of trust:

> If you are among the people, then gain your supporters by building trust. The trusted man is one who does not speak the first thing that comes to mind; and he will become a leader. A man of means has a good name, and his face is benign. People will praise him even without his knowledge. On the other hand, he whose heart obeys his belly asks for contempt of himself in the place

of love. His heart is naked. His body is unanointed. The great-hearted is a gift of God. He who is ruled by his appetite belongs to the enemy. (Hord & Lee, 1995, pp. 26)

In accordance with this passage, Patience is trusted because she listens, she is humble among them, and the people have spoken amongst themselves of her "good name." They believe she is not motivated by greed or self-interest—her heart does not "obey her belly"—but the interests of Others, their interests. I witnessed the affection and trust among the people she worked with from village to village. The question becomes: Once trust is gained and a new discourse is possible, what are the alternative actions offered by these rights activists that lead to sustained change? First, we understand that when the girls and women are released from the shrine they are not left alone. Patience continues:

> *We help them go to school for professional training if that is what they want to do* (looks intently into my eyes)
>
> *All this is not a one-day affair*
> *When they are released, we go with them to their homes*
> *And we continue to go back to see how they are adjusting*
>
> (She holds her hand up and counts with finger.)
>
> *We counsel the family, the household, and the community who fear the girls are still Trokosi and should remain as outcasts* (raises her voice)
>
> *We must counsel the Trokosi and the non-Trokosi because the fear is very powerful*
>
> (Counting with her finger again she almost sings the list.)
>
> *We follow them for about two years to be sure they are socially integrated, economically independent, psychologically adjusted, and healthy. We encourage them to think on their own and for themselves* (softly but with determination).
>
> *The priest does not need to think for them anymore*
>
> *We even study all aspects of their body movements and facial expressions to observe* (raises her head and smiles).
>
> *They are happy.*
>
> *During this time of tracking we keep profiles of the women. We check*

in on all the factors (pause) *health, finances, social adjustments, and so forth*

We want them to realize they can be independent (hands together in a fist and voice raised).

When they have a problem (pause), *they don't have to wait for someone to come.*

They can take care of it themselves.

Once the priests were able to engender trust, the conversation began, and then the possibility of an alternative logic became possible and, finally, plausible. What evolves from the meeting between priest and rights activist is more than compromise and negotiation; it is creating something not done before, creating a generative cultural formation—that is, an alternative practice and belief now valued and shared anew. It is a different way of being. The religion remains, but reformed and consciously changed from a reevaluation of the past to save its future and preserve the core of its meaning. The practices must be changed within the discourse of rights and freedom to save the religion. But to remake cultural practice means that the point between what was and what the activists hope the religion will become requires creating the connection between past and future, the connection that constitutes what is to be done *now*. As Patience says: "All this is not a one-day affair"; it is a long-term commitment.

Kwame Nkrumah, the intellectual, socialist philosopher, and the first president of Ghana after independence, stated: "Indeed, for the African, everything that exists, exists as a complex of forces in tension. ... It is out of tension that being is born. Becoming is tension, and being is the child of that tension of opposed forces and tendencies" (Eze, 1998, pp. 90–92). This "being" that is "born" is based on the relentless labor—the indigenous, critical methodology—of local human rights activism that was in opposition to the practices of the Trokosi shrine. Nkrumah reminds us that we begin with these tensions, these opposing forces, for change and for rebirth to occur. Here, tension is not simply the differing ideological beliefs between the priests and the activists on first contact, but how these tensions were manifest and enacted through persistent and continued visitations by the activists to the shrines. Each encounter that was constituted by tension was a move closer to Nkrumah's rebirth.

I observed the dedication of Patience and the other activists at ING through their comings and goings and coming back again and again with the commitment to give the Troxovi/Trokosi the knowledge that they possessed a *self.* I witnessed ING activists do the work of gifting these women and girls with the tools toward independent living while helping them reenter their communities against the forces of a long-held stigma. I witnessed the infinitely human right of selfhood come slowly and methodically into being.

> *Some believe that we do not know the Trokosi system because we have not lived there and that we are outsiders* (shakes her head).
>
> *This is not true*
>
> *We have lived there*
>
> *We are not outsiders*
>
> *We have Trokosi relatives*
>
> (hands raised and speaking in an empathic tone)
>
> *The village people should not think we are just city people trying to go in and change the system.*
>
> (moves in to make sure I am listening to this point)
>
> *We have people who are victims of the system on our team* (with emphasis).
>
> *So we know what we are doing.*
>
> *We have been there talking to people one-on-one.*

The position of being both an "insider" and "outsider" suggests that one possesses a certain kind of knowledge or authority regarding the relational dynamics of two contrasting or competing worlds. It also implies that the insider/outsider can move between these worlds with difficulty or ease, translating and often enacting their divergent codes, costumes, laws, etc. Therefore, the assumption of a certain authority of knowledge is also based on the experience and history of what it means to be *affected* corporally and emotionally by what happens or has happened in those contrasting worlds and, moreover, to have survived them. It is important for the activists to make it known to the Troxovi/Trokosi, as well as the priests, that they are not just outsiders but are "from where they are from," not only in knowledge but from experiencing through body and feelings what it is to be of a place—to know the people, to eat the food, to speak the language, to walk the same paths for water, to share the same memories of the place.

This being *from* the same place conjoined with being *of* a different place is an interesting paradox. Being from the same place provided an authority of knowledge of what goes on in the same place and the unique feelings about it, that is, "I care and know about what goes on here." But being of a different place provides an authority of knowledge of what the alternatives or other possibilities of what the same place could be: "I care and know about another way to be." I do not mean to privilege a one-way direction of change; that is, the outsider domain always wants to change the insider domain or vice versa.

The point is that the insider/outsider position does garner hybrid knowledge or specialized knowledge that creates the space of different and new realities (Anzaldúa, 1987; hooks, 1989; Madison, 1998, 2005). Ghanaians in exile most penetratingly experience the insider/outsider phenomenon from a slightly different perspective than these rights activists, but nonetheless relevant to this discussion. Ghanaian poet Abena P. A. Busia states:

> In every instance, my various identifications—as scholar, as poet, as Black, as female, as African, an exile, as an Afro-Saxon living in Afro-America—are always present. Even in my identification as Ghanaian, which I stated so boldly at the start, I am the child of a woman whose people are patrilineal who married a man whose people are matrilineal. Am I thus doubly claimed, or doubly disposed? None of these categories is mutually exclusive. They coexist and are the boundaries within which I must exist or which I have come to cross every waking moment. (1993, p. 209)

Many of the activists who work with ING choose not to leave the country. They stay in Ghana working for human rights. However, when they leave the city to go to the villages—taking with them their new ideas about an ancient religion and a revered cultural practice—they are often regarded as foreigners, as outsiders.

I have witnessed the "various identifications" that Busia describes: Patience and her colleagues move in and out between

English in the city and Ewe and Twi in the villages; between the faster body rhythms of the city and the slower, deliberate strength demanded of village life; between their philosophical interchanges on human rights at meetings and conferences and their flesh to flesh embodied interchanges of food, story, and companionship in the village. It is in these "waking moments" that I have witnessed the multiple identities of Ghanaian people in Ghana doing the work for themselves on their land.

The final section of the narrative is a poetic treatise on *difference* and how to embrace what is innately human about difference for the sake of making a radical and revolutionary *difference* for the life of another. It reflects the value of both the anti-humanist and humanist philosophy. In the anti-humanist tradition, this section further shows us that humankind is *produced by* discourse, events, and history. And, in the humanist tradition, the narrative shows us that humankind are *producers of* discourse, events, and history, especially when one human being communicates a yearning to another and thereby creates a dialogical alchemy that, in turn, sets forth alternative ways of being.

I said my thanks to Patience and slowly reached over to turn off the tape recorder when she raised her hand very gently to indicate that there was one more thing she wanted to say:

One thing about human beings (pause) *they are not like machines*

In this work you learn a lot about human beings

And one thing you learn is that they all behave differently

You learn how the environment changes them and then you begin to develop relationships with them (pause) *even if you believe in different things*

You get to know them very well and you learn all about them

And you respect them even if you have different ideas from them/you respect them

(sitting up in her seat and moving closer to the edge)

We see ourselves really helping them.

When I play a part in this person's life to make it better.

(Smiling, she rests her hands together on her lap.)

I am happy.

Thank you Patience.

You are welcome Soyini.

As I am about to leave the room, my friend Wisdom Mensah, program director of ING, enters. Wisdom is an invaluable resource for me, helping me understand all sides of the issues and what it meant to witness human rights in action as I watch him go into the field negotiating with stakeholders on all sides, counseling rights activists, and working with Reverend Pimpong in setting the record straight against the attacks by certain traditionalists against ING. Wisdom informs me that Mrs. Okudzeto, the head of the ING Trokosi Vocational Training School, is outside and wants to come in and say hello.

I met Mrs. Okudzeto several months before when I went to visit the school where they teach the newly freed Troxovi/Trokoi how to read and write as well as provide vocational training in dressmaking, cosmetology, catering, batik, weaving,[4] and soap making. Mrs. Okudzeto carries herself with unwavering confidence; she is outspoken and cheerful, with a witty sense of humor. Before I met her, Wisdom mentioned how much she loved the girls at the school and how she was such a "very efficient" head master.

I am pleased that Mrs. Okudzeto has arrived because I wanted to speak with her about a gentleman who had come by my flat about two weeks ago to tell me that any Ghanaian who was against the Trokosi practice was against their ancestors and their heritage. He said the activists were spreading lies about the abuses in the shrines because "the fact is the girls are treated honorably, like queens." He went on to say: "The people that want to stop the practice are spreading lies in order to get European and American money." He then stated emphatically: "Trokosi will never come to an end and if any one tries to stop it, they will stop it over my dead body!"

When I told Mrs. Okudzeto about the visitor, her response was a mixture of exasperation and irritation:

We should eradicate all outmoded customs

(turns in toward me with a very serious, intense look).

That man says these women are carriers of the society?

He says they are queens?

He says we honor them?

He says they are special women?

That is what he tells you (with a small ironic, resentful laugh)*?!*

Hmm, Hmm But they are not!

The girls themselves will tell you they have been treated like slaves!

He says those of us who want to stop the Trokosi practice will only stop it over his dead body? (laughing ironically)

Well, he is going to die soon!!!

He says the women that go through the shrines are only going there as an education for training to teach them purity and to prepare them to have children for the gods?

(raises her hands up in astonished disbelief)

They don't teach them anything in the shrines except you wake up in the morning and go to the bush to farm you gather firewood

They don't learn anything!

Do they teach them how to read, to write? No!

They don't teach them anything!

(irritation is building)

They would rather sexually abuse them!

These are the people who are trying to suppress women in this country?

(shaking her head in disdain)

I am with these girls and they have been sexually abused a lot!

The African symbol of *sankofa* is a majestic bird whose commanding body is positioned forward while its long elegant neck dramatically circles backward gazing into the past. *Sankofa* symbolizes the significance of the past and tradition in order to move toward the present and future. The man who came to see me referred to the *sankofa* symbol and explained that his mission was to "uphold and defend African culture and religion against those who want to denigrate and destroy our traditions." He did not distinguish between the shrines that were abusive and those that were not. His defense of tradition was in many ways contrary to the organization Afrikania or Afrikan Renaissance Mission, a well-known traditional organization in Ghana that openly exposes and condemns the abusive "breakaway shrines" while also identifying itself explicitly as being of the *sankofa* faith in their mission as defenders, teachers, and celebrants of African tradition. My visitor was more concerned about defending the Troxovi/Trokosi institution from its critics, without exception, than he was about women and girls being maltreated in certain shrines. This was also the case for several other defenders of the institution of Troxovi/Trokosi. For the visitor to say "over my dead body" was not an uncommon charge for those who believe that criticizing African tradition (particularly African religious tradition) was an abomination.

In Ghana, I came to understand more than ever (for better and for worse) that tradition is the life breath of the past and the very ground on which the present stands and the future is even possible. Traditional religion is evidence of the past but, more, it is also the hope, creation, and embodiment of a *generation of people*. Tradition is evidence. It is the sacred materialization of what those who came before belief, valued, and yearned. I learned that to defy cultural and religious tradition is to defy the sacred debt we owe to the ancestor. It is to defy the sacred being of our kinship. But I also had to ask: What happens when tradition does harm? What of those who did defy tradition and dare to oppose it and want to change it? How did Mrs. Okudzeto and other rights activists begin to believe differently and work for change? In Kwame Gyekye's important and classic book *Tradition and Modernity* he eloquently addresses this question:

> To say that a belief or practice is handed down to a generation is to say that it is bequeathed to the generation, passed on to it. But what this really means is that the belief or practice is placed at the disposal of the new generation in the expectation that the generation would preserve it. But the preservation of it, in part or in whole, would depend very much on the attitude the new generation adopts toward it and would not necessarily be automatic, as the word "transmit" would suggest. If we look back across the line, we find that some of the cultural values created ...

are dropped by subsequent generations, or they simply sink into oblivion—winnnowed away by time. Those values were, for one reason or another, not accepted, maintained, or preserved by subsequent generations. This means that the continuity and survival of a pristine cultural product depends on the normative considerations that will be brought to bear on it by a subsequent generation. The forebears—the previous generation—do not "transmit" their cultural creation as such; what they do, rather is to place theme at the disposal of subsequent generation of people. But the subsequent generations may on normative or other rational grounds, either accept, refine, or preserve them or spurn, depreciate them, abandon them. The desire or intention of a subsequent generation to preserve or abandon inherited cultural products often results from some kind of *evaluation* of those cultural products and the tradition they lead to. *Such critical evaluations are essential for the growth and revitalization of cultural tradition.* (Gyekye, 1997, p. 221, emphasis added)

I experienced in Ghana that "evaluation" of the kind that invokes *alternatives* within one's own culture and society is primarily an admixture of:

1. Serious reflection. I am compelled, often by my circumstances or a particular situation, to contemplate and evaluate where and how I live, and, in turn, the workings of my life and my environment. What is guiding and determining the world of my being? I begin to dream of possible alternatives.

2. Mobility. I move from the micro space of my own world to witness another world and way of being. My world is not all there is. I discover how Others live. I experience their movements, ways of speaking, productions, and their futures as different from my own. I witness alternative experiences.

3. Disturbance. I feel the weight of a lingering and substantial discontent. I am not at ease or at peace within my environment. I begin to resent the workings of my world and feel disconnected to it.

4. Language. I embrace a new language. I begin to formulate the words out of which I can now name and describe

my discontent and the doomed future of my own world. I now speak about alternative ways of being within my own world and alternative futures. Language orders, generates, and materializes my lingering discontent as well as new reflections and hopes for a different world and way of being.

5. Comrades. I am emboldened by like minds and comrades. I can now speak, act, and feel with others who substantiate and inspire my hope for alternatives. Together, we act for change.

So, what does it mean when the evaluation must now move to change? Mrs. Okudzeto has evaluated the tradition as an "outmoded practice," and she, like Reverand Pimpong, Wisdom, Patience, and so many others, take evaluation a step further. She is an activist and her evaluation generates praxis:

The school is helping the girls to feel free inside themselves

(joyfully with pride and confidence)

We teach them to use the potential within themselves

When they come to the school they can not read

They can not write

(softly)

They don't know about the things around them

We try to make them feel free and to go out and see things for themselves—how life is

We teach them they can work with their own hands

They can create with their own hands

They can live with dignity and love

They must feel free and they have the right to feel happy

(almost pleading with her hands to her chest)

Last week we took them out into the city.

They went to the airport / to the harbour / to the zoo in the city!

For many of them that was the first time they'd been to the city

(small laughter)

They saw a two-story building.

It is good exposure to them

Some of them, even when they finish the course (pause) *they don't want to go back home*

They want to stay with me

(smiling, raising her hands and placing them near her heart)

The school is changing their lives

They feel safe and worthy

Some of them are now on their own

(nodding her heard, her eyes widen, and her voice rises)

They are making their own life

The Location of Poverty

I have been traveling back and forth across the Atlantic to Ghana, West Africa, since 1998. I remain struck by the abiding harm some religious traditions around the world have on the life and freedom of others, particularly women and girls. I am also struck by how often these same traditions are revered and glorified by some members of the culture in the face of the blatant abuse the traditions impose on the female body. But I am more struck by something else that I believing is equally, if not more, unjust and life threatening, but certainly more convoluted and disguised: how the history and present of global politics and power operate in affecting people across the world, particularly in the global south. I refer specifically to the injustice of the location of poverty.[5]

It is at this point where the politics of poverty must enter the conversation. My work with Ghanaian human rights activism and my experiences with Troxovi/Trokosi were complicated even further when I came into contact with what seemed to be an ingrained ideology of phallocentrism[6] and male domination that was inseparable from the stark reality of wretched poverty. It is often difficult to summarize Troxovi/Trokosi, because how it is practiced, even what it is called, is contingent on the *economy of its location*. I include here an excerpt from my field journal in March 1999:

Dear Journal,

This is becoming yet another classic case of human rights and its relationship to poverty. As I travel through the areas where Troxovi/Trokosi is practiced, I am struck by how the maltreatment of women and girls is in direct correlation with the economic and material conditions of the area. What has "Development" over the past decades accomplished here? Sometimes one can only feel rage. Arturo Escabar's work on Development speaks to the question. I paste his words here on this page.

> *Whatever these traditional ways might have been, and without idealizing them, it is true that massive poverty in the modern sense appeared only when the spread of the market economy broke down community ties and deprived millions of people from access to land, water and other resources. With the consolidation of Capitalism, systematic pauperization became inevitable. (Escobar, 1995, p. 22)*

In the poorest areas, the areas that are more remote and distanced from the city and where piped water, electricity, education are scarce or inaccessible, the treatment of women and girls is more severe and their labor more demanding. It is clear to me that the Trokosi/Toxovi Institution is not one monolithic or unified cultural practice. What it is and how it is performed across the various shrines is very different and, again, contingent on the level of the economy in the area. There is a tension here between oppression from male dominance and oppression from poverty— the colonial past complicates each within discreetly differing force fields.—March 22, 1999

Regrettably, in some conversations, poverty is becoming wearisome and sexism is too easily separated from the political economy. The point is that traditional patriarchy and phallocentrism alone do not account for the consequences of poverty or "determine relations of production and reproduction" that exploit the lives and labor of African women:

Patriarchal relations do not determine the material basis of the relations of production and reproduction. What is revealed here is that an examination of only the patriarchal relations of both precapitalist and colonial capitalist societies will not explain how women's exploitation and oppression were shaped by the historical limits, changes and differences of these societies. The cultural, familial and political reality of African women was restructured with the introduction of commodity production based on monopoly of the means of production, racist ideology, and a policy of separate political and economic development. Under colonial capitalism African women experienced three forms of exploitation based on African Women's position in production, African women's position in the family and African Women's racial position in colonial society. (Courville, 1993, p. 42)

Here Courville echoes the position of postcolonial writers in asserting that with the onset of the colonial epoch, African women were now exploited by the "coexistence of dual political systems, dual patriarchal systems and dual modes of production" yet, they were not identical dualities (p. 41). The existence of a colonial capitalist mode of production was of a different kind and degree of production than it was under the traditional African patriarchal mode of production. Although African women lived under the oppressive and exploitive forces of male control, they still had a certain amount of power within the familial household (Allman, Geiger, & Musisi 2002). The family was "the source of their social standing and their limited protection within the society, and the site and foundation for collective action to express their dissatisfaction and bring about change" (Courville, 1993, p. 36). Therefore, from a more *local commodity production* to foreign *monopoly colonial capitalism*, "colonialism was the process of the forced and violent integration of the African continent into the world capitalist system" (p. 36).

Major factors that combined to bring forth colonial domination were: (1) military intervention; (2) the transformation of African economies into monetary economies; (3) the intrusion and exploitation of imperialist colonial trade; and (4) foreign investment in the development of infrastructure and metropolitanism (Ake, 1981; Mudimbe, 1988). Compounding these forces were the colonial policies of indirect rule in which "the colonial state controlled and supervised the separate political and economic development of the colonizer" and, as a result sealed the "underdevelopment of the colonized" (Ake, 1981, p. 32).

The oppressive constraints on African women from antiquity to independence were a factor of *both* traditional African society *and* colonial capitalism. African women were constrained under traditional African patriarchy, yet, under the very nature of these laws (by which the patriarchal society existed), they were still able to carve out for themselves precarious elements of independence. However, this troubled and fragile independence was, in many circumstances, diminished with the intrusion of colonial capitalism. Therefore, the idea that colonialism brought "progress" to a "backward" continent by introducing technology, culture, and infrastructural development becomes an assertion riddled with falsehoods, contradictions, and contingencies, as does the idea by some Afrocentrists of a traditional African culture based on egalitarian bliss and a spiritual utopia. How does this history of traditional patriarchy and colonial capitalism speak to present-day poverty and human rights? How does it "seal the 'underdevelopment of the continent'"? Drawing from the work of Claude Ake, Courville summarizes the contemporary economic and social effects of colonial capitalism and patriarchy:

> The economic relations were characterized by an aggregation of disparate modes of production, dependence on external trade and technology, disarticulation of resources, development of export commodities, market imperfections, and limited indigenous capital to mobilize for investment and development. The social relations of the colonial society were based on disparate aggregations of African and European patriarchies accompanied by racially structured domination and subordination. (Courville, 1993, p. 40)

Ake list the very foundations on which present-day poverty rests: trade, technology, natural resources, indigenous capital, the market, and modes of production. Each of these domains combines to form a political economy that breed poverty and sets a climate for human rights offenses. In the face of global capitalism and poverty, indigenous human rights activists carry the legacy of a colonial past that makes their work even harder.

Conclusion: My Wish List

In this chapter, indigenous methods of human rights defense are narrated as a "performance in print" (Nfah-Abbenyi, 1997) and as a subaltern praxis in the determination to bring about change in the troubled time and space and on the contested land where these Ghanaian activists live and choose to remain. Against the representations and effects of popular discourse, African people are more than victims and abusers of human rights who are enlightened and/or saved by Western ideology and benevolence.

I enter the day-to-day labor "on the ground" with those in their own country working for human rights and who choose to face the added struggle of going against the forces of tradition and economic forces. The questions that now begin to surface are: What does it mean for our scholarly projects to seek out and present the theoretical offerings and scholarly arguments from those not popularly known, but profoundly worthy? What does it mean to seek out and present the "doings" and the work "done" of indigenous activism in locations that are some of the most contested in the world? These are the guiding questions that constitute my work as a critical performance ethnographer and that undergird this chapter. These questions also enliven my ever-growing *wish list*. This wish list not only enumerates the direction I tried to follow in this chapter, but the direction in which I continue to work toward in the future.

Wish List

First. We do not become senselessly enthralled with critical theory, nor do we become dour theory bashers. Instead, we learn critical theory thoughtfully, rigorously, and purposefully for the politically charged objective of clarifying unproductive confusion and precisely naming what could be otherwise dangerously imprecise.

Second. We resist theoretical feudalism by not assigning the power of interpretation *exclusively* to a few lords of knowledge in privileged, expected, and anticipated towers of ivory or babble. The form of this kind of theorizing that is taking place in certain circles is undemocratic and the contents have become repetitive clichés. We seek theory from near and far, the expected and the unexpected, from the tower and from the ground so theory remains relevant, useful, interesting, and generative. Knowing all these different theories demands hard, rigorous work, but these troubled times demand it even more.

Third. We do not speak *For* Others when we can *Listen* while Others speak.

Fourth. We do not not speak while *only* humbly listening to the Other speak. Listening does not mean *not* speaking; it means paying attention to when it is the right time to speak. At that time, speak to and from the tower *and* the ground, even if *your voice shakes.*[7]

Fifth. We practice at home what we preach on paper and in the field. We work to become more generous with each other *within* the academy as we work for a politics of global generosity. I wish that we are generous with each other at every opportunity and when there are no opportunities, we create them. I wish that academic generosity (of information, influence, resources, and praise) becomes as important to us as academic freedom.

Patience's deep and simple clarity is the point: When I play a part in this person's life to make it better, I am happy.

Notes

1. An expanded version of the arguments in this chapter will appear in Denzin, Lincoln, and Smith, Eds., In press, *The Handbook of Critical and Indigenous Methodologies*, Sage Publications.

2. Many traditionalist refer to Troxovi/Trokosi as an institution, whereas others regard it as a practice; I use practice and institution interchangeably throughout the chapter.

3. International Needs Ghana is now International Needs Network-Ghana.

4. Sleeping mats are very common in many parts of the developing world. They are used for sleeping (in the house or outside) as floor coverings, and sometimes as prayer mats. They range in appearance from plain straw to having colorful designs of varying sorts.

5. What I call "the location of poverty" is a supplement to the notion of a "location of culture." In Ghana, looking at Trokosi, it is impossible to understand culture without considering the systems of poverty that affect and in many ways determine it.

6. I consciously use the term phallocentrism here to echo bell hooks's (1989) notion of the phallic as sexually centered male domination over the female

body without necessarily having structural or material power or membership within the national or dominant political system.

7. I refer here to one of my favorite bumper stickers: "Speak the truth, even if your voice shakes."

References

Ake, C. 1981. *A political economy of Africa*. New York: Longman.

Alexander, B. K. 2006. *Performing black masculinity: Race, culture, and queer identity*. New York: AltiMira Press.

Allman, J., Geiger, S., & Nakanyike, M., Eds. 2002. *Women in African colonial histories*. Bloomington: University of Indiana Press.

Aubrey, L. 1997. *The politics of development cooperation: NGOs, gender and partnership in Kenya*. London: Routledge.

Anzaldúa, G. 1987. *Borderlands/la frontera: The new mesitza*. San Francisco: Spinsters/Aunt Lute.

Bauman, R. 1977. *Verbal art as performance*. Rowley, MA: Newbury House

Busia, A. 1993. Performance, transcription and the language of the self: Interrogating indentity as a post-colonial poet. In S. M. James & A. B. Busua (Eds.), *Theorizing black feminisms: The visionary pragmatism of black women*, pp. 203–13. London: Routledge.

Conquergood, D. 2002. Performance studies: Interventions and radical research. *The Drama Review* 46(1):145–56.

Courville, C. 1993. Re-examing patriarchy as a mode of production: The case of Zimbabwe. In S. M. James & A. B. Busia (Eds.), *Theorizing black feminisms: The visionary programtism of black women*, pp. 31–43. London and New York: Routledge.

Denzin, N. K. 2001. *Interpretive interactionism*, 2nd ed. Thousand Oaks, CA: Sage.

Denzin, N. K. 2003. *Performance ethnography: Critical pedagogy and the politics of culture*. Thousand Oaks, CA: Sage.

Escobar, A. 1995. *Encountering development: The making and unmaking of the third world*. Princeton, NJ: Princeton University Press.

Eze, E. C. 1998. *African philosophy*. London. Blackwell Publishers.

Gyekye, K. 1997. *Tradition and modernity*. Oxford: Oxford University Press.

Hamera, J. 2006. *Dancing communities: Performance, difference, and connection in the global city*. New York: Palgrave.

hooks, b. 1989. *Talking back: Thinking feminist, thinking black*. Boston: South End Press.

Hord, L. F., & J. S. Lee, Eds. 1995. The teachings of Ptahhoptep. In F. L. Hord & J. S. Lee (Eds.), *I am because we are: Reading in black philosophy*, pp. 24–31. Amherst: University of Massachusetts Press.

Langellier, K. M., & E. E. Peterson. 2004. *Storytelling in daily life: Performing narrative*. Philadelphia: Temple University Press.

Madison, D. S. 1998. That was my occupation: Oral narrative, performance, and black feminist thought. In D. Pollock (Ed.), *Exceptional spaces: Essays in performance and history*, pp. 319–42. Chapel Hill: University of North Carolina Press.

Madison, D. S. 2005. *Critical ethnography: Method, ethics, and performance*. Thousand Oaks, CA: Sage.

Mudimbe, V. Y. 1988. *The invention of Africa*. Bloomington: Indiana University Press.

Nfah-Abbenyi, J. 1997. *Gender in African women's writing: Identity, sexuality, and difference*. Bloomington. Indiana University Press.

Nkrumah, K. 1964. *Consciencism: Philosophy and ideology for de-colonization*. London: Zed Books.

Ogundipe-Leslie, M. 1993. African women, culture and another development. In S. M. James & A. B. Busia (Eds.), *Theorizing Black feminisms: The visionary pragmatism of Black women*, pp. 105–20. New York: Routledge.

Okpewho I., C. B. Davies, & A. Mazuri. 2001. *The African Diaspora: African origins and New World identities*. Bloomington. Indiana University Press.

Pollock, D. 1990. Telling the told: Performing like a family. *The Oral History Review* 18(2):1–35.

Pollock, D. 1999. *Telling bodies performing birth: Everyday narratives of childbirth*. New York: Columbia University Press.

From Politicized Knowledge to Standardized Knowing

The Trickle-Down Effect in Schools

Christopher Darius Stonebanks
Bishop's University, Canada

Apple (2004) has his fictional encounter of two community members meeting on a street corner in their generalized ghetto discussing the success of North American schools and agreeing that, "Yes, schools work … for them" (p. 60). Kincheloe (2003) has his encounters with "brilliant" teachers and student teachers who relay their frustrations of wanting to do "good work" in a top-down institutionalized system that rewards mediocrity and discourages teachers and student teachers who take active research approaches in schools to elicit progressive change. After working in the teacher education field since 1996 and in schools since 1991, to the Apple and Kincheloe examples I add my own modest knowledge.

Unfortunately, if you are not looking at this from a research corroboration point of view, my own experience of witnessing new teachers enter or preparing to enter the field of education is one predominantly filled with frustration that echoes the preceding authors' statements. I also find myself talking with these brilliant teachers and student teachers who all too often find themselves in schools where there is a general disconnect between the education they are acquiring within their university studies and the practices that are being implemented in the so-called real world of teaching (Morrison & Marshall, 2003; Rinaldo, 2005).

For the teacher and student teacher who want to move away from the ever-prevalent banking model of education (Freire, 2005) through their own professional commitment to researching new approaches to, for instance, curriculum content, there continue to be significant barriers to changing the manner in which schools function. Foremost to my own research interest and this chapter are the obstacles created by political forces that manipulate the media's portrayal of everything from current and historic events to the individuals involved in the events (as well as the public persecution of the teachers that provide a counterinterpretation of these events) and how that shapes teachers' decisions to promote research-based classrooms (Kincheloe, 2003; Steinberg & Kincheloe, 2005) and elicit transformative change. As Apple, among many, notes, the manner in which schools propagate "knowledge" has been historically intertwined with politics and ideology and continues to function in this manner:

> It has become increasingly evident that the formal corpus of school knowledge found in, say, most history books and social studies texts and materials has, over the years, presented a somewhat biased view of the true nature of the amount and possible use of internecine strife in which groups in this country and others have engaged. Our side is good; their side is bad. "We" are peace loving and want to end strife; "they" are warlike and aim to dominate. (Apple, 2004, p. 80)

Despite the education teachers receive in their undergraduate studies, such as multicultural considerations, much of the research they review regarding "past" injustices are either still continued in our schools or propagated within a different context. For example, "Indian country," "shock and awe," "dead or alive," and even "war on terror" are examples of recent language by the "coalition" leaders of the West with regard to the expanding military actions in the Middle East. Despite the connections public scholars like Tariq Ali, Noam Chomsky, and Howard Zinn, or the wide variety of other authors and researchers (Ivie, 2005; Lobe, 2004; Pfaff, 2007; Stonebanks, 2004; Sullivan, 2003) make between the ideology that facilitated manifest destiny and the tragic results to the indigenous of North America, the general North American public seems to demonstrate little concern about the historic or current implications of such language and actions. Although intellectuals—such as Zinn, Chomsky, and Ward Churchill—

have provided in-depth and respected research to support their analysis of North American history, little of their work, or similar opposition to grand-narrative (Lyotard, 1979/1984) qualitative research, has permeated the public education sphere, thus limiting critical responses to such terminology. Whereas, as Chomsky (1992) notes, assertions regarding public figures in popular media such as "Quaddifi is a terrorist or Khomeini is a murderer" is tacitly accepted by both "experts" and the public, counternarrative critical statements regarding privileged members of North America's public sphere, both historic and current, brings about intense scrutiny and, quite often, scorn.

This chapter examines to what extent political pressure through the media exerts control over educational policy and educators' curriculum and thus denies respected counternarrative qualitative research to enter public schools. To comprehend how these forces influence student teachers and teachers, it is important to understand that in North America, the majority of our student teachers come from the "power blocs" (Kincheloe & Steinberg, 1997) of our society. Perhaps it is through the intriguing responses I receive from my education students when they read works by such authors as Apple (2004) and Kincheloe (2003) in my Curriculum Development course that we can reveal some causes as to why the education system has not really changed. Faced with these and similar readings that suggest public schools, teachers, and Western education may not be the locations of objective truths, many students appear genuinely surprised.

Despite the varied responses that I have witnessed since I began my teacher education career in 1996, with very few exceptions, all of the students who wish to enter "our most important profession" (Hunter, 1994, p. 245) do so with an overwhelming unifying belief in themselves that "I am a teacher, I want to do good work" (Kincheloe, 2003, p. 1). For the majority of the class, these readings and the discussions that stem from them become a troubling perspective that had not been part of their initial driving reasons to become teachers; to their credit, for many students, these ideas are deeply pondered as they imagine themselves as future teachers.

Some of the students believe that many of these readings

dealing with terms like "hidden curriculum," "power blocs," "critical pedagogy," etc., are "much ado about nothing" and that schools function in a manner that has served Western society well and will and should continue to do so for years to come. Many of these students will enter their "field experience" and have their perspectives validated when they see schools function just as they remembered and have their cooperating teacher tell them things like "all that 'theoretical stuff' you learn in university is nothing compared to 'real education' you will receive in the schools."

For a minority, like myself during my own studies, there is a moment, similar to Macedo (2005) describing a sixteen-year-old African American student who upon reading Freire's *Pedagogy of the Oppressed* (2005) states, "I want to meet the man who wrote this. He is talking about me" (p. 23), where they have read texts that finally speak to their own experiences. For these students, when they enter their field experience the "theory stuff" they read about in university is utilized within their own continuing research to better explain and navigate the social injustices that inspired them to become teachers. In this context, some will have cooperating teachers and supervisors who they can communicate with, but many will use the experience and think, "the main thing that helped me in becoming the teacher I am was all of the horrible or ineffectual teachers I observed" (Gill, 1998, p. 2).

Between these seeming polar opposites there are, of course, multiple complex variances of reactions; however, for the sake of brevity, I am fairly confident in stating that for the majority of the class, the mass that does not either immediately connect with the readings or reject outright their calls for social justice, the not-so-simple act of rethinking schools and the knowledge that is part of these institutions (the same schools that provided them with so much comfort) can be fairly troubling: "Many individuals often have trouble empathizing with students harmed by such negative educational dynamics because schooling in their experience has played such a positive role in their own lives" (Kincheloe, 2007, p. 16).

In a tradition reminiscent of the "Look to your left and to your right, one among the three will fail this course" scene from *The Paper Chase* (Bridges, 1973), one of my mentors during my

Ph.D. studies and lecturing days at McGill University's Department of Education was reputed to ask first-year undergraduates why they wanted to become teachers and when they excitedly raised their hands, he would growl, "and don't say it's because you like kids or schools!" This would then evoke a mass lowering of hands. Reflecting on this experience a year or so after the fact, student teachers saw the humor in the encounter and recognized the veteran professor's desire to let them know that although liking your future students and/or liking your own school experience are of course important contributors to your career choice, there's much more to teaching than simply "liking." However, after a number of years of working with first-year undergraduate students, many student-teachers *do* enter the field of education because so much of what makes up our schools, from the smell of a fresh box of crayons to wanting to see students experience an "aha!" moment has deep, personal meaning to them. Many of these students enter the profession because schools were, among many things, locations of personal learning, growth, and security. Many enter the profession because they want to reproduce the positives they personally experienced. All of which are optimistic sentiments of wanting to be a good teacher. However, for this majority, change, and the research that necessitates informed and transparent change, was not part of their initial motivators for becoming teachers.

Educators like Gill (1998), who declares, "I became a teacher because I detested school—hated just about every minute of it" (p. 1), or me enter the field of education because, although we had positive experiences, they were more often negative. For some of us (and we certainly do not come from a single theoretical position), the feelings of security and belonging that many of my student teachers express as their career choice reasoning were absent in our lives as students. We think of change and research toward change, not reproduction and status quo when we consider our future selves working in schools. Change in our schools, however, has not been and still is not an easy endeavor, and the powerfully persuasive forces of an increasingly right-wing-driven media make it difficult for counternarratives to even be considered in our schools.

• • •

Ms. Coning. We're talking about you.
Want to join on KXL 750?

—Faulconer & Coning Freeman, 2005, p. 323

"We're talking about you." This is the e-mail text that a U.S. teacher, Ayesha Coning Freeman, received from her local talk radio show regarding a lesson on the Palestinian-Israeli conflict. As she read the e-mail, her students were preparing for their mock United Nations project of developing a proposal for "a peace plan to end the conflict" (p. 323). While her students talked about peaceful, transformative change, the radio show talked about how the teacher was "indoctrinating her students to be anti-American," how the teacher "looked Arab," how she "must be a Muslim," how "the FBI needed to look into" her background, and ultimately why she should not be a teacher (p. 323). Despite the teacher's commitment to providing age-appropriate, multiple relevant primary perspectives and an ultimate challenge to her students to develop a *peaceful solution*, she was nonetheless attacked publicly for her research and teaching efforts.

One wonders if radio shows, like KXL 750's, supposed commitment to exemplary education standards includes a "calling out" of history teachers who do not take into account current research. For example, the mounting body of evidence shows that the North Vietnamese attack on U.S. destroyers during the now-questioned 1964 Gulf of Tonkin incident was manufactured to draw the U.S. deeper into that conflict. Would these same radio talk show jockeys chastize the teachers who, perhaps, if such lessons were given, questioned whether the U.S.'s tragic involvement in Iraq through the country's premature acceptance of government "facts" may have been avoided? However, even in Canada, teaching about wars, like the Vietnam War, in anything other than "our side is good; their side is bad" (Apple, 2004, p. 80) terms is rarely done.

• • •

How often, when thinking about how to teach contem-
porary issues like the Iraq War or civil rights advocacy, or
historical events such as the Vietnam War or the Native
American experience, do teachers feel a bit of hesitation?

—Faulconer & Coning Freeman, p. 323

Moving away from the standard curriculum developed by the educational authorities the teacher works for is a risk and calls for extra effort in research and development that requires transparency and accountability (Walker, 1990). McLaren (2007) observes that the continuous efforts of the "leaders of the dominant capitalist states" (p. 289), through the support of the atmosphere of an endless "war on terror," have developed laws to suppress teacher deviation from state-approved curriculum. "In 2006, the governor of Florida, Jeb Bush, approved a law (known as the Florida Education Omnibus Bill) barring the teaching of "revisionist" history in Florida public schools, including 'postmodern viewpoints of relative truth'" (p. 291). What exactly constituted "revisionist" history in this political climate is truly troubling, and political acts such as this, that McLaren connects with a "cult of anti-intellectualism," driven by an ideology of "we equate good, they equate bad" sends a powerful warning to teachers to set aside the counternarrative perspectives they studied and researched and simply follow the grand narrative set forth by "leaders" like Governor Bush.

Through the example of the recent deaths of former U.S. presidents Gerald Ford and Ronald Reagan, McLaren (2007) also points out that the prevalent anti-intellectual culture perpetuated through the corporate media dissuades consumers to consider anything but the standardized narrative of reflecting about their terms in office with anything but accolades. With a media that controls the content of "facts," McLaren ponders, "(a)fter the deaths of these two 'great' presidents, how many classroom discussions in the nation's schools centered around egregious foreign and domestic policies? One wonders if the Florida Education Omnibus Bill is even necessary" (pp. 291–92). For the teacher committed to transformative change, the current atmosphere in North America makes deviating from the standardized truths difficult enough; for the student teacher and teacher who never thought about his or her professional career in such terms, these threatening barriers are more than enough to make you want to simply avoid controversy. Consider what Ayesha Coning Freeman's media experience with her well-researched curriculum on the Palestinian-Israeli conflict says to other teachers who consider moving away from the "tried and true" curriculum: "An experience like Ayesha's causes a powerful ripple effect: other teachers become concerned for their own professional safety and quickly examine their curriculum for anything that might make them vulnerable to similar onslaught" (Faulconer & Coning Freeman, p. 324).

This ripple effect among peers has an especially powerful consequence on those within the field who may be bordering on entering the dysconcious (King, 1991) state of considering their role and obligations as a teacher within the pressures of their school and community. In this context, through their research and studies, the student teacher or teacher may have moved from the unconscious understanding of issues such as racism, social inequalities, and/or justice to the conscious comprehension of the issues and then, depending on circumstance, to the dysconscious state in which the teacher decides to accept "a form of racism that tacitly accepts dominant White norms and privileges. It is not the *absence* of consciousness (that is, not unconsciousness) but an *impaired* consciousness or distorted way of thinking about race as compared to, for example, critical consciousness" (King, p. 135).

For these teachers, the pressures of scorn and exclusion from the kinds of teachers Gill described or the pressures of conforming to a curriculum that has always existed and is sanctified by political powers or the pressures of public condemnation by corporate media from moving away from the "sound bite" is enough to make them want to return to the safe confines of the standardized/traditional school that originally inspired them. Giving these teachers the benefit of the doubt that they want to do "good work," the decision to enter a dysconscious phase of their career is not based on maliciousness but on succumbing to the historic pressures (Apple, 2004) to conform and the relative safety that comes with it.

Adding to the pressures of the ripple effect is the trickle-down effect that we witnessed in the post-9/11 era. In this trickle-down effect, political forces have used their influence to publicly silence prominent academics who do not tow the line with dominant "truths." In a recent guest lecture visit to Shirley Steinberg's Media Literacy class within McGill University's Department of Integrated Studies in Education, I discussed the possible effects that the public demonization of an academic like Ward Churchill had on teachers' decision making to research and develop curriculum that provided for counternarrative voices. Scanning the predominantly young student teachers in the auditorium, I saw many receptive faces; of particular note were the four or five students who started to nod their heads. Churchill, an established academic at the University of Colorado at Boulder who wrote extensively on present and historic indigenous social justice issues, came under immense attack after writing "On the Justice of Roosting Chickens" (2003) in which he argued that 9/11 was, in part, a result of U.S. foreign policy and that those killed in the attacks of 9/11 were not, given the West's concepts of "collateral damage," innocent victims.

As I have already written (Stonebanks & Wootton, In press), much could be said about criticizing Churchill for perceived insensitivity during a horrific period in recent U.S. history. However, the analysis of the content beyond the very superficial assessment given to Churchill's comparison to the victims of 9/11 as being "little Eichmanns" (and what that actually means) was not evident at all. The political and media attack on Churchill resulted in, among other things, a denial of his indigenousness, the removal of his livelihood, and the promotion of grave shadows of doubt on the extensive body of research he had carried out in regard to indigenous issues, in particular, on such important subjects as the genocide of Native peoples in the Americas (1998).

The use of the term "trickle-down" effect is meant to bring to mind the same images of the transfer of knowledge through a "top-down" approach that appears to permeate advocates of standardized knowledge and curriculum. I use this term to evoke in students the question as to whether there is a purposeful attempt to publicly silence academics like Churchill or former professor Norman Finkelstein, whose scholarship gave greater academic nuance to the Israeli-Palestinian conflict, and create an academic ripple effect of fear so that that self-censorship takes care of professors who may otherwise expose their pre-service teachers to information that deviates from a power bloc construction of truth. In these scenarios, the climate and politics of fear and anti-intellectualism ensure that other forms of knowing (e.g., counternarratives to the grand narrative), are silenced by either ensuring that potential students who are open to critical perspectives do not receive information, keeping them unconscious, or through self-censorship and maintaining dysconciousness. Furthermore, it would seem that these countercritical education practices are effective, given that schools are replete with teachers who, despite participating in progressive educations filled with courses that used concepts such as "critical," "social justice," and "multiculturalism," maintain the status quo; perhaps nothing better illustrates this than when schools observe national holidays or historical dates of significance.

As a student and when I worked in elementary schools, I was always somewhat wary at these times of the year, and as a parent I often find myself holding my breath when my young children say, "You know what we learned in school today?" Some "fun facts," like that reindeer fly, are of little damage (although this could be argued); others, like what Villaverde and Kincheloe (2005) refer to as the "the enigma of Thanksgiving" can have more profound considerations about the manner in which we view knowledge—how it is attained by student teachers and teachers and how it is disseminated.

$$\bullet \ \bullet \ \bullet$$

Thanksgiving is one of the many enigmatic celebrations in the North American pantheon of holidays. A large part of myth and historical erasure, Thanksgiving celebrations and school lessons paint a picture of American Indian–English settler relations that is quite misleading. Such a depiction is important because Thanksgiving serves the central role of providing a national origin myth. From the traditional

> *morality play of settler–Indian interactions, students gain an ideological understanding of America specially blessed by God, America forged by civilizing both the savages and the wilderness in which they resided, America as the representation of order in the sea of indigenous chaos—an ethnocentric vision of nation and self.*
>
> —Villaverde & Kincheloe, 2005, p. 149

A number of years ago when my wife took our children to the community fall festival, they returned with the familiar stories of animals, food, pumpkins, and wonderful student teachers animating art activities for the youth. Among the art projects children could participate in was the making of stereotypical black and white Pilgrim hats. Not that we believe there is something insidious about the making of old Puritan headwear, but we could not help but notice how the U.S. celebration of myth-making had permeated the Canadian context, probably because of the overwhelming influence U.S. social studies content has on Canadian curriculum (Clark, 2004). (It should be noted that, in Canada, our version of Thanksgiving is not tied to the Plymouth settlers.) When later I asked the students why they chose to make Pilgrim hats, these genuinely caring and earnest students said that it just seemed like the thing to do; it was what they could readily find; it seemed harmless; and, ultimately, *it seemed normal.* Pressing a little harder, I asked what they knew about the settlers of the Plymouth Colony, and they responded that they honestly knew nothing. They did not know that they had been chronicled as "giving thanks to God for the smallpox plague ... that devastated the Native population," that they were "often seen as grave robbers who relied on Indian generosity," and that within half a year of settlement, they had "killed a large percentage of Indians living in their proximity" (Villaverde & Kincheloe, 2005, p. 149). After learning this, I wondered how they felt about paying homage to these people and also if, at some future date, these or any teacher would raise their hand at a staff curriculum planning meeting and ask the simple question, "Why are we *really* doing this?"

• • •

Indeed, school curriculum with the morality play between settler-Native replete with Squanto and the planting of corn is for the most part a twentieth century phenomenon.
—Villaverde & Kincheloe, 2005, p. 149

Allow me to consider the requisite "morality plays" that I, as a non-Christian, had to perform during my own North American school experience (such as the above-mentioned Thanksgiving Day play or the Nativity plays). Recognizing that "pedagogical practices are always moral and political. The political always performative. The performative is always pedagogical" (Denzin, 2007, p. 128), these actions involve, on the one hand, little critical analysis as to why they are being performed in schools and, on the other hand, play an important role in the maintaining of the power bloc narrative.

Of course, this is not to say that there are not performative, political, and pedagogical counternarratives. Although not on academic or aesthetic par with indigenous artists who tackle these issues, like Shirley Cheechoo's (1993) play, "Path with No Moccasins," which dealt with her residential school experience, or Sherman Alexie's (1993) poems and stories that capture what we imagine are encounters between himself and his second-grade missionary teacher, writing, "'indians, indians, indians.' She said it without capitalization. She called me 'indian, indian, indian'" (Alexie, 1993, p. 173), the Thanksgiving Day play segment from the 1993 "black comedy" film *Addams Family Values* (Sonnenfeld, 1993), for me encapsulates the minority experience of "participating" in these types of "ethnocentric vision of nation and self" (Villaverde & Kincheloe, 2005, p. 149).

The very title, connecting the ghoulish Addams family with the often-used political term "family values" must have been meant to draw comparisons to the increasing call by right-wing groups, through this term, to promote their so-called conservative agenda. In this particular scene, the summer camp outcasts, meaning the religious, visual, disabled, etc., minorities, are cast as the Indians; the popular children, meaning the white, Christian, privileged, abled, etc., are cast as the Pilgrims. The camp leader,

Gary, who penned and produced the piece, introduces the play by noting that Thanksgiving is "the most important day in our shared history." Anarchy ensues when the protagonist, the macabre Wednesday, deviates from the script at the point where she is supposed to accept the Pilgrims' invitation to the feast:

> Wednesday (as Pocahontas): You have taken the land which is rightfully ours. Years from now, my people will be forced to live in mobile homes on reservations. Your people will wear cardigans and drink highballs. We will sell our bracelets by the roadsides. You will play golf and enjoy hot hors d'oeuvres. My people will have pain and degradation. Your people will have stick shifts. The gods of my tribe have spoken. They have said, "Do not trust the pilgrims, especially Sarah Miller."
>
> Becky (as Sarah Miller): Gary, she's changing the words!
>
> Wednesday (as Pocahontas): And for all these reasons, I have decided to scalp you and burn your village to the ground.

Perhaps the response by Becky, the young blond girl who is meant to represent the unquestioned dominant power bloc, best sums up the fear for this group, that we are "changing the words" to their grand narrative. Changing the narrative in schools has been documented; I thoroughly enjoy reviewing and reenacting "the hooks" from Bigelow (1999) and Sweeny's (1999) curriculum on rethinking Columbus.

• • •

I begin my class by stealing a student's purse. I announce to the class that the purse is mine, obviously, because look who has it. Most students are fair-minded. They saw me take the purse off the desk so they protest: "That's not yours, it's Nikki's. You took it, we saw you." I brush these objections aside and reiterate that it is, too, mine and to prove it I'll show all the things I have inside. I unzip the bag and remove a brush or a comb, maybe a pair of dark glasses. A tube, or whatever it's called, of lipstick works best: "This is my lipstick," I say. "There, that proves it is my purse."

—Bigelow, 1999, p. 101

Each time we explored Bigelow and Sweeny's work, my undergraduate student teachers seemed to thoroughly enjoy the creative manner in which the author/teachers evoked critical thought in their students. As well, with a bit of research on Columbus and the suffering his actions brought on indigenous peoples, the vast majority are products of their own education and are overwhelmed that they had no idea who this man really was beyond the "in 1842 Columbus sailed the ocean blue" mantra. With so much homage paid to this man (i.e., countless street names carry Columbus or Christophe Colombe in my province of Quebec), where and how does a teacher go about separating the myth from the actual person? Imagine beginning a lesson or a unit on Columbus with a quote from Zinn, in which one letter from Columbus reads, "They would make fine servants ... With fifty men we could subjugate them all and make them do whatever we want" (2003, p. 1). I agree with Bigelow, most students are fair-minded. So, with this rather important initial perspective into Columbus's mind, what would young students make of this man? Would they name streets after him? Would these facts, the actual written words of Columbus in his own hand, be considered revisionist history in Jeb Bush's schools, and thus inappropriate?

Again, it's important to note that I have yet to encounter a student teacher who has stated that this was indeed what they learned in their school experience. Although it could be argued that many of these student teachers had teachers who did not engage in research and were truly unconscious of this information. However, what role does Chomsky's (1992) statement regarding what we risk saying in public spaces have on teachers' inclusion of perspectives in their curriculum? Does a teacher risk anything when he or she says in class "Khomeini is a terrorist," as opposed to saying, as Native protestors at a Columbus Day parade put it, "Christopher Columbus, America's First Terrorist" (Abourezk, 2004, paragraph 3). Giroux (2002) wrote that, post-9/11, "the political reality that is beginning to emerge from this shattering crisis increasingly points to a set of narrow choices that are being largely set by the jingoistic right wing and fueled by the dominant media" (p. 9). In a pre-9/11 context, with the exceptions of the Bigelows and Sweenys of the teaching world, schools did not take critical research approaches to figures and episodes in history. Considering, for example, that the history surrounding Native issues in North America are largely glossed over with a positive spin or ignored (Stonebanks, 2008), what hope can we have in schools critically examining current issues? If the past is taboo for critical examination, can we expect that teachers and students will be encouraged to research the present?

Mayer (2007) comments that the arts continue to be the one form of communication (and education) that allows for dissenting narratives. Reviewing artistic text and performances from *The Colbert Report* on Comedy Central to Joseph Heller's *Catch-22*, Mayer observes that comedy takes risks where few others dare to go, although from political satirist Bill Maher's "coward" incident,[1] we may infer that an adequate distance from the event be given for mainstream comedic timing, conjuring up that image of the comedian on stage glancing at an unresponsive or hostile audience and uttering, "too soon?"

In education, it seems that it is always "too soon," and I watch in amazement how every so often artists, like the comedy troupe of the CBC's *This Hour Has 22 Minutes*, dare to make observations that are deeply poignant and reflective about the time in which we are living. In an undergraduate social studies class, we discussed a newspaper article that reported on the hullabaloo that ensued because the Canadian War Museum had a display that read "Strategic Bombing: An Enduring Controversy," in which it explained that the allied bombing of civilians during World War II has been contested for its effectiveness in reducing the German military. Reading the perspective of the historians who argued its accuracy and of the relatives of Canadian bomber pilots, the majority of undergrads, when considering their prospective students being exposed to this debate responded, "Well, you have to support the troops." Given that most, if not all, social studies curriculum in North America advocates the development of involved citizens in a democratic society, I question how this stance actually supports the troops. "Afghanistan is a subject of deep national concern. Few satirists have seen fit to tackle it" (Mayer, 2007), Mayer points out and remarks that *This Hour Has 22 Minutes* was one of the few that tackled it in 2006, through a skit where a news anchor discusses Canada's military involvement in Afghanistan with a politician and a pundit.

Military analyst: "I think when talking about the situation in Afghanistan, the key thing you must understand is that I support our troops"

CBC Host: "Agreed. There can be no meaningful discussion of this issue unless Canadians understand that I, also, support the troops."

Conservative Member of Parliment: "Indeed. I support both your support of the troops, and would like to add my own support to the support of the troops that you previously supported."

The skit continues with each member of the panel trying to out-support the other, and, in the end, Canada's involvement in Afghanistan is never discussed. How much of our schools' curriculum include this kind of superficial, bumper-sticker inspired patriotism to our democratic system? Are we really supporting our troops when we, in effect, say nothing? As the son of a father who served in combat three times in the British army, this was a discussion we had often pre- and post-9/11. My father's experienced perspective was that the only meaningful discussions were those that involved not treating human life in casual terms. Without the benefit of higher education, but with the perspective of having lived a rich life, he was more than aware of the essence of cautionary statements, like Giroux (2002) warning against our choices "being largely set by the jingoistic right wing and fueled by the dominant media" (p. 9). By no stretch of the imagination was my father a pacifist, but he taught me while I was very young to question anyone's motives that might send others to war. Democratic responsibility, then, involves a critical search for knowledge so that when choices are made, they are done so by informed, educated citizens and not through a standardized, top-down approach that risks misinformation. In my experience working with many brilliant teachers and student teachers, few would argue against this kind of rationale, yet the curriculum in our schools is caught in the quagmire of reproducing the same injustices and miseducation.

• • •

It is with that uncomfortabilty that we will teach.
—Steinberg, 2007, p. x

In Steinberg's preface (2007) to Kincheloe and McLaren's *Critical Pedagogy: Where Are We Now?*, she remarks that the process of making changes in schools and the professional practice of being critical in pedagogy as often an "uncomfortable" one. And it is. This is a particularly hard statement for the majority of student teachers who enter the profession for reasons of "comfort." The long hours, the low pay, the demands by parents, peers, etc., may be difficult but they are quickly overlooked for such comforts as a vibrant classroom, receptive students, and the title of "teacher." Returning to the safety of the never-ending "back to the basic" notions may give comfort to those student teachers who seemingly flourished in this environment, but it is an intolerable prospective of a life as a cog in the top-down process for others who want to research, learn, and teach for change. In the post-9/11 culture of fear, the uncomfortable path is a risky one, strewn with barriers at all levels. The comfortable path includes the security of repetition but also, given the education that student teachers now receive, involves purposeful dysconciousness. One is a path of vision. The other a prepackaged view. My guidance to student teachers: Make your own path with your students and be wary of comfort.

Note

1. In 2001, Bill Maher was the host of the ABC late-night television show *Politically Incorrect*, which utilized a roundtable discussion format featuring four guests from various segments of public culture (music, film, television, politics, athletics, etc.) debating the issues of the day. On the September 17, 2001, episode, Maher said he agreed with one of his guests, conservative author Dinesh D'Souza, that the 9/11 terrorists were "not cowards." Maher went on to say: "We have been cowards lobbing cruise missiles from 2,000 miles away. That's cowardly. Staying in the airplane when it hits the building, say what you want about it, it's not cowardly." His statement drew widespread criticism, especially from sponsors of the show such as FedEx and Sears (both of which pulled their advertisements from the show), as well as from White House Press Secretary Ari Fleischer. Fleischer lambasted Maher for his remarks on the show, stating in part that Americans "need to watch what they say, watch what they do. This is not a time for remarks like that; there never is" (Office of the Press Secretary, September 26, 2001). *Politically Incorrect* was eventually cancelled on June 16, 2002. Maher has since gone on to host the successful *Real Time with Bill Maher* talk show on HBO (2003–present).

References

Abourzek, K. 2004. On Columbus Day, a different view of "discovery." *Lincoln Journal Star*. Oct 12. http://www.journalstar.com/articles/2004/10/12/local/doc416b61b4be60f936438266.txt (accessed June 13, 2007).

Alexie, S. 1993. *The Lone Ranger and Tonto fistfight in heaven*. New York: The Atlantic Monthly Press.

Apple, M. 2004. *Ideology and curriculum*. New York: RoutledgeFalmer.

Bigelow, W. 1999. Discovering Columbus: Rethinking the past. In I. Shor & C. Pari (Eds.), *Education is politics*, pp. 100–9. Portsmouth, NH: Boynton/Cook Publisher.

Bridges, J., Director. 1973. *The paper chase* [motion picture]. Available from Twentieth Century-Fox Film Corporation.

Chomsky, N. 1992. *Manufacturing consent: Noam Chomsky and the media*. Directed by P. Wintonick & M. Achbar. Humanist Broadcasting Foundation. http://freedocumentaries.org/film.php?id=138 (accessed January 12, 2007).

Churchill, W. 1998. *A little matter of genocide: Holocaust and denial in the Americas 1492 to the present*. San Francisco: City Lights Books.

Churchill, W. 2003. *On the justice of roosting chickens: Consequences of American conquest and carnage*. Oakland, CA: AK Press.

Cheechoo, S. 1993. *Path with no moccasins: A play*. West Bay, Ontario, 48 pages.

Clark, P. 2004. The historical context of social studies in English Canada. In A. Sears & I. Wright (Eds.), *Challenges & prospects for Canadian social studies*, pp. 17–37. Vancouver, Canada: Pacific Educational Press.

Denzin, N. K. 2007. The politics and ethic of performance pedagogy. In P. McLaren & J. Kincheloe (Eds.), *Critical pedagogy: Where are we now?*, pp. 127–42. New York: Peter Lang.

Faulconer, T., & A. Coning Freeman. 2005. Teachers, classroom controversy, and the media. *Social Education* 69(6):323–27.

Freire, P., Ed. 2005. *Pedagogy of the oppressed: 30th anniversary*. New York: Continuum.

Gill, V. 1998. *The ten commandments of good teaching*. Thousand Oaks, CA: Corwin Press.

Giroux, H. 2002. Terrorism and the fate of democracy after September 11. *Cultural Studies & Critical Methodologies* 2(1):9–14.

Hunter, M. 1994. *Enhancing teaching*. New York: MacMillan.

Ivie, R. L. 2005. Savagery in democracy's empire. *Third World Quarterly* 26(1):55–65.

Kincheloe, J. 2003. *Teachers as researchers: Qualitative inquiry as a path to empowerment.* New York: RoutledgeFalmer.

Kincheloe, J. 2007. Critical pedagogy in the twenty-first century. In P. McLaren & J. Kincheloe (Eds.), *Critical pedagogy: Where are we now?*, pp. 9–42. New York: Peter Lang.

Kincheloe, J., & S. R. Steinberg. 1997. *Changing multiculturalism.* London: Open University Press.

King, J. E. 1991.Dysconscious racism: Ideology, identity, and the miseducation of teachers. *Journal of Negro Education* 60(2):133–46.

Lobe, J. 2004. Prisoner abuse calls into question America's position of moral "exceptionalism." *Foreign Policy in Focus.* May 19. http://www.fpif.org/fpiftxt/621 (accessed June 13, 2007).

Lyotard, J-F. 1979/1984. *The postmodern condition: A report on knowledge.* Trans. G. Bennington & B. Massumi]. Minneapolis: University of Minnesota Press.

Mayer, A. 2007. Fighting words: How satire gives us a better understanding of armed conflict. *Canadian Broadcasting Corporation News.ca.* November 8. http://www.cbc.ca/arts/media/fightingwords.html (accessed December 5, 2007).

Macedo, D. 2005. Introduction. In P. Freire (Ed.), *Pedagogy of the oppressed: 30th anniversary*, pp. 11–27. New York: Continuum.

McLaren, P. 2007. The future of the past. In P. McLaren & J. Kincheloe (Eds.), *Critical pedagogy: Where are we now?*, pp. 289–314. New York: Peter Lang.

Morrison, K., & C. Marshall. 2003. Universities and public schools: Are we disconnected? *Phi Delta Kappan* 85(4):292–97.

Pfaff, W. 2007. Manifest destiny: A new direction for America. *New York Review of Books* 54(2):54–59.

Office of the Press Secretary. 2001, September 26. Press briefing by Ari Fleischer. Washington, DC: The White House.

Rinaldo, V. 2005. Today's practitioner is both qualitative and quantitative researcher. *High School Journal* 89(1):72–77.

Sonnenfeld, B, Director. 1993. *Addams Family Values* [motion picture]. Available from Orion Pictures Corporation.

Steinberg, S., & J. Kincheloe. 2005. *Students as researchers: Creating classrooms that matter.* New York: RoutledgeFalmer.

Steinberg, S. 2007. Preface: Where are we now? In P. McLaren & J. Kincheloe (Eds.), *Critical pedagogy: Where are we now?*, pp. viiii–x. New York: Peter Lang.

Stonebanks, C. D. 2004. Consequences of perceived ethnic identities (reflection of an elementary school incident). In J. Kincheloe & S. Steinberg (Eds.), *The miseducation of the West: The hidden curriculum of Western-Muslim relations*, pp. 87–102. New York: Greenwood.

Stonebanks, C. D. 2008. *James Bay Cree students and higher education: Issues of identity and culture shock*. Rotterdam, Netherlands: Sense Publishers.

Stonebanks, C. D., & K. Wootton. In press. The backlash on "roosting chickens": The continued atmosphere of suppressing indigenous knowledge. *Cultural Studies & Critical Methodologies*.

Sullivan, C. 2003. Manifest destiny rides again; justifying plunder. *Counter-Punch*. February 12. http://www.counterpunch.org/sullivan02122003.html (accessed June 13, 2007).

Sweeny, M. 1999. Columbus, a hero? Rethinking Columbus in an elementary classroom. In I. Shor & C. Pari (Eds.), *Education is politics*, pp. 110–19. Portsmouth, NH: Boynton/Cook Publisher.

Villaverde, L., & J. Kincheloe. 2005. Engaging students as researchers: Researching and teaching Thanksgiving in the elementary classroom. In S. Steinberg & J. Kincheloe (Eds.), *Students as researchers: Creating classrooms that matter*, pp. 149–66. New York: RoutledgeFalmer.

Walker, D. 1990. *Fundamentals of curriculum*. Toronto: Harcourt Brace Jovanovich.

Zinn, H. 2003. *A people's history of the United States: 1492–present*. New York: HarperCollins.

Heartbeats

Exploring the Power of Qualitative Research Expressed as Auto/Ethnographic Performance Texts

Mary E. Weems
John Carroll University

Carolyne J. White
Rutgers University, Newark

Lois Melina
Gonzaga University, Spokane, Washington

Phoenix deCarteret
Monash University, Australia

Ruth Nicole Brown
University of Illinois, Urbana-Champaign

Clarence Shelley
University of Illinois, Urbana-Champaign

Jonathan Wyatt
Oxford University, UK

Jackie Goode
University of Nottingham, UK

Tim Bond
University of Bristol, UK

Patricia Alvarez McHatton
University of South Florida, Tampa

Lois Ann Scheidt
Indiana University, Bloomington

*[T]he line of words fingers your own heart. It invades
arteries, and enters the heart on a flood of breath; it presses
the moving rims of thick valves; it palpates the dark muscle
strong as horses, feeling for something, it knows not what.*

—Annie Dillard, 1989

Proem

Mary

Carolyne volunteers to help me facilitate a pre-conference work-shop titled "Heartbeats: Writing Performance Texts," at the second annual International Congress of Qualitative Inquiry, at the University of Illinois in Urbana-Champaign. This learn-ing community-based pre-conference workshop is for qualitative researchers from all disciplines who are interested in exploring nontraditional ways of expressing the results of their research.

After sharing my imagination-intellect theory (Weems, 2003) and the importance of developing it from both a personal and professional perspective, we read examples of our auto/ethno-graphic work. I explain my approach to writing or creating from the space between the conscious and unconscious, and the impor-tance of freeing up the heart-mind to allow thoughts and ideas to flow from a more creative, and passionate, place.

Like Annie Dillard (1989, p. 20), I know that "[t]he line of words fingers your own heart," that there is an inextricable link between thinking and feeling, that being connected with the heartbeat of our passion for research, for other ways of know-ing, for social justice, for living our lives fully makes a significant difference in the world. Too often, the push for objectivity, for keeping a distance between the researcher and the researched, for denying our feelings either kills our ability to effectively com-municate or prompts us to write about our lived experience as if it happened to someone else.

The problem with this approach is that for too many it sucks the life out of us, and our work comes out anemic, too pat, as dry as day-old cold bread without butter. During this workshop, we create a non-conference-like space for inviting an ad hoc community of men and women from all over the world to explore what happens when people with similar goals take time to relax, listen to music, and respond to visual imagery, objects, and each other.

Changing the space starts with my asking Carolyne to join me in bringing artifacts from home to redecorate a typical university conference room. We bring incense, candles, fabric, objects including boxes, ribbon, art museum postcards, black and white images from magazines, and personal photographs of family members. We move all of the stuff we don't need to the side (projector, podium, etc.), and take the chairs out of their straight rows, form a circle of chairs in the front of the room, and make sure the remaining ones are in complete disarray. I put some Miles Davis on the CD player and we smile our "This is going to be a powerful experience" smiles and wait for the participants to arrive.

We greet each person as he or she enters and begin sharing our intention for the workshop. People come who had signed up for the conference. People come who had signed up for other workshops and decided to switch to ours; people come who had heard about our work and wanted to meet us. The circle is full of good vibe and the spirit of *We deserve a break today*. We introduce ourselves and give a brief overview of the workshop. I explain that we will write with a focus on "not thinking" about what we write, and that the individual writings will be prompted by various things in the room, including selections of music. The goal is to link it to a lived experience, either during a research project or in our personal lives.

Next, we move around the circle, each saying where we are-from and what drew us to this space. Our intimate talk generates a learning community as we learn what we have in common and about some of our differences, which include race, gender, age, ethnicity, religion, and language.

I feel the room relaxing and know it is time for our first writing. I ask each person to take some time to connect with an object and/or image in the room. I encourage each to select an artifact that reminds them of something in their lives and to bring it back to their chairs and write without thinking until I say stop. I select a song to play as a backdrop and say "Go!" Once each person has selected something, I give them ten to fifteen minutes to write. Next, volunteers share what they have written.

Clarence Shelley, friend, colleague, and one of the participants, is so impressed with the collective work that he asks me during a short break if we'd like to try and collect the writings to use in an article about the pre-conference workshop. I ask if anyone is willing, and a majority agree. We talk a bit about the importance of collaboration, which is at the heart of Carolyne's work, and decide to submit the finished text for publication.

Knowing better than to ask participants to send me their writings after the conference, I collect the handwritten drafts and type them up a couple of months later. I forward the drafts to the participants and ask each to edit them and add a line or two about their experience. What follows are the edited drafts, and comments of participants who chose to add a note to their poems.

• • •

Carolyne

Like so many things in life, writing is made painful when I try to control it, especially painful when I try to control it in a room by myself—do battle with negative critics who sit on my shoulder, as I sit alone, outnumbered. Is it any wonder that I avoid writing. In this workshop, I am inspired with positive energy, co-writers surround me, I am held in the flow of our vibe, a vibe so powerful negative critics that stop me can't enter.

"What Is Love …?"

I wake to

"You will not read Mary's poem!" from that fear voice in my head.

It wants me to live small,

wanted me to remain in the Arizona house, my first house,

on half an acre of mountain land

where I buried Jackson.

The house was to keep me safe.

Love moves me off that land.

Love among people on Havana streets, families on bicycles,
a man who puts down grass clippers just to speak, seek heart
connection, know and be known.
Love inspires me to dream a people connected life in Newark.
Sal's love finds me a place to live on James Street.
Neighbors' love welcomes, embraces
Mary's love gets me settled.
Jazzie gives Dalmation love freely on city sidewalks,
moves strangers to wish her "Good morning."
My students' love for urban children fills our classroom,
inspires them to work hard, inspires me to persist.
Love moves through fear.

• • •

Lois

"On Coming across a Butterfly"

Here you are again, my
child, right
where I need you, as you always
are, reminding me
to Love myself, not get caught
up in my head, where I feel
most comfortable, especially here,
at a research conference, oh my!
But we have an agreement, you and I:
you will let me know
when you want my attention, and here
you are. What stuns me is how often
I have failed to notice
you, and how close
you are to me all the time,
waiting, ready

to emerge,
on wings of love.

• • •

Phoenix

I picked up a cookie from the morning tea tray to use as a prompt for the writing exercise. The tray beckoned me with the simplicity of sharing what it suggested was ahead. I had only recently arrived from regional Australia and had missed meals over several days. I was hungry, but too unsettled to eat. On the way to the Heartbeats Workshop I was swimming with disparate impressions that rushed in walking through an unfamiliar town. A surreal vulnerability settled in me. Finding the rhythm of heartbeats to write seemed unlikely, until the session began. Over the few short hours of the workshop vulnerability was replaced by the possibilities of fellowship that came with the sharing of experiences and tenderly written words. A room of strangers became a room where connections were braided from listening to embodied experiences. Similarly, when research participants share their stories with me it is also a contact zone of difference, where simple, everyday things offer the gift of possibility.

"Hungry for Connection"

Cookie or a biscuit? What is this crumbly cracked

creation. Lightly browned, cold but there it is

somewhere close to home. Too round and cut to

perfection. Not like home. If it were warm, straight

from the oven with whispers of coconut or vanilla

and bits that break off at the edges maybe then,
but for now it will do.
Food consumes me, strange that food consumes
me. Feeds me signals of difference, of elsewhere,
consumes me with feelings of elsewhere. Will food bring
the elsewhere home, elsewhere, where else can be home,
where else can home be?
To digest difference, that's why I left home.

• • •

Ruth's Note

I do not remember the prompt for this particular writing exercise. I was in the moment. I do know that the moment facilitated by Mary, and Carolyne encouraged us all to not be controlled by our thoughts. For me, this meant taking nothing for granted. I could not rely on my writing routine and rituals of self-doubt. Instead, I could be free to write, think, and feel. Because the room smelled familiar with the incense burning and because everything was intentionally out of place (like the chairs, table, etc.) just the way I like to be in the world, I wrote freely. Well, I wrote semi-freely, as I was not completely able to shake off every fear or demon of self-doubt. It was not easy. Yet, I took comfort in doing what was asked of me without fear or judgment and was surprised by what I created in concert with at once familiar people (not strangers). Rereading "What Is Love?" several months later, I am further inspired to write more about the relationship between my black feminist practice working with young black girls (acts of love) and hip hop (because "chicken noodle soup" was what a lot of the girls brought with them to our meetings).

"What Is Love?"

Unknown
Indiscernible
Translated
But how? And for what
purpose?
But we need it
2 live
2 breathe
4 as long as
we are this
kind of human
it feels good
like a validation

like you are
all that you need
and the world
shines because
of it.
Looking like
a smile
big, wide
full.
Smelling like
chocolate
thick, brown and
sweet.
Tasting like
cotton candy on
a rainy day a la Nikki Giovanni.
Love is
the precursor
to great sex
either because
you think the world of the
one you're with
or just happen
to feel so damn
good about
yourself while
looking in
the mirror,
now that's sexy.
Love is
creation
giving birth
it's embodied by

something inspired
by you and
God too.
Brother Talib said,
just to get by
people use all
kinds of drugs
when all we
really need is love (and I think he's right).
So love is everything.
Could it be nothing?
Could love be absence?
(what I privilege that until
this point I only thought of its
presence)
I certainly do not feel
love listening to commercial
Hip-Hop.
Oh wait.
T-Pain sang
I'm in love with a stripper
and thus the girls I work with
equate strippin' with love.
Ahhh, yes ... so love is Ms. New Booty
They either have one (presence)
Or don't (absence).
Love is carpet munching? (oral sex the girls translate for me)
Love is the chickenhead (a dance) but not a chickenhead (a
person).
Love is grinding up on some boy
in the club & girls have to choose while boys stand
against the wall real cool
2 be chosen (so they tell me).

Love is
not in
this modern
day radio-played Hip-Hop.
Sorry T-Pain I
ain't buyin
what you call and sell as
love.
Love is misunderstood
misused
miscommunicated
it's a language we
are speaking
that must be translated
not on our back either. And
because I can't stop thinking about it,
Who loves women of color?
and our daughters?
Who loves?
A necessary black girlhood, gone but not forgotten.
Love can bring it back.

• • •

Clarence

As I recall, the prompt I used was a photo of two young—at least adolescent—black boys sitting on a dock or landing staring down into water. The photo was especially poignant because it was in black and white.

"Untitled"

What can I do for him?

this young black boy looking to the future and for the past?

What can I offer him to keep him soft and safe from the fear, the shame

and the pain to come?

Searching for stars in the water is such a luxury,

and dreams die hard and take flesh with them.

Hopefully someday he'll pull down clouds to use for cloaks

across the world's mud puddles.

And where is the man in the water?

So, the young black boy

may never be a man

because he has not been allowed to be a boy ... How will he know?

Where is the man in the water?

Look beyond the fear, the pain, the loss

the anger. He is there; waiting. You must find him.

He is there—find him

that is your salvation!

And the tears won't hurt you.

• • •

Jonathan

I remember the feel of the room as I walked in. The colors. The sounds. The sense of warmth. Quite early into the workshop Mary and Carolyne gave us the invitation to use the music—jazz— Miles Davis?—as a stimulus to write about love. (Did they? Or was "love" my choice?) As I wrote, alongside others in a group of about twelve people, there was quiet except for the music. I remember having browsed the room looking for something that captured me amongst the postcards and other artifacts, but I don't remember choosing. I remember only the jazz. I'm not a jazz listener, but something in it drew me. I tried to pay attention to the feel of it in my body and how it made me think, how it moved me to words. I tried to trust the music, trust my body, trust myself.

"Untitled"

Love is muffled
Love is
Love sweeps up a scale
Changes tone, slightly
Is heard with other instruments
Discordant now
Harmonious then
Goes silent for a time
Then struggles to be heard
Before blasting, strident, bold.
Playful, confident, flirtatious
Love is close, intimate, next to my skin
Love is low
Love is
Holds its note, holding on, holding on
Pierces
Love pierces
Love bounces, dances, shakes its hips
Love longs
We listen to love
But become distracted
We hear love
But it is smothered
By what? A saxophone?
Which takes over
We like that too
Maybe it is love
Too
Another aspect,
Knowing
Worldly
Wise

. . .

Jackie

I'm attending a workshop. I have a vivid memory of a workshop I attended many years ago. Through no fault of the leader or the other participants, I left it feeling exposed and diminished. So workshops make me nervous; aware of my own "performance anxiety" in the face of others' creativity; conscious of the rarity, these days, of formally being in the position of "learner," and of the risks involved in learning. But we are asked simply to choose an object and respond to it. So far so good. I can do "responding." I choose. I respond. I write:

"Looking inside"

I love artifacts. Things that have been made.

That stimulate the senses. That I can hold.

This one has form, color, pattern, texture and a strange design on it that I can't readily decipher. This is also a part of its attraction.

It demands intellectual as well as sensual engagement—
a mystery to solve: delicious! It has a clasp. It can be opened. I can look inside.

What will it hold?

How long can I hang on to the promise, the anticipation?

Shall I be disappointed?

Well, maybe. But if it's empty, that means there's a space I can put something in—a treasure. Carolyne used the word "sustenance" this morning. So important.

In my imagination, I can put in this box
whatever I need to sustain me, and take that away from here with me. I'm ready to open it now. ... Seeds! It's seeds!

How fantastic! The promise of new life. Of growth.

It's a real treasure box.

• • •

Tim

The workshop provided an opportunity for reflection: a welcome pause from the pressures of travel across the Atlantic, the busy-ness of meeting people and highly charged discussions. As I turned my attention inward I felt sharp pangs of missing my wife Jan and our kids, Zoe and Sam, all of whom had remained in the UK. I remembered times before children when Jan and I had been freer to travel together and enjoy the urgency of our pleasure in each other's company. Fifteen years later, our relationship has deepened and expanded to embrace our children but, in that moment, I experienced the losses, struggles, and rewards of sustaining a relationship over time. I felt proud of what I was missing so acutely: but the pangs of a short separation reminded me of the precariousness of relationship and of life. The words that flowed spontaneously from deep inside me are both a lament and a celebration prompted by asking:

"What Is Love?"

Love is eyes that smile, at each other

Arms that embrace each other

Walking together in animated chatter

Silently enjoying time [not "this"] together

Weeping when passion is lost

Crying with joy at tenderness revived [not "reserved"]

Love is?

Impossible

Unachievable

Unsustainable

Bliss

• • •

Patty

I step out of the elevator to the soft melodic tones of Miles Davis and the faint scent of incense. Intrigued, I follow the sounds and fragrance down the hallway like a child, hoping they will lead me to my destination. I peek into the room filled with artifacts and wonder what part they will play in the work ahead, excited to find it is indeed the place for me. As I move throughout the room I see a photograph of Che Guevara and thoughts of my mother surge to my consciousness unbidden. Surprised, I move on only to return several times to the photo as the room begins to fill. Mary entices us into lowering our defenses, asking us to explore the artifacts, find one that calls to us, and allow the feelings to guide the words. The time was right for remembering. I return to the photograph of Che and the words flow unbidden.

"Che y Mami"

I feel a connection Che

He holds a piece of her spirit

I remember her speaking of him

What a man-most handsome

she had ever seen at a rally

que guapo

exudes sexuality.

I never heard her speak that way before

But then again I don't think I ever

Really knew her

When I see him I think of her

In all her youthful exuberance

Mami y Che

She marched the streets in opposition

To what

I don't remember

Did I not listen?

And when I was ready to listen

She was too tired to speak

Che y Mami

Was there a passionate soul within

Her soul

Did it struggle to get out once she
Came here?
How did that change her?
Her youth was filled with adventure
Cuba in its hey day
Jewel of the Caribbean
All dimmed as time passed by
More than age, more than growing
Older, it was as if a shadow
Slowly squelched what light she had
Mami y Che
With time the shadow began to consumed me as well
And I fought I had to fight
Fight no no no separate
Separate, separate

To survive I heard once
An animal in a trap will chew
Its leg off to be set free
I was free but suffer the
Phantom pains of an amputee
The limb is still there
She's still there
Che y Mami
I feel her more when, know her
Better when I see his image
It reminds me of the girl she was
Rather than the woman she came to be
She died 2 years ago
Did I grieve, I don't think so
And I felt guilt until I realized
That I had done my grieving a long
Time ago

So life went on and now when
I see Che
Grief wells up again not for her
As was in the end
But as she was in the beginning
Mami y Che

• • •

Lois

"City—1920"

Beat of passage.
Snap of flag.
Structure of facade.
Bells on horse and trolley.
Formality of track.
Bright sun and deep shade.
The gargoyle experiences it all.

• • •

Mary

"Fantasy Island"

I grew up on Black & white movies
Step N' Fetchit skinnin' and grinnin'
Mammy suckling white folks.

I remember laughin at Buckwheat, The Little Rascals
I wish Cotton was a monkey. Watchin' Rochester
serve Jack Benny, no black people
in commercials.

Today in spite of hip hop's political re-construction
of the doo rag, I can't see a Black face
with a rag on her head and not think:
Aunt Jemima on the pancake box.

Even though that box is smaller,
like opportunities for Black youth,
her face lighter, the politically correct shade of Black
in the media. Even though the rag's been
replaced by a carefully constructed straight doo,
her black mouth, not too wide a smile

I still want the stereotype
to die so I can move
through the media without
mammy on my back

like a huge mountain weighing me down like a tear—
the one the world refuses to cry.

Coda

We share our work here in the hope that more qualitative researchers will create opportunities to collaborate in this way. We believe
in the power of community and collaboration through the arts to
change the world one-audience member, one-heartbeat at a time.

References

Dillard, A. 1989. *The writing life.* New York: Harper & Row.

Weems, M. E. 2003. *Public education and the imagination-intellect: I
speak from the wound in my mouth.* New York: Peter Lang.

12 Cancer and Death

A Love Story in Many Voices

Leah Vande Berg and Nick Trujillo
California State University, Sacramento

with Kimo Ah Yun, Janis Andersen, Sylvia Fox, Rona Halualani, Janellen Hill, Thom McCain, Juliane Mora, Carol Pagelson, Laurie St. Aubin, Jillian Tullis Owen, Morrie Vande Berg, and David Zuckerman

My wife, Leah, was diagnosed with Stage IV ovarian cancer in October 2003. She endured surgery and a year of chemotherapy before dying on Monday, December 13, 2004, the day before my forty-ninth birthday. We recorded our thoughts throughout the ordeal. This chapter narrates our love story of cancer and death and includes the voices of many friends and relatives who shared the experience.

A Stomach Ache in October

I do not recall exactly when I felt the pain in my abdomen. I sensed a dull ache there for a couple of weeks, though I thought it was a bladder infection.

Then the pain intensified. One morning, while walking with Nick and our dogs Hawkeye and Ebbet, I felt a searing pain in my abdomen. I could not continue, and we had to go home.

I called my personal care physician. He said the pain could indicate appendicitis and I should go to the emergency room where they could run tests and get the results immediately.

Nick was preparing to teach his afternoon classes, and I told him that I needed to go to the hospital. He asked if I needed a ride, but I said I could drive. I kissed him goodbye and took something to read.

...

I don't know how long Leah felt pain before she sought medical attention. Knowing her tendency to gut out everything, she probably experienced discomfort for a month.

But when she couldn't continue our walk that morning, I knew something was wrong. Leah rarely complained, and she called in sick just a few times in her career.

She went to the hospital for tests, and I assumed she'd receive medication for a bladder infection or intestinal problem.

I came home from my evening class around eight-thirty. Leah had left a message that she was still at the hospital.

The hospital operator took a while to connect me.

"Mr. Nickers," Leah said calmly, using the nickname she coined years earlier. "They think I have cancer."

The Shock of a Lifetime

At the hospital I had a mammogram and an x-ray. I also underwent my first CT scan, which felt like rolling into a giant tunnel. About an hour later, a young resident came in and said the CT showed masses in my abdomen that might be cancer.

Nick arrived shortly thereafter, white as a ghost. The staff gynecologist, who had a Dutch name and piercing blue eyes, did a pelvic exam. He said they thought that I had Stage IV ovarian cancer, with tumors in the abdomen, on the liver, and possibly surrounding the heart.

I was frozen in time as the doctor went over the diagnosis. I felt as though I was outside of my body and this was happening to someone else.

Nick asked the doctor if we could go to the ocean that weekend, and he said, "If she were my wife, I would go tomorrow morning."

We went home, sat on the couch, and cuddled with the dogs. In many ways, Nick is more emotional than I am, and he hugged me and cried. I was in too great a shock to be crying.

It is difficult to express what I felt. I was not at all in denial. It was not a diagnosis to argue with, because I had been in pain and clearly something was wrong. However, I was calm because I believed that God would lift me up.

The next morning I thought it was a bad dream, until I felt my tummy.

• • •

It was a late afternoon and I was returning several DVDs to the local video store. I was engaging in a bad habit at the time: driving while also playing my voice messages. One was from Nick. As soon as I heard Nick's voice, I cringed.

"Rona, I hate to tell you this through voice mail but Leah has been diagnosed with ovarian cancer. ..." As Nick's words kept playing, I pressed the brake of my car and almost crashed into the side. I couldn't believe what I was hearing. I must have played the same message ten times in the video store parking lot.

The rest of the evening, I was somber and couldn't get my mind off of the news. I made calls to my family—my mother is a registered nurse and my brother is a cancer care/oncology consultant—to find out some information about the diagnosis. My mother warned me about ovarian cancer—"things may not be good, Rona"—and my brother gave me the sobering statistics. "Rona," he said, hearing my panic, "these are statistics. Leah is more than a statistic. Everybody is different. Anything is possible." (Leah's former student, Rona)

• • •

When my wife told me over the phone that she might have cancer, I felt like the wind was knocked out of me. I ran two red lights on the way to the hospital, even though it was five minutes away and wasn't an emergency.

Leah sat in bed talking to a doctor. She wasn't crying and didn't even seem that upset. She kept saying, "How interesting."

"Oh Miss Leah," I said. "This is not interesting."

Time stopped as he went over the diagnosis. It sounded like a death sentence.

The doctor left the room, and I looked at Leah. She smiled softly, and my eyes filled with tears. She might have been in shock, but I attributed her stoic reaction to her Calvinist upbringing. Calm, even as she learns about her life-threatening disease.

Neither one of us could sleep that night. I lay next to Leah and rattled off silent Hail Marys, even though as a mostly fallen

Catholic I don't really believe that God or Mary answers our prayers. But repeating the ritual gave me comfort, and I figured if anyone could heal a feminist with cancer, it would be a goddess.

Before we left for the coast the next day, I made phone calls and sent e-mails about Leah's diagnosis to friends and relatives. We knew rumors would fly once the word got out about her cancer, so we tried to control the information as much as possible.

• • •

The news and the seriousness of Leah's cancer crept up to a place where it sent horror throughout my being. I didn't see it coming—it just hit me one moment and from then on I was different. I'm not one to think the worst and in fact minimize bad news as much as possible. So the nature of the bad news didn't hit me all at once. I will say, however, that the loss of my mom just a few years earlier to ovarian cancer gave me knowledge and history of the disease that tempered my hope with fear and doubt in spite of the remarkable strength that Leah gave to me. (Our friend, Jan)

When I read Nick's e-mail about the news, I only remember yelling FUCK! (Our friend, Thom)

Surgery and Recovery

When we returned from the coast, Nick and I met the surgeon. He went over the scan, answered our questions, and made us feel that we were partners in the treatment. He explained that he would remove my uterus, ovaries, fallopian tubes, the lining surrounding the abdomen, and possibly part of the intestine, depending on how much the cancer had spread.

I went to school and told my students I had cancer and could not finish the semester. I asked them to think carefully about the fact that life is short and about how they spend their time and treat other people. Some of my students cried. I did not cry, but I had a couple of tears.

It was still dark when we arrived at the hospital the morning of surgery. An Admissions official took some information and led us to the pre-surgery area. I thought I would get to stay longer with Nick, but we had to part at the door to pre-op. He kissed me goodbye and said he loved me and would see me in a few hours.

The nurse came in and told me the doctor had arrived.

"We are going to give you some saline solution now," the anesthesiologist said.

Those were the last words I remember.

• • •

In my pre-op prayer, I usually thank God for the day, for the hospital and staff and for medical arts. I ask that God give the surgeon discernment and that the patient awakens with the most minimal discomfort. No two prayers are alike because they are specific to the patient's situation. I prayed for Leah, and I prayed for Nick while he waited through the surgery. Silently I prayed for myself that I would be encouraging and affirming. It's hard to say this, but sometimes I "just have a feeling" about some people—whether they will recover or not—and I had a feeling about Leah. It was not good. I do not want to transfer this feeling to the patient, and I really want to be wrong but seldom am. (Leah's pastor, Carol)

• • •

Leah's surgery was scheduled for the week before her fifty-fourth birthday. I didn't sleep much the night before, but I was wide-awake when we headed for the hospital. When I kissed Leah goodbye in the hallway near pre-op, I honestly wondered if I would ever see her again.

The surgeon said to stay in the waiting room for a half hour in case anything went wrong, but then to go home and wait for his call. He said it could take up to seven hours.

I went back to the house and played Tom Petty's "I Won't Back Down" and Sonny Terry and Brownie McGhee's version of "Jesus Gonna Make It Alright." Even in a sleep-deprived state, I recognized the irony of a fallen Catholic thinking about being at the gates of hell and hoping Jesus would make it all right.

The surgeon finally called and I dashed to the hospital. He told me he had good news and bad news. That's a line you want to hear in a joke, not about your wife's major surgery. The good news was that it was an "optimal debulking," meaning he removed most of the cancer and didn't have to remove any intestines. The bad news was that it was carcinosarcoma, the worst kind of cancer, and certain to grow back.

When they finally admitted Leah into her room, she was groggy, but she opened her eyes and saw me.

"How is the liver?" Leah asked.

I told her it was fine, not wanting to go into details and wanting to be completely positive at that moment.

• • •

I have a vague memory of trying to sit up after surgery. The next thing I remember is being in a hospital room. Nick was holding my hand and saying it was okay.

I floated in and out of consciousness. I was in pain and had all kinds of tubes hooked up to me. I felt that I had elephant legs because they were swollen from edema.

I had to start walking the next day because the sooner I started walking, the sooner my bowels would start moving, and I could go home. Walking was exceedingly difficult and painful. Initially I needed help because I could not push both IV stands while I walked.

On the third day, the bag draining post-surgical fluid filled. A nurse came, and he shook the bag to get air bubbles out. It burst open and spewed blood and cancerous liquid all over me.

The food was awful. Everything seemed to be red or yellow, the color of blood or urine.

The room was stark and antiseptic. Fortunately I was being flooded with cards and flowers, which made the room more cheery. Nick also put up pictures of the ocean and of the dogs. I thought, *I'm going to beat this disease and walk on the beach for many more days.*

Nick came two or three times a day, and every night he was there, holding my hand. Several friends also visited and brought books and magazines. It was tiring but wonderful, because sitting there was lonely.

My dad and brother arrived from the Midwest a couple days before my birthday. They had not seen me all swelled up, and I think it was déjà vu for them, having seen my mom in the hospital before she died of congestive heart failure twenty years earlier.

• • •

I had spent the days leading up to Leah's surgery thinking of a gift to buy her. I notice that Miss Leah does not wear a cross necklace, but that she is very religious. While she is in surgery I go shopping by myself in jewelry stores to find a cross necklace for her. I find something I think is perfect for her that is simple and elegant. I give it to her in the hospital. She opens it up and immediately puts it around her neck.

We are alone in the room and I comment on the number of flowers she has in her room. She is amazed by the graciousness of others. We talk about the book she is reading, laugh about hospital food, and make fun of Nick. Even during the worst of times we could always find ways to have fun laughing at Nick's expense. I was deeply touched by Leah. I never saw her again without wearing the cross necklace that I gave her. My wife now wears Miss Leah's cross necklace. I think of her every time I see it. (Our friend and colleague, Kimo)

• • •

Leah's half of the room was smaller than a prison cell and cramped with machines. I should have insisted on a bigger room, but I was so thankful she survived surgery that I didn't even think about the post-surgical situation.

On the first day, the stimulator that massaged her calves stopped working, an omen of things to come. I retrieved a nurse. She fumbled with buttons, but nothing helped until she smacked it with her clenched fist.

One night all four machines hooked to Leah stopped working, and it took an hour to find a nurse who could fix them. Leah was very distressed, and I yelled at the nurses and wrote a nasty letter to the chief-of-staff.

Although I never received a reply, the experience led me to take an active role in Leah's care. Whenever machines malfunctioned, I adjusted the shutoff valve on the IVs, smacked the calf stimulator, and pulled the catheter bag to keep fluid draining. I probably violated hospital policy doing these things myself, but at least they were getting done.

Leah felt very lonely and powerless at the hospital. I'm sure it was one of the longest weeks of her life.

• • •

Nick told us that Leah was getting restless in the hospital and visitors were welcome. I could think of no better way of brightening Leah's spirits than bringing her some of the most heavenly chocolate cookies from a French bakery not far from the hospital.

Leah was resting when I arrived, but rallied to welcome me. Leah looked like Leah, except her legs were swollen. We talked about the appallingly uninteresting walls of her hospital room, baseball, and the crappy hospital food. Little did I know that all Leah could eat was broth. What a fool I was for thinking that a woman who just had a radical surgical procedure in her abdomen could eat freakin' chocolate cookies.

Leah was courteous when she declined my offer of chocolate comfort. I could see Leah's energy was beginning to fade, so I hugged her goodbye and sheepishly left with my cookies. (Leah's former student, Jillian)

Coming Home

The day before my birthday, I passed gas walking down the hallway. I was never so happy to pass gas in my lifetime, because I would be able to leave that little ward of horrors.

I went home the next day. Nick, my dad and brother, and I had dinner together. I even sat at the table. I was home with my family on my birthday.

I said, "Thank you good and gracious God. Thank you for this glorious day!"

• • •

When Leah came home, friends continued to ask if they could do anything, like mow the lawn or wash dishes. I declined most offers, because I'd have to tell them where to put the dishes anyway. Besides, doing chores provided me with a sense of normalcy.

In retrospect, I should have asked people to help out, for their sake. They really wanted to feel they were doing something tangible for Leah. I did, however, ask Jillian and Juliane to keep Leah company when I taught.

• • •

After Leah was released to go home, she insisted that Nick return to work. I was available on the days he taught and was happy to help. The first day I went over, she was sitting on the couch and eating solid food, and she was extremely optimistic about her recovery. We talked for a while and then I asked if there was anything that I could do: vacuum, wash dishes, laundry? She refused at first, but I managed to convince her that as one of five children in a large active family, I was used to doing chores.

I straightened the kitchen, swept the floor, vacuumed the carpet, and washed a few loads of laundry. Leah woke up after a nap and was happy to see what I had accomplished. She talked about her family and how far away they were and how she and Nick had always been self-sufficient. I told her that times like this were when she needed to let people help her.

"Focus on your body, your health and your relationships," I said. "Everything else will get taken care of."

From that day on, she allowed me to clean, make her meals, take the dogs for walks, change the sheets and do laundry. I think it helped her to conserve her energy for fighting the cancer. (Leah's former student, Juliane)

Chemo Reality

About a month after surgery, I met my oncologist. She put me on a very aggressive regimen of three chemotherapy drugs every four weeks.

The chemo infusion suite actually is a cheery place. The oncology nurses were wonderfully compassionate, truly competent people with a calling. You sit in a reclining chair and they cover you with warmed-up flannel sheets.

The first treatment took about eight hours. When they finished, I felt pretty liquid logged and really tired, but not yet nauseous.

The next day I felt as though I had the worst flu ever and had been run over by a Mack truck. I stayed on the couch and took anti-nausea drugs.

I drank nonalcoholic ginger beer and tea, which have a soothing effect on the stomach. Some friends with cancer also used marijuana. I did not want to smoke, so a colleague made organic pot brownies for me. Even though I was not hungry, the brownies gave me the munchies and I could keep up my regular eating.

I cut my hair short so it would not be a huge shock when I lost it. After two treatments, large clumps fell out, and I asked Nick to shave my head. I became completely bald and looked emaciated, like people in camps from World War Two.

It was weird losing hair *everywhere* on my body. Even when you shave you have a little stubble, but that was gone. I felt as though I were a newborn. I used lotion to keep my skin soft. Nick and I went a long time without having sex. We could have had oral sex, but my mouth was sore from the treatments. Cancer puts a crimp in your sex life for a while. A long while.

• • •

On her first day of chemotherapy, Leah expressed concern about catching a cold.

"I wouldn't worry about the flu," the nurse said and laughed. "You have cancer!"

We were welcomed to the world of cancer jokes.

Leah remained very upbeat during chemotherapy. She maintained her trademark smile and every day she said, "Have I told you how much I love you today?"

I tried to make some time for myself as she continued her treatments. I mostly gave up golf and tennis, but I took long walks with the dogs during Leah's couch time in Week One. Doing something physical in nature cleared my head and helped me think about anything besides her cancer. The walking also helped me keep my weight down, as I was eating some of those organic brownies with Leah.

Our sex life ended with her diagnosis. We were married for almost twenty years and she went through menopause, so we had gone without sex for weeks at a time. But after surgery Leah was in pain and during chemo she was nauseous and weak. After she recovered from her last treatment, we finally made love. But Leah couldn't get into a comfortable position, and I have to admit to feeling uneasy when I saw her completely hairless. Neither one of us had an orgasm, and we did not try again.

I continued to send "Leah Updates" through e-mail, though these updates evolved from clinical descriptions of her condition to very personal disclosures about our emotions. Friends forwarded my messages to other friends, and soon there were a couple of hundred people on the "Leah Update" list.

• • •

At first, I found Nick's e-mails about Leah distasteful. They seemed too private to share with so many people in such a public way. I would be more private about this. But as time progressed, I changed my mind and found them a beautiful way to share the joys and sorrows of core life struggles, and I found Leah's energy in the group that shared her news. I feel that Leah lives more visibly to me through the stronger friendship ties she gave me as we shared her passage together. (Our friend, Janellen)

Back with a Vengeance

The chemo drugs kept shrinking the tumors. When I finished the eighth and final treatment in June, I felt great. The doctor said I needed a break from chemo for my body and heart.

I decided to return to full-time teaching that fall. I cannot think of anything I would rather do. Teaching is my mission.

In August I had an occasional upset stomach. I assumed that my body was getting tired of everything I had been taking. Then, two weeks after school began, I went in for my first CT scan after stopping chemo. The news was a body blow. The cancer was back in less than three months. The lesion on the liver had grown. I had spots in my abdomen. I had a mass growing between my kidney and my ureter.

I was angry it returned so quickly. I always like to think that if I do everything right, I am in control. But I am not in control of this disease. I realized that I would not be able to finish teaching, and I finally let myself feel sad and discouraged rather than optimistic and hopeful.

When the chemotherapy worked so well, I believed that God was using modern medicine to heal me. When it came back so soon, it seemed that the answer was, "No, I don't have any further plans for you here." But I never lost my faith.

• • •

Leah woke me up after her oncologist called about the CAT scan. She looked mad. I thought I had done something wrong, until Leah told me her cancer had returned.

I started to cry, but then jumped out of bed to be with her. We held each other for what seemed like a year. Neither one of us withdrew, not knowing how much time we'd have together.

After we finished, she hugged her terrier Hawkeye. "I hope whoever you meet next is a dog person," she said to me and sobbed. She cried more that morning than during the entire previous year.

Leah read student papers and worked on a report to distract herself from the bad news and/or tie up loose ends. I mostly sat and stared in silence.

• • •

I began a new regimen of chemotherapy in late September, but after eight months of treatments, my veins were very brittle. I needed to have a port put in, though it took a while to get used to that Borg-like implantation.

By the one-year anniversary of my diagnosis in October, I was not well. My stomach was distended, I needed a blood transfusion because of a low blood count, and I had to take laxatives to keep my bowels moving because of a hernia. Then I had to have a stent inserted because a tumor was preventing my kidney from draining.

The day before my birthday, I felt nine months pregnant. I called my surgeon's office and the nurse practitioner tapped my stomach. She sterilized the spot, stuck a needle in, and an hour later they had drained four quarts of fluid. It was a wonderful sense of relief to be able to stand upright and breathe.

I opened presents on the morning of my birthday. So many flowers arrived that the house looked like a florist shop.

• • •

Leah's birthday fell on a day when Nick was teaching, and he asked if I would go by the house. I brought flowers and gifts and an assortment of small desserts that she and Nick could sample. I told her that whatever she needed, she was to ask me for and I would be happy to help. She asked me to rub her legs.

In response to the treatments that she was receiving, her body was producing fluids that collected in her legs. The only way to reduce the swelling was to massage the legs so that the lymph nodes could remove the fluid.

I did not tell her that it felt awkward at first to place my hands on her body. I sat at the end of the couch with her legs across my lap as I had many times before with my mother, sisters, and close female friends. But somehow this was different. She was my professor, my mentor, my teaching supervisor, and the chair of my committee. And she was sick. I started at her feet and squeezed as I moved my hands up over her ankle, rubbing and pushing the fluid up her legs from the bottom up. Then I moved up over the knee to her thigh and pushed the fluid higher to the hip and groin where it could be absorbed by the lymph nodes.

We talked about how she was feeling and about my progress in the program. She wanted to know how I was doing. On her birthday, while she was suffering from the effects of chemotherapy and an untrained masseuse, she wanted to know how I was doing. I rubbed her legs. It was the least I could do to help. (Leah's former student, Juliane)

• • •

By early November, life had become really hard. We saw the oncologist and agreed that the new chemotherapy was not working. I decided to stop treatments because they were not making the quality of my life any better.

From then on, I found it difficult to wake up cheerful. We spend most of our lives mentally in the future, thinking about what is next. It was hard for me to think about there being no next. My dad and stepmother came in early November. I think he was blown away at how ill I had become. Then my brother, sister-in-law, and their kids came for an early Christmas in mid-November. Nick made a complete Christmas dinner, and I taught my niece how to make the pecan tassies my mom and I made before Christmas.

I was happy to see everyone, but it was surreal because they were coming to say goodbye. I will not get to see them again. I felt as though I were floating along.

• • •

The day Leah discontinued her treatments, we took a long drive. We talked about how some people die suddenly from heart attacks and car wrecks and don't get to cherish even their final hours. Leah said she wanted to enjoy her last few months with me and the dogs and with her closest friends and relatives.

We scheduled visiting times for her dad and stepmom, her brother, sister-in-law and the kids, her best friends, her students, and my mom. Everyone put on a good face, but it was so sad to watch Leah say goodbye to them for the last time.

I had refused to think much about Leah's death, but as she deteriorated I considered the inevitable. I feared she would hang on for months, paralyzed and barely conscious. I prayed for her to go quickly at the end.

• • •

The last time I saw Leah was around her birthday. Little did I know she had only weeks to live. I remember being very sad to see how she had declined. Her face was pale, gray shadows consumed it. She was hugely swollen from the disease, and very uncomfortable. She looked scared to me, and it broke my heart.

The morning I left to go home we sat at the table. The morning crossword puzzle sat on the table, neatly folded, ready for us to dig in to. Neither of us had the heart. For me, I was thinking I would rather leave with the completed puzzle from the day before than start a puzzle that even in the best of times we'd struggle with. We didn't need any more struggles.

The clock over the mantle ticked away, and soon it was time for me to leave for the airport. Nick and Leah both walked me out, and hugged me good-bye, like they had done dozens of times before. I could not let myself think this was the last time I would see Leah, nevertheless, I cried all the way to the airport. (Our friend, Laurie)

The Last Week

I love Nick, the dogs, my family and friends, and I am sad that I will not get to share the rest of their lives. On the other hand, every day I wake up and ask myself, "What am I still doing here?" I feel good for about an hour, and then I go lie down and sleep my life away. Right now I am having a hard time swallowing. I get tired walking from the bedroom to the bathroom. If I am just going to be a vegetable on the couch, I might as well be a vegetable for a short time.

Nick and I had a fight about my unwillingness to recognize my current situation. I am trying to realize how dangerous it is for me to do many things. I have to say I cannot do some things and ask him to do them for me. He needs for me to acknowledge that I am dying. I do not seem to be facing this reality terribly well.

• • •

I thought Leah was going to die the night of Sunday, December 5th. Earlier that week, she gasped once every twenty seconds and her whole body convulsed for a moment every thirty or so minutes. But that night she lay calmly in bed, and when she fell asleep she reached for someone or something with both arms. She also seemed to talk to someone, though I couldn't understand her.

I had read about the near-death experiences of people who said their spirits floated above their bodies and deceased relatives appeared as escorts. As Leah reached up, I looked around the room, searching for God, an angel, the spirit of Leah's mother, a beam of light, for any sign that she was being called.

"Do you see your Mom?" I whispered in her ear. "Do you see God?"

Leah didn't respond.

I stayed awake for most of the night holding her hand. I told her the dogs and I would be fine and it was okay for her to go. I was very surprised that she was still breathing in the morning.

For several days, Leah didn't get out of bed except to go to the bathroom. But on Friday, she woke up restless.

"I don't know why I'm so tired," she said, and pushed the covers off the bed. She got up and lay on the couch for most of the day. She expressed uncharacteristic frustration with me, even at the dogs.

She said she was hungry for chicken salad, but I hadn't shopped for days. I called Jillian and asked her to buy food.

When I returned to the living room, Leah asked if the

chicken was organic, as we had been eating more organic foods the past few years. I should have told her yes, but I said I didn't know. She became upset and insisted that she'd only eat organic chicken.

Jillian came with the food, and I asked her to stay with Leah while I took the dogs for a walk to calm down. I didn't want to fight with Leah, even though she seemed determined to win one last argument.

• • •

When I arrived, Leah called me into the living room and asked if the chicken was organic. I told her it wasn't, and she said it needed to be organic.

"It's not that difficult," she said. "I do it all the time."

Nick took the dogs for a walk and I stayed with Leah. "I don't know why Nick thinks I'm going to die," she said, out of nowhere. I paused, not knowing what to say. Then I told her that Nick was concerned because she was sleeping so much. It was pretty clear that she was not accepting of the fact that she was dying. (Leah's former student, Jillian)

• • •

I don't know why Nick thinks I'm dying. … I'll feel better if I lie down.

• • •

Leah's aggravation continued into Friday evening. She tossed in bed and groaned in pain. At one point she stumbled toward the bathroom. I guided her to the toilet and pulled down her pajama bottoms. Before she sat down, two globs of feces plopped to the floor. I stared for a moment, startled by the sight and surprised anything could come out after she had eaten so little. When she finished, I pulled her to a standing position and wiped her butt.

She also threw up several times. I called hospice for guidance. They weren't scheduled to deliver the hospital bed and morphine drip until the next week. They told me to go to the emergency pharmacy and get new anti-nausea medication that would dissolve in Leah's mouth.

I called Kimo and asked him to get the drugs, because I couldn't leave her by herself.

While I waited for Kimo, Leah continued to moan. I could clean up her vomit and wipe her ass, but I couldn't stop her pain. I felt completely helpless. Every second was excruciating.

I called hospice one last time, and they agreed that Leah should go to emergency.

• • •

By the time I got to their house with the medication, it was 1:30 in the morning, and it was obvious that the meds weren't going to help her. She was in a lot of pain. The ambulance came to transport her, and they put her on a gurney. She had her eyes closed and I walked over and held her hand. She did not even know I was there and had no energy at this point.

Nick said, "Miss Leah, Kimo's here. He's holding your hand."

Like she got power from some mystical force, she opened her eyes, turned and looked at me, somehow managed to lift herself slightly up off the gurney, reached out for me, and gave me the biggest hug that I've ever had. At that moment, I knew it was no longer about her; it was about her telling me that things were going to be okay. (Our friend and colleague, Kimo)

• • •

Leah entered the ER around two o'clock in the morning on Saturday and was placed in the same cubicle where she received the diagnosis the previous year. The nurses hooked up a morphine drip, which relieved the pain but made her more nauseous. She threw up mucous, blood, and tissue that looked like coffee grounds and smelled like a dog's yeast infection. I stood over her with a plastic container, catching most of the gunk that spewed from her mouth.

When the shift changed near dawn, a new doctor came.

"I'm sorry about your mother," he said.

When I told him she was my wife, he apologized and said he didn't check the chart.

"Don't worry about it," I said. "She looks like my grandmother."

I told Leah whenever visitors came into the room, but she couldn't keep her eyes open for more than a second.

• • •

By the time I got to the hospital it was probably after eleven on Saturday night. Nick was by Leah's bedside, and he told her that I was there. She stirred a little, but didn't say anything. At that point, she was heavily medicated on morphine and coughing up a lot of blood and tissue. I spoke to her a little, but mostly spent my time trying to give what comfort I could to her and to Nick. We talked about the irony—I guess that's the right word—of Nick being the first person to visit my wife and newborn daughter in the very same hospital just months before.

One tries to say something comforting and wise in such circumstances, but what can be said at that point? My wife tells me that when her father died, the best thing that anyone said to her was that they can't possibly know how she must feel. I said that, and brought Nick some food so that he could have some strength as he sat with Leah. After a while, I whispered some words of peace to her and then left. (Our friend and colleague, Dave)

• • •

On Sunday, Leah's condition deteriorated further. I brought in a CD unit and played Christmas music and a Sacramento Choral Society disc recorded when Leah was a soprano in the chorus. Whenever the female sopranos sang, Leah twitched her eyes and moved her mouth.

I stayed next to her all night long, unable to sleep as her gasping and tremors intensified. I said everything I could to help her die. I told her that I loved her, I'd take care of the boys, there wasn't anything left for her to do, it wasn't her fault, it was okay to go, to look for her mom. I even lied at midnight on December 13th and told her it was my birthday, as she promised to hang on for that occasion.

During one moment of sleep-deprived delirium, I considered smothering her with a pillow to relieve her struggle. I yelled at God for not taking her sooner, but then the vestiges of my Catholicism resurfaced and I realized it was Satan who was tormenting me with the ultimate paradox: kill my wife to end her suffering, and then be haunted with the memory for the rest of my life. I prayed, I cried, I swore, and I sang, fueled by adrenaline and feeling every possible emotion.

In the wee hours of Monday morning, I experienced a moment of serenity and summoned Leah's attention. "Leah?" I said, and repeated her name. "I have to tell you something. I want you to know that I love you." Leah twitched her eyes.

"Uv ü," she whispered, barely audible.

I kissed her forehead and wept.

At six o'clock in the morning, our friend Sylvia returned. Two nurses arrived to turn Leah to prevent bedsores. When they moved Leah, she became very distressed. Her eyes bulged open and her neck stretched, and for a ghastly moment she looked like E.T. from the Spielberg movie.

I held her hand, but she remained agitated even after the nurses left the room. Her breathing shifted to a higher octave but in a minor chord.

"Something is different," I said.

Sylvia backed away as I stroked Leah's hair and coached her to die. I told her it wasn't her fault, I was so proud of her, and that she could do this. Her gasps shortened, until I noticed only faint reflexes in her mouth and throat.

At a few minutes past seven o'clock, Leah took one last micro-gasp and then became completely calm. She probably was dead for five minutes before I went to the nurses' station and asked for assistance.

· · ·

Some nurses' aides came in to move Leah, to avoid bedsores—in more lucid moments I realized the absurdity of needing to move someone so close to death—and it distressed Leah a lot. Her blue, blue eyes opened up wide, panicked, and she turned, not seeing anything in the room.

Nick rushed to her other side, soothing her through words, stroking her hair, her arm, her hands, telling her how much he loved her, that it was okay to let go, reminding her that they had talked about everything, that "the boys" were okay. I stepped back by then, not wanting to intrude, but not wanting to abandon Nick if he needed me. Each silence between breaths took longer, longer, with Nick softly talking to her the whole time, a murmur of loving words. Finally, there were long silences between the harsh, hard sounds of those last, final breaths. When she took her last breath, we just sat with her for a while, quiet, waiting. (Our friend and colleague, Sylvia)

• • •

Kimo arrived about a half hour later. Sylvia said goodbye to Leah and to us, while I continued to hold Leah's hand. Kimo said he would always remember Leah's blue eyes.

I told him that her eyes were still crystal clear, a condition I never understood given what her body went through. I propped open Leah's left eyelid.

"Look at how clear they still are," I said.

Kimo took a glance and sat back down. I closed her eyelid.

"And you didn't look at your grandmother's body?" Kimo said and smiled, a reference to my refusal to look at my grandmother's body in the casket because I don't want that to be my last memory of a loved one.

"Things have changed a little," I said and smiled.

A doctor came in around eight o'clock to make the official pronouncement. Kimo and I stayed with Leah until nearly nine o'clock, when a man from the crematorium came to take her. He looked like a character from "The Sopranos."

"I'm sorry for your loss," he said softly.

Kimo helped me to my car and gave me one last hug. I spent the day on the phone telling family members the news and finalizing her memorial service. I couldn't believe she was actually gone.

I still can't.

• • •

I talked with Leah a couple of years ago about her spiritual life, and she said she was not worried about her walk with the Lord because he promised he would abide with her no matter what the circumstances. I am sure she and her mom are among the singers who are singing with choirs and praising the Lord. (Leah's father, Morrie)

Life Goes On

I wonder what Nick's life is going to be like. I know he will be fine after I die. He is a young man with another thirty or forty years. I am sorry I will not be here with him. I hope he meets somebody who will love him and take care of him and be kind and is wonderful with animals.

• • •

Over three years have passed since Leah's death. I'm still moved by the experience, and I'm surprised at how positive that experience was. Of course I can close my eyes and see her last breath, though that image did not haunt me as I thought it might. I never want to relive the experience, but I am stronger and kinder for having done so. I hung on for many moments of brutally sad grief, but now feel more joy than ever before. I will always miss her, but life does indeed go on. And I know that some day I will meet somebody who loves me and who is kind and is wonderful with animals.

Most of all, I will always remember how my friends supported me during that time, friends who participated fully in our love story of cancer and death.

CODA

Let's Get Personal

First-Generation Autoethnographers Reflect on Writing Personal Narratives

Carolyn Ellis
University of South Florida, Tampa

Arthur P. Bochner
University of South Florida, Tampa

Norman K. Denzin
University of Illinois, Urbana-Champaign

H. L. (Bud) Goodall, Jr.
Arizona State University, Tempe

Ron Pelias
Southern Illinois University, Carbondale

Laurel Richardson
The Ohio State University, Columbus

Carolyn Ellis: Welcome to "Let's Get Personal: First-Generation Autoethnographers Reflect on Writing Personal Narratives." The participants on this panel are Ron Pelias, Art Bochner, Laurel Richardson, Bud Goodall, and Norman Denzin, who has put this conference together. I will be both panel member and moderator, because our moderator has another commitment. We're immodestly calling ourselves "first-generation autoethnographers," denoting that we're among those who've been on the front lines writing and talking about personal narratives.

I have given each participant a copy of seven questions. Each question has several parts; each part could easily take up the whole session. It's not so much that the questions are difficult; it's that I'm holding each participant to a one-minute answer per question. That impossible task kept me up most of the night thinking about how I was going to make that work. I also asked participants to be spontaneous and to resist writing out and reading the answers, but, of course, all of us—including me—have jotted a few notes. We're not *that* spontaneous. Besides, the one-minute limit has put a lot of pressure on us to say something significant in just a few words. I'm used to easing into an answer, warming up, and I'm sure others are as well.

Let's start with Question 1, which is about personal history and then move to Question 2, on presentation of self. We may have to skip Question 3 on evidence and truth, Question 4 on evaluation, and Question 5 on ethics to have time to address the last two sets of questions, which to me are the most important: Question Six is about the current state of autoethnography, and Question Seven concerns our major challenges and goals as autoethnographers. (Like students who want to do it right, the panelists ask questions about procedures. Then Carolyn reads the first set of questions.)

Round 1

Personal History

Carolyn: Discuss your experience with writing personal narratives or autoethnography. For example, what was the first personal narrative you wrote? When and why did you write it? What was your experience with publishing it? Discuss other personal narratives that followed this one. Feel free to address any part of this set of questions. Ron, would you begin?

Ron Pelias: Thanks, Carolyn. One minute—here we go! First thing that struck me when I read this particular question was feeling the need to draw a distinction between personal narrative and autoethnography. I have been working with personal narratives in my role as a theatre director since the early eighties. I don't think that work, however, ever took on explicitly the burden that I think autoethnography does, which is to use the self to explicate culture. The selves one encounters in personal narratives are, of course, culturally situated, but the goal of performing personal narratives wasn't seen as a method for evoking cultural insights.

The first piece that I wrote that I would say made a bid for autoethnography was a piece called "The Critical Life." I first presented it at a pre-conference workshop with Carolyn Ellis. I was lucky to have both Carolyn and Buddy Goodall give me some feedback. I raced home, did revisions, and sent it out to *Communication Education.* This piece tracks one day in the life of the academic. It looks at how prevalent criticism is in our daily routines. After the editor read it, he said, "I kind of like this, but it's not quite scholarly enough and what we really need to do is beef this piece up with a good theoretical introduction." I sighed. This was in 1999 and a number of wonderfully eloquent justifications for autoethnography had already been written. So I said, "No, I don't think I want to do that." I thought that was going to be the end of it. A couple of weeks later, the editor responded, "What if I get some people to respond to the essay, and we'll let you have the essay the way you wrote it?" So I said, "Okay, fine." He gathered together several scholars to respond to "The Critical Life." It appeared as a forum where people tried to make some kind of sense of the piece and weigh in on whether or not such a piece should appear in a scholarly journal.

Carolyn: Well done, and done within a minute (laughter).

Art Bochner: I'm not sure that I abide by any hard and fast distinctions between personal narratives and autoethnography. When we write and/or perform personal narratives, they begin to circulate into the culture of the academy and outside the academy as well, evoking diverse reactions and responses. As a result, a cultural dialog is initiated, and what began as a personal narrative ends up as an autoethnographic one. In other words, personal narratives become autoethnographies. So, in this manner, it occurs to me that the first autoethnography I ever wrote was a letter to my college sweetheart after we broke up and as far as I know it was never published (laughter).

Academically speaking, the first autoethnography that has my name attached to it is a piece that Norman published in *Qualitative Inquiry*, titled "It's about Time: Narrative and the Divided Self." I talked extensively about this article yesterday in the autoethnography workshop. I first presented a much briefer version of this story at a NCA [National Communication Association] convention in 1995. I had been invited by the vice-president of NCA to be on a panel on social theory. At the time, I was heavily immersed in reading Richard Rorty, and I was particularly impressed by Rorty's statement that if you compare what has been accomplished in the realm of social justice by the social novelists with the achievements of the social theorists you come out decidedly on the side of the social novelists.

I wanted to show how a story can function as a theory or theoretical statement. So I presented my own autoethnographic story about my father's death and its meaning in relation to the divided self of the academy—between the derogated personal and the embraced academic self. I used the story to expose what I later called the "institutional depression" that circulates through the academy as a result of this split between the academic and the personal. One of the nicest experiences I had in relation to this particular piece was an e-mail I got shortly after by somebody I didn't know. A retired professor in Massachusetts from another field wrote and laid out what was evoked for him by that piece. He had retired early from his position as a professor of sociology, and he told me that my story touched a wound that had festered for years. He concluded his letter with the line, "I would not have retired if I had thought there was an opportunity to bring the personal into the academy."

Laurel Richardson: I'm going to take two minutes from everybody else. (The audience laughs, and Carolyn says okay.)

The divided self. Much of my life I did divide myself. I wrote poetry under the name of Laurel Richardson, and I wrote academic stuff under the name of Laurel Walum, and then after awhile Laurel Walum Richardson and Laurel Richardson Walum, but there was a real division. At one point I thought, "Wait! This is not healthy for me or the universe. I'm not going to live divided any longer." (A self divided against itself cannot stand itself?)

Let me go back a bit in my writing history. The first paper I wrote after graduate school was not an autoethnography ... was it? It was called "Women and Science: Why So Few?" Not an autoethnography. Of course not (laughter). It was soundly rejected by the ASR [*American Sociological Review*] editor with one sentence. I know it by heart: "This was obviously written by a woman because no one but a woman would be interested."

Norman's writing about epiphanies has been influential to my thinking, in general, and as I was trying to answer the questions Carolyn has posed, I realized that I move into autoethnography following an ephiphanic event. That epiphanic event, for me, is always tied to my being situated into a speaking position of power. So my first "real" autoethnography was my Presidential Address for the North Central Sociological Association. I called it "The Collective Story." In that piece, I wrote that I didn't know what to write, how to write, or who to write it for. The crisis of representation had hit me personally. I couldn't write, and talking about it was bringing together the poet and the sociologist.

The second time I felt that strong position of power was at a SSSI [Society for the Study of Symbolic Interaction] Couch-Stone meeting in Des Moines. I'd been given a featured place on the program—scheduled to do a performance in a bar. I sat on the bar and performed "Vespers," a piece that explored my alienation from my mother. It was published in a literary magazine (*The Chicago Review*) and became the culminating piece in my anthology, *Fields of Play: Constructing an Academic Life*. Being "featured" gave me a place of power.

The third place of power I felt was when I was the distinguished lecturer for SSSI. I wrote "Paradigms Lost" about a car accident, my coma and my inability to have words, my physical pain and loss. I was very concerned that I reached people—and I still am—who have that kind of trauma. People who have lost voice, who have lost neurons, who have lost their old familiar abilities. I wrote a hopeful story about the reclaiming of the possibility to return.

As an entitled full professor at a major research university, I want to use that position to validate the personal within the academy. If I don't use this position of power, who am I? If not now ... if not then ... when? If I'm not for me, who will be?

Carolyn: What strikes me is how much influence everyone on this panel and others have had on my being able to write autoethnography. Two names that keep appearing as I think through my own autoethnography are Norman Denzin and Mitch Allen, the editor of Left Coast Press. Mitch is not at this session, but his spirit is certainly with us. He has been instrumental in providing publishing outlets and support for autoethnography.

My first project was *Final Negotiations*, about the illness and death of my first husband. I started it in 1985, but I didn't publish it until 1995. Still, it provided the context for everything else that emerged. By the way, Mitch was an important reviewer of that book.

The other significant project for me was a paper called "Systematic Sociological Introspection," which advocated for the usefulness of introspection and doing the kind of work we are doing. It was published in 1991. Norm was a reviewer on that paper.

My first published autoethnography was written with Art, my second and *last* husband (laughter). I wasn't sure that chapter really counted because it was in a volume that I edited with Mike Flaherty, called *Investigating Subjectivity*, published by Mitch while he was at Sage. Does it count if I was the person who decided to put it in there?

My first "real" publication ... I'm finally getting to it ... was "There Are Survivors," about my brother's death. It had originally been part of the longer book, *Final Negotiations*. But Art and Laurel convinced me to publish it separately. I then, of course, sent it to Norman Denzin, who published it in *The Sociological Quarterly.* That was really the beginning for me. It's interesting when I look back at that because Sherryl Kleinman wrote a sociological analysis of that piece that was published in the same volume. Similar to Ron's experience, I think having a response helped legitimate my piece being in the journal.

My next published piece was "Speaking of Dying," about the death of a friend of mine. Andy Fontana heard me give it at a conference and then asked for it for *Symbolic Interaction,* so it was a pretty easy publication. That piece was published under the subheading of "short story," indicating that it wasn't really an article. But I didn't care because at least my work was getting out in the world.

Then I published a piece on race in the first issue of QI [*Qualitative Inquiry*], Norman's journal. When QI came out, I felt, oh this is heaven, what a gift! So, what I learned from all of this is that it's really important to have people out there providing feedback and places to publish and acting as your guardian angels. I'm very fortunate to have had many of those.

Bud Goodall: In 1983, I was trolling in the academic backwaters of Huntsville, Alabama, at a science and engineering university that didn't really even carry journals that were in my field. One day I received a note from the library that said there was an issue of something called *Communication Monographs* that I might want to look at. So I went to the library and there was this article called "Organizational Communication as Cultural Performance" by my friend Nick Trujillo and Mike Pacanowsky. I thought when I read it ... hmmm ... because all of a sudden this opened the door to doing the sort of cultural analysis via narrative that I had always wanted to do, but I had never seen an opening before.

So I started writing. I had been trained at Penn State in creative and biographical writing as well as communication, so this was sort of rediscovering my roots. I sent a paper off about a computer software startup company to none other than Nick Trujillo and Mike Pacanowsky, who hosted a conference on Alternative Approaches to Organizational Communication that summer in Alta, Utah, and, to my surprise, they accepted the paper. Actually, I should also say this: If it weren't for Nick I wouldn't know I was writing ethnography. It wasn't until after I read my paper that I was told that was what I was doing. I said, "What? I thought I was being a creative writer." Nick said, "No, we call that ethnography." I said, "Oh, ok." And he said, "There're some books you probably need to read" (laughter).

So, anyway, that paper—that story—became the first part of a book called *Casing a Promised Land*, which was published by Southern Illinois University Press in 1989. I want to tell you this part of that story of its publication only because it's a cautionary and funny tale: I sent it to every academic press in America and it was rejected by all of them. I had pretty much given up on ever being able to publish it and then I got a phone call one afternoon from the editor, Kenny Withers, who said, "I've decided to publish your book." I said, "Why? You've already rejected it." And he said, "Well, I know, but Penguin just bought the paperback rights to a book we published ten years ago called *Boswell's Clap*, which was about the sexual problems of literary men, for $100,000" (laughter). He says, "I have to show a loss for next year and yours is a book that nobody's gonna buy, so I'm going to publish it." So, here's the moral to that story: We are gathered here in this room today in part because of Boswell's sexual indiscretions.

I have always thought that when I write personal narrative—autoethnography is a fancier term than I am used to, but I can carry it as well—I believe firmly in the power of personal narrative. I think that it gives us a wonderful opportunity to use creative nonfiction as an outlet for our work to reach broader public audiences and when we get to the end of the session today I'm going to say that's the future I envision for us. Thank you.

Norman Denzin: When we think of autoethnography, we need to mark 1987 as the year that really gets it into the literature as a formal term, as a formal methodology. So, in that sense we are talking about a genre that is twenty years old. Each of us came into that genre before or after 1987 for our history. I think each person has said here that what has been critical to each one of our histories has been our relationships with each other. Having sessions like this and having congresses like this, and having persons organize sessions like this is absolutely central to the evolution of the genre and to giving new voice to persons in the academy.

My particular entrance into the genre is on two levels. First, coming through sociology in the sixties and not being taught anything about qualitative methodology, we would read anthropology accounts and some sociological accounts about participant observation. But to think that sociologists would write in the first person was completely taboo. When I did what became the alcoholic and recovering alcoholic books, I decided as I was doing that project that I was going to have to be in the project because I was the person doing the observing during the ethnography. But I was just going to disguise myself because I still didn't have the freedom to—I hadn't given myself the freedom to—write that narrative in the first person. But I'm on every page of those two books. So that was sort of a disguised entry into ethnography written through the personal, but using the genre of the day to hide behind various accounts. I used the theoretical apparatus of the book to hide myself.

It was after that book that Michal McCall and Patricia Clough and others of us started doing sessions on postmodern motherhood. A number of us and many of us on this panel also came to the Midwest sociological meetings and the SSSI meetings. We decided we were going to do first-person narratives through our mothers about working our way through our childhoods and our adulthoods. I was the only male on the panel so I wrote about my mother and they wrote about their mothers and about being mothers themselves. Out of that came two or three papers. One of them was called, "I Love Lucy," which was an important piece for me. Another was called "That Psychiatrist," which was a dialog that I had with my mother after I had gone through a treatment center and gotten on the path to recovery and she just couldn't accept that trajectory for me. I recorded and wrote a telephone conversation I had with her.

Then I wrote a piece that was built on everyone here that was called "Two-Stepping in the Nineties," which was an important piece for me. This was the early nineties and we had done a series of these panels and Laurel's book was out there, Carolyn's book was out there, and Art's work was out there. We were starting to coalesce this sense that the personal narrative written through the autoethnographic was a legitimate form, and so "Two-Stepping in the Nineties" sought to recover that moment when I two-stepped with my mother. Dancing with the old Victrola radio in the dining room and she taught me how to two-step. That piece was about my mother's death and about Laurel's mother's death and trying to come to grips with the fact that I learned of my mother's death by phone call because she excluded everybody in the family from her death. You know in the personal narrative there is a way to recover my own relationship to myself as my mother, and I went through Carolyn and Laurel to get to that spot. There's a space in Laurel's book where she talks about where she was the moment her mother died, and I started my two-stepping piece where I was when my mother died.

So, you can see that this was a deeply personal and political project for each of us, and we empower each other. I'll pick that notion of empowerment up later, but in my mind one of the lessons this group gives down to the next generation is a platform to work from. Now we want to be coming to sessions where we can be in the audience and you can tell us about your experiences.

Round 2

Carolyn: We're ready now for Question Two, which reads:

Presentation of Selves

What selves do you allow to become present in your work and what selves do you leave out? What selves do you become by virtue of having written autoethnographically?

Norman: I don't want to talk about two.

Carolyn: You don't want to talk about two (laughter)? Okay, Ron you're next.

Ron: I'm responding to the question: What selves do you allow to become present in your work and what selves do you leave out?

My immediate response is that I'm absolutely the worst person to try and answer this question, in part, because you never quite know what a reader's going to do with your work, never quite know how they're going to take it. I was surprised to find after publishing "The Critical Life," the piece I was referencing a few minutes ago, a number of people thought of me as a cynical, bitter academic. They thought, why are you hanging around if that's how you feel? What writing that essay did for me, however, was allow me to get rid of some of the weight that I was feeling at that time about criticism in the academy and how it was functioning. But I was read as bitter and cynical. That really surprised me.

The other point that I would like to make is that the one self that I present in highly limited ways is my relationship with my partner. I simply don't have permission to write about her. What's ironic about that is that the more I write, the more present that absence becomes.

Art: I just want to look briefly at the last part of this question. As I understand it the last part of the question was, what selves do you become by virtue of having written autoethnographically? What's really important to me is something Mark Freeman, a psychologist who has written quite a bit about narrative and autobiography, calls the "narrative challenge." He also created a term called "narrative integrity," which to Freeman is the notion that before we act we consider what story we might be writing ourselves into. Narrative is particularly interesting to me in terms of time, looking back on the past as we do from the perspective of the present, but pushing into the future, that is, who we want to become. So when we write autoethnographically, the reflexive consequence is a story which you want to be able to tell later on about yourself and your actions. For example, when my mother was sick and declining into dementia, it was very important for me to consider what I could do to help her, to support her, to be an other for her, to take into account what story I would be able to tell about this time in my life after she died. So for me, both in the writing of autoethnography and the living of narrative integrity, the question is what story do you want to become? I think that's empowering in the sense that it opens up choices to us that we might not otherwise consider.

Laurel: I love following Art because he's so good. I love to write because I don't know who's going to be there when I start the writing—all those people, all those voices, all those experiences that make up me. I'm not quite sure who's coming to play on the computer. I give myself a great deal of freedom to write. One of the things I love about writing is how I can be in the present and the past and future at the same time. I can be writing about now, but suddenly I'm six years old again, and that's okay, and then I'm writing about someplace else that I haven't yet been. Sometimes it's the voice I have right now, the smarter more reflexive grown woman, and sometimes it's the child voice, or the younger woman. All of this brings me great pleasure in the writing process. But the writing is not the same as publishing. So, I do allow whoever is going to be inside of me to come forth because by criticizing that writing part of the self, by censoring whoever it is who wants to come and play on the computer I'm not going to be able to write a truthful narrative or a full story. That doesn't mean I'm going to publish all of that, though, because the next task calls forth a different kind of self—a critical, literary, analytical self who wants to rearrange things so that people want to read what I've written. They might not want to read my two-year-old voice (laughter) … although I'm working on a long autoethnographic project where I'm growing myself up. It does start with my three-year-old voice; the voice changes as I get older. It's a real writing stretch for me. And, like Ron, I don't talk about my marriage except playfully. I don't talk much about my children, and then only with their express permission. I don't really talk a lot about my spiritual life, but the writing to me is a spiritual practice. Thank you.

Carolyn: Similar to what other people have said, when I start to write I never know what self I'm going to write. What I try to do is write as many selves as I can possibly write, and then question those and rewrite those as well. I tend to try to write as much as I can in the beginning as uncensored as I possibly can, but then what gets into print doesn't have the worst thing about me nor does it have the best thing about me. I still have to live in this world, and I don't want you to think I'm too weird. I also don't want my presentation to look too self-serving. So there is some censorship that goes on along the way. I feel like I don't have a whole lot to hide about my life now like I have in the past and I'm sad about that (laughter). But it still doesn't seem like writing gets any easier ethically. Now I'm involved in trying to write about my childhood, and I'm caught up in the ethical issues of writing about other people who were part of that world. I feel as if I'm just as confused about the ethics of writing the self as I've ever been.

Also, my experience has been that when you write and publish a story, you become the story on the page. Other people see you as that story, and you start to see yourself as that story. You start to see your experience as what you've written down. What I'm trying to do now, and advocating in what I write, is to go back to published texts and revise them. That we re-exam them from our position now to examine how we might see them differently or how we might pick up different aspects than we did the first time through. So, this revision has become important to me in thinking about the selves that I put on the paper.

Bud: I guess I feel a little differently. I've written myself into being. I have literally created myself in the prose that I have written, and in the talks that I have given, and in the classes that I've taught, and in the conversations that I've had. And I embrace that. For me, it's about voice. It's about developing a voice because your voice is your character. It's how you deploy it through language on a page. It's what goes in and out of the accounts that we weave. I also think, too, that one of the things that I've learned in this ripe old age of mine, particularly as a result of my last book, which was painfully self-analytic, is that to live in this world you need to be able to hold the light and the dark in both hands. They're part of the same thing. Unless you're willing to open up to that, you're going to have trouble with voice and you're going to have trouble with life. So, for me, the boundary issue is that I waited thirty years after my parents were dead to write about them, and I had very good reasons for that in a lot of ways. And I had very bad reasons for that in a lot of ways because I was running away from something that I had experienced that I couldn't really put words to. Once I decided to engage that and once I decided that I was going to open it up and look at my complicity in their demise, and write through that experience, I could own it. I had a story about it that both enriched my life and made it possible for me to hand it on to my son, for example, instead of giving him the half-truths and the lies that I had grown up with. So, my lesson about this is that voice is character. Don't be afraid of the dark and the darkest part of the light, open it up.

Norman: I'm going to answer Question Two now. My most recent project is called *Flags in the Window: Dispatches from the War Zone,* and it's a series of short pieces that I wrote over the last four years about the Bush administration. It's political autoethnography, unlike what I wrote during the Vietnam War, when my publications never recorded the fact that there was a war going on—that I lived through it. We didn't write about that stuff in the sixties and seventies, and I have huge guilt about that. So, I decided, the next major war, I'm going to write myself into it. Then autoethnography turned political becomes a vehicle for inserting myself into history, into the history of this insane administration. In Joan Didion's recent book, *The Year of Magical Thinking,* she talks about how she held herself together during this nightmare, thirteen-month period when her husband and her daughter both died. Her use of the words "magical thinking" indicated that she would put things together that didn't belong together. She would engage in all sorts of odd rituals to make it seem like she was still sane and that somehow things were still happening in an ordinary way. Well, I've had six years of magical thinking under Bush (laughter), so I go on trying to act like I knew what was going on—collecting stacks of newspapers, finding all sorts of political magazines, finding every anti-Bush book I could. I've got a room full of anti-Bush books. *Flags in the Window* is a series of essays that was sort of like: "6th of November, week 85 of the war ..." And so on. What was the news headline in the *New York Times* on week 85 of the war? And that's the way I would start the piece. And then I would go through the major news items like in a bulletin. "Rumsfeld says, 'War is over, victory is imminent.'" Or, "Bush says ...'whatever'" (laughter). There are fourteen of these autoethnographic political pieces. That's where I've gone most recently, is to use the genre for political purposes to make a series of stances about, following Joan Didion, somehow making sense of this insane period we're all living through. So, when it's over, *Flags from the Window* is one man's political autoethnography that's an intervention, which would say anybody else could have written that intervention. "Day 55 of the war ... week 67 of the war ... week ... whatever." We put all of those together and we somehow have intervened in this moment. So, that's my stance.

Round 3

Carolyn: Because of time constraints, we're going to skip to questions six and seven and answer them together. These questions read:

Current State of Autoethnography

How would you characterize the current state of autoethnography? For example, what are its strengths and tensions? What have we done right? What have we done wrong? Why do you think autoethnography grew in popularity in the last two decades? Do you think there is a "backlash" against autoethnography? If so, describe it and discuss why it might be happening.

Challenges and Goals

What are the major challenges autoethnographers face in the next decade? What work needs to be done? In what new directions do we need to go? What would you most like to see happen in autoethnography politically, practically, and/or academically and intellectually? Where do you see your work heading? Talk about the current state of autoethnography and challenges and goals for the future, where you think we're headed in the future. Ron, would you begin?

Ron: When I start thinking about the current state of ethnography, the first thing I want to say very quickly is that it's never been healthier. And, I would quickly add, it's never been healthier in part because of the labor of the people sitting to my right. The work that they have done has been absolutely amazing. Thinking about this question invites us, however, to consider the backlash against autoethnography that is happening. There surely are people across a number of our disciplines who still find little use for autoethnography or for qualitative methods in general. Autoethnography is often held up as the demon example of why all qualitative methods are bad. Such arguments are clearly disciplinary policing moves. But I want to insert quickly that throughout this conference we've been talking about different evaluative criteria. Policing is exactly what we're doing, too. There's no escaping in academic circles what we want to rule in and what we want to rule out. When I evaluate an autoethnographic paper for QI or in my classes, for example, I am policing what I think should be going on.

Perhaps what's a little bit more disturbing to me is the backlash within our own circles. It seems to me that criticism comes in a couple different forms. The first argument out there is that we are engaged in sacrificing the Other for a self-indulgent self, that we're engaged in navel-gazing. This argument misses a couple kinds of points. First, the navel tells the story of our first connection to another (laughter). Second, it seems to forget that the self is always constituted in our interactions with others. The other argument that plays itself out is the insufficiency of literary craft. Perhaps there's some truth to this concern. Most of us have not been trained in literary circles. Autoethnography calls on the evocative to write what hasn't appeared in our scholarship before. The question we should be asking is not if our writing is as good as the best novelists and poets (though it may be beneficial for us to strive for that), but if we are sufficiently skilled with our literary craft to do what needs to be done in scholarly circles—to uncover and to make present what has not been written before.

Skipping to the next question and looking into my crystal ball, the first thing I see is all the damage Bush has done. It's going to take years to recover from the Bush years, and it's going to take considerable labor just to get us back to where we were before he was elected. That's a pretty scary thought right there. Given that, our task is to couple the critical with autoethnography much more frequently than we currently do. I think we must become more rhetorically savvy advocates, or to borrow from Soyini Madison's keynote address, we must become "dangerous ethnographers."

Art: The last part of Question Six on backlash toward autoethnography was the only one of these questions that I actually wrote out a response to, and I did it this morning. It's not very poetic. I was concerned that this issue appealed to a certain sort of rage within me that I try to exert some control over. It seems to me that especially within the congress here, we have a great deal of diversity, diverse interests in cultural studies, critical ethnography, indigenous ethnography, autoethnography, the politics of evidence. And one of the very difficult questions we face is bringing those diverse interests together into a supportive environment, an environment that will help us to grow and nurture our interests in qualitative research.

There exists, however, even among the culture of qualitative researchers, a fairly large segment who I believe are still imprisoned by the illusion of the distortive framework of what Richard Rorty called "the circus tent of epistemology." They still thrash aimlessly about with the conviction that the project of the social sciences must take the form of representations that correspond to a world separate from themselves. They refuse to concede the point, that, in principle, our grasp of things lies in the way we are in touch with the world, what Heidegger referred to as "being-in-the-world," and Merleau-Ponty called "being-to-the-world." Consequently, they leave untouched and unfettered an account of a researcher's knowledge that is distinct from the world and often unwittingly reintroduce a mediational depiction of knowledge that accepts the Cartesian dualism that postmodernism demands we put to rest once and for all.

The critics of autoethnography, backlash if you prefer, express what I often perceive to be an indignant and self-righteous reaction to what they deem to be a relativism, or nonrealism gone wild. They remain in the grip of what I like to call the "science illusion," or what Freud might have called "science-envy" (laughter). They see those of us who flirt with autoethnography as destroying the civilization of inquiry, giving comfort to the enemy, apparently anti-representationalism, or being out of touch with reality. On the whole, they react out of fear—fear that our representations may in principle be confined to what is under our skin and in our minds. Perhaps unwittingly, they regress to a concealed form of foundationalism. As therapy for such fears, they appeal again and again to what I call "method-o-centricism," an oppressive doctrine that disciplines and punishes those who would want to experiment with something new and different under the sun.

Laurel: I retract, I am not happy following Art (laughter). Because he's just too good. My colleagues are going to talk about the state of the world, but I think at the moment I'm going to focus locally. I think it's really important that we provide institutional support and journals and more and more journals—thank you, Norm—for people who are working in this genre, places for them to publish because it's important if they're going to be academics that they have the institutional support and that they can depend on those of us who have academic sinecure to support them. Community is the most important thing.

I made a note to myself, "ethnographer's work is never done." And that's what I think is true. So, where am I in my own work? I just recently moved deeper and deeper into my own self, revealing more and more about who it is I am, who it is I might be moving away from. There is nothing to be feared. I have nothing to fear from any university. I'm in a privileged (and again powerful) position (because I am independent of university judgments). So, my work is getting deeper and deeper, and more self–revelatory. My new book (*Last Writes: A Daybook for a Dying Friend*) reveals so much of me that I didn't know I would be willing to reveal, and having finished it, I am moved further. Another thing that I am really pressing for in terms of autoethnography is that we enlarge our palette. There are many ways to express ourselves, to display our knowledge and understanding.

In the workshop on Writing Lives and Deaths, for example, that I did here, the members worked as community to express emotions, to make sense of diverse material. The presentations of the workshop attendees said more than words might have said. Gestures spoke—hugs, stances, dances. Along these lines of expanding past the written word, I think about the amazing dissertations of dancers, photographers, sculptures. Indeed, my own journey is taking me into visual arts, including the making of altered books, a process in which the reader literally interacts with author by altering the pages. The text is reborn. So, my concern with autoethnography is that we expand our identities and communities. Some of us are writers; some performers; some artists. Some of us experiment, discovering new stuff about ourselves and our worlds through deploying different ways of knowing and telling.

All of us are creators of social and cultural understandings. And a wonderful thing is that we don't have to be wonderful dancers. (A cell phone rings.)

Carolyn: It's yours, Laurel (laughter).

Laurel: (fumbling with turning off cell phone) … and we don't have to be technological whiz kids either. Anyway, that's what I wanted to get at—that we have the whole practical and the political worlds about us and we can tap deep down into ourselves becoming as full as we can be. We're out in the world; we know there's more in the world than just the book that we're writing.

Carolyn: I agree with Ron that I don't think we've ever been in better shape. I also don't think we've ever had more critiques than we have now. I tend to see these critiques, not as symbolizing backlash, but as symbolizing that people are paying attention. Some critiques are coming from within, but I'm hoping that serves to strengthen what we do rather than break us down. That's my hope.

I teach a class on autoethnography, and the last couple of weeks of the class the students and I looked at critiques of autoethnography. We read about a dozen of them. It was very interesting to read them side by side. They came from at least three places. We got the social science critique, which went something like: "You're not realist enough, your data are suspect, you're atheoretical, you're not analytic, you need systematic analysis of data. There's too much emphasis on the literary, the aesthetic, the emotional, the therapeutic—now the therapeutic really drives them nuts (laughter). You're not legitimate, it's not social science."

Then we also got poststructuralist critiques, which said: "You're too realist, there's not enough analysis." But unlike the social scientists, they don't want more data, they want more text. They mentioned the impossibility of knowing the self; that we're kind of naive realists who think we can reveal the secret self. Like social scientists, they also think there's not enough theory in what we do. They say we're trying to be too linear and we're not problematizing the self enough.

The third set of critiques came from aesthetic literary corners. One of the critiques said: "You're too concerned with being accepted as science. You're too concerned about being legitimate in the academy." And as long as we have those kinds of concerns, how in the world can we ever write aesthetically? So, their critique was that we don't write well enough; we're not aesthetic. They want more texts, but they want us to connect more with literary texts rather than the theoretical texts some of the poststructuralists were talking about. They, too, think that we are naive realists.

You can start to see how some of these critiques connect and overlap and some of them are coming from opposite places. After thinking about them, I started to feel like, hey, we must be doing something right here. Each of my students picked a critique to respond to. As part of their assignment, I asked them: "Is there a way we can talk back and show that we're listening, that we're paying attention, rather than just defending our position or attacking back?" Granted in the class we did defend and attack, but once we got that out of our systems, we tried to step back and ask: "What can we learn from this?" To be honest, I learned a lot from these critiques. At first, I may have just distanced myself from them, but I tried to take a second look. I'm starting to think more about aesthetic writing, for example, and problematizing the self. Of course, I know that we don't have contained selves that we reveal. But sometimes in our writing it might sound like that's what we're saying. What I want is for all of us to keep talking with each other. And not just be off in our own private classroom, complaining that "they" don't understand what we do, and how dare they and so on. But, instead, to really try to talk across these boundaries, especially with people who are doing this kind of work and others who are doing other kinds of interpretive and qualitative research. That's my naive optimism perhaps, but that's the way I am (laughter).

Where are we heading? I have several thoughts here. One, I love writing the traumatic, and I'm pulled to this dark side. I love the dark side, and I don't intend to stop writing about it. But I would like to see us expand a little and write about more things, such as what Norman's talking about—writing about the political and critical self—and the mundane self and so forth. Second, I'd like to see us put more emphasis on how we put meaning together, rather than how it all falls apart around us. Good autoethnographies do that already, but I would sometimes like to start with the meaning construction.

Now, what I think is the real challenge here, and I have thought this for some years now, and I continue to think about it, is that I don't know what happens after the second generation of autoethnographers comes through. I can't help but feel very optimistic seeing all of you here. Doing a workshop on autoethnography and having people come to take part in that, going to other places to give talks and seeing that there are people there who do this a whole lot better than I do. All this makes me really happy to think about the future. But what I think is the challenge is that I do not believe we're getting enough of our students into universities where there are Ph.D. programs where they can teach other people to do this who will then carry it on in the academy. That, to me, has been a roadblock that I've never been able to figure out quite what to do about. So, that's something I'd like for us to think about and talk about.

Bud: Gosh, I guess in all of this I'm moved to say something about what Norman says. I, too, have been writing about the war; he's been gracious in accepting some of my pieces. But I also have used my writing about the war in a different way, and that is to get the attention of people in Washington. So, it is now that I am a U.S. State Department international speaker on counterterrorism and public diplomacy. They send me to Europe to conferences and I can present a critique of the Bush administration, which is only possible because the State Department is made up primarily of liberals.

Okay, now, that would never have happened to me if my writing, my autoethnographic writing about the war, hadn't come to the attention of people who saw in it something that they couldn't get out of their think tanks or inside the beltway. And so one of the things, one of the messages that I give to people (and I see some of our students here and they've heard this from me before), is yes, it's important to have legitimacy inside the academy, you can't give that up. But now that the novelty of autoethnography has worn off—and I think it has worn off—we have to demonstrate that we're capable of giving something both to the academy and to the more general publics that pay us university salaries to live this great life. And so by engaging the larger questions, by not being afraid to take on poverty, disease, welfare, war, the abuse of women, and to write about that not just *in* the academy but also *outside* the academy, I think is the challenge that we face for the future.

Sometimes when I say that I think people get the wrong impression—they think what I'm saying is that I'm devaluing academic publication, but I'm not. That's still our bread and butter, and thank God we've got Norman Denzin, who's been visionary in terms of creating journals and space for this sort of thing. Thank God we've got performers in the room who are taking risks with this. Thank God we've got people like you who are willing to engage this kind of material and say, "You know what? It's risky, there's no certainty in it, we don't know what the rewards are going to be, but we find in it a worth and value that we can't ignore." That's what's going to carry us forward, I think, in the future.

But it's also going to take some practical things. How well do we train generations of writers in the practicalities of being a writer? About getting a literary agent? Writing a literary inquiry? Putting together a blog? Putting together a website? These are things that should be part and parcel of the enterprise that we call academic preparation for a future. Because unless we give our students those tools, unless we cultivate that, it's like throwing someone into a very competitive, highly competitive market without any skill other than that they can write and they want to have a voice, and in this day and age that's just not quite enough. So, what do we do? We nurture the young.

I'm gonna use one of our students, Karen Stewart, who's sitting here and I'm going to pick on her a little bit. She's an excellent writer, she shows up in a methods course of mine, a course in creative nonfiction as a method of inquiry. She writes an Alzheimer's story that just blew me away. I had never seen anything quite like it. And I didn't know what to do with it. I gave her little comments here and there, you know, like "Did you think about doing this with this?" and so forth and so on. But I knew who could do something with it and so I encouraged her to send it to Carolyn. And Carolyn's comments then came back to Karen. And so it's a network of relationships, and it is in that kind of informal exchange that we can put forward the best ideas that we have. And I encourage us to continue to do that.

Norman: I think we have to move in three or four directions at the same time, and some of these directions will come up tomorrow in the session on tenure and promotion. The first thing I think is that we're going to have to struggle with the issue of insularity of discourses. So, there's a new handbook out on narrative. Okay? By Jean Clandinin, a beautiful handbook (*The Handbook of Narrative Inquiry: Mapping a Methodology*). Is there a chapter on autoethnography in that book? Is autoethnography in the index of that book? The answer to both questions is no. Okay, how did she do a handbook on narrative that excludes autoethnography? Insularity of discourses. Okay, was that her responsibility? We have a responsibility, a moral responsibility as an association. Our responsibility is to position our discourse in such a way that she couldn't have ignored it.

Second example, critical race theory. Okay, critical race theory privileges first-person narratives. Case studies, lived experiences of stories of discrimination under the capitalist legal system. Okay, you go to a collection of papers on critical race theory. Is there a paper on autoethnography? Is there a discussion of how autoethnography could inform critical race theory? Or go to autoethnography and say, is there a series of papers on how critical race theory could inform autoethnography? So we could stitch our work more deeply into the dimensions that Soyini was talking about last night about race, capital, and class. Now, they're separate discourses, they're discordant discourses, so it's time to take stock, twenty years later. Where are we in relationship to these other discourses about narrative, autobiography, autoethnography, critical ethnography, and so forth? Let's now start to go the next generation in those discourses.

If we do that, then I think we can start to take up the next issue, which is legitimating this set of discourses within the academy. Now, I'm aware of three tenure cases this year where people are being turned back for tenure by campus committees and deans, promotions committees, because they're doing first-person narratives and autoethnography. And they're being turned back by people who don't have a clue about this work and who are passing judgments on this work.

Now, how do we counter this, to make it easier for this next generation so those of you here can go through the system with the full weight of this last twenty-five years behind you? How we do that I think is our next challenge. Those are the two main points that I wanted to make.

Also, we need a new journal and I think Carolyn and Art need to take this up. We need a journal of autoethnography. You can't say no. (The audience cheers.)

Art: This reminds me of the end of the big session last year (see Ellis et al., 2007), the final session in a big room with a lot of people, and one of the things I said there … and it comes out of my own personal experience, too. At my age, you know, running for office at NCA and doing these sorts of things wasn't all that appealing, believe me. There are a number of people in the audience at the associate or full-professor level; I see a lot of gray hair out there as well as up here. I'm glad that Norman brought this up, and it is a transition to tomorrow's session as well. I agree with him and think we have a moral responsibility to this community to serve, to serve our young scholars, to serve our students, and to participate in our universities. Get on college tenure committees, develop qualitative networks of qualitative researchers across disciplines that meet occasionally to talk about mutual interests in their work, but also to strategize with regard to hiring practices, tenuring practices, and so forth. And I think that that is something that we really have to address. And each of us has to look inside of ourselves as well as at what we can do as a congress to say this is an agenda for us, and what we do in this regard is going to be very important to our future. I don't have a crystal ball about what's going to be in ten or fifteen years, but I think we can make something happen by participating in the system and not leaving it to others to decide what our future is.

Carolyn: Anybody else want to add anything? You know how these sessions always extend to fill up whatever time you have? Well, we have two minutes ...

Laurel: Is that right?

Carolyn: Yes. Is there anybody in the audience who has a burning desire to say something? Respond? Raise an issue that didn't get raised here? Yes? Stand and do it.

Audience member (woman): This is just a comment and it's a thank you to all of you. I want to say thank you very much from the other side of the world. I have an opportunity because you do this kind of writing.

Carolyn: Thank you all for coming (big applause).

Reference

Ellis, C., A. P. Bochner, N. K. Denzin, Y. S. Lincoln, J. M. Morse, R. J. Pelias, & L. Richardson 2007. Coda: Talking and thinking about qualitative research. In N. K. Denzin & M. D. Giardina (Eds.), *Ethical futures in qualitative research: Decolonizing the politics of knowledge*, pp. 229–67. Walnut Creek, CA: Left Coast Press.

INDEX

Editors

Norman K. Denzin is Distinguished Professor of Communications, College of Communications Scholar, and Research Professor of Communications, Sociology, and Humanities at the University of Illinois, Urbana-Champaign. One of the world's foremost authorities on qualitative research and cultural criticism, Denzin is the author or editor of more than two dozen books, including *Performance Ethnography, Reading Race, Interpretive Ethnography, The Cinematic Society, Images of Postmodern Society, The Recovering Alcoholic, The Alcoholic Self,* and *Searching for Yellowstone.* He is past editor of *The Sociological Quarterly,* coeditor of the landmark *Handbook of Qualitative Research* (1st, 2nd, and 3rd editions, Sage Publications, with Yvonna S. Lincoln), editor of the *Handbook of Critical and Indigenous Methodologies* (forthcoming, Sage, with Yvonna S. Lincoln and Linda Tuhiwai Smith), editor of *Contesting Empire/Globalizing Dissent: Cultural Studies after 9/11* (Paradigm, 2006, with Michael D. Giardina), editor of *Qualitative Inquiry and the Conservative Challenge: Confronting Methodological Fundamentalism* (Left Coast Press, 2006, with Michel D. Giardina), editor of *Ethical Futures in Qualitative Research: Decolonizing the Politics of Knowledge* (Left Coast Press, 2007, with Michael D. Giardina), coeditor of *Qualitative Inquiry,* founding editor of *Cultural Studies/Critical Methodologies,* editor of *Studies in Symbolic Interaction,* and *Cultural Critique* series editor for Peter Lang Publishing. He is also the founding director of the International Association for Qualitative Inquiry.

Michael D. Giardina is visiting assistant professor of advertising and cultural studies at the University of Illinois, Urbana-Champaign. He is the author of *From Soccer Moms to NASCAR Dads: Sport, Culture, and Politics since 9/11* (Paradigm, forthcoming) and *Sporting Pedagogies: Performing Culture & Identity in the Global Arena* (Peter Lang, 2005), which received the 2006 "Most Outstanding Book" award from the North American Society for the Sociology of Sport. He is also the editor of *Globalizing Cultural Studies: Methodological Interventions in Theory, Method and Policy* (Peter Lang, 2007, with Cameron McCarthy, Aisha Durham, Laura Engel, Alice Filmer, and Miguel Malagreca) and *Youth Culture & Sport: Identity, Power, and Politics* (Routledge, 2007, with Michele K. Donnelly). His works on globalization, cultural studies, qualitative inquiry, and the racial logics of late-capitalism have also appeared in journals such as *Harvard Educational Review, Cultural Studies/Critical Methodologies, Journal of Sport & Social Issues*, and *Qualitative Inquiry*. With Joshua I. Newman, he is completing a book titled *Consuming NASCAR Nation: Sport, Spectacle, and the Politics of Neoliberalism*.

Contributors

David Altheide is Regents' Professor, School of Justice and Social Inquiry, at Arizona State University, Tempe. He is the author or editor of more than ten books, including most recently *Terrorism and the Politics of Fear* (AltaMira, 2006) and *Creating Fear: News and the Construction of Crises* (Transaction, 2002), both of which received Charles Horton Cooley Awards from the Society for the Study of Symbolic Interaction (in 2007 and 2004 respectively). In 2005, he received the George Herbert Mead Award for Lifetime Achievement from the Society for the Study of Symbolic Interaction.

Patricia Alvarez McHatton is an assistant professor in the Department of Special Education at the University of South Florida, Tampa. Her research interests include preparing culturally competent educators, experiential learning and service learning, perceptions of school belonging by culturally and linguistically diverse students, and issues of stigma and discrimination for culturally and linguistically diverse families and students.

Wendy Austin is Canada Research Chair of Relational Ethics in Health Care and professor of nursing at the University of Alberta, Canada. She is the author of *First Love: The Adolescent Experience of Amour* (Peter Lang, 2003), and editor (with M. A. Boyd) of *Psychiatric Nursing for Canadian Practice* (Lippincott, Williams, & Wilkins, 2006). She has also published numerous articles in journals such as *Nursing Ethics, Advances in Nursing Science, Ethics & Behaviour,* and *Journal of Psychosocial Nursing.* Her research program centers on exploring the core elements of relational ethics and their application in particular health-care environments.

Arthur P. Bochner is professor of communication and co-director of the Institute for Human Interpretive Studies at the University of South Florida, Tampa. He has written extensively on ethnography, autoethnography, and narrative inquiry, and has published such books as *Ethnographically Speaking: Autoethnography, Literature, and Aesthetics* (AltaMira, 2002, with Caroyln Ellis), *Composing Ethnography: Alternative Forms of Qualitative Writing* (AltaMira, 1996, with Carolyn Ellis), and *Understanding Family Communication* (Gorsuch, 1990/1995, with Janet Yerby and Nancy Buerkele-Rothfuss). His work has also appeared in journals such as *Qualitative Inquiry, Journal of Contemporary Ethnography, Communication Theory,* and *Studies in Symbolic Interaction.* He is the current vice-president of the National Communication Association.

Tim Bond is a Professorial Teaching Fellow at the University of Bristol, UK. He specializes in counseling, ethics, and qualitative research methods. He has researched and published extensively about professional ethics. He is the author of many books, including *Standards and Ethics for Counseling in Action* (Sage, 2000), *Integrative Counseling Skills in Action* (Sage, 2004, with Susan Culley), and the forthcoming *Confidentiality and Record Keeping: Recording Confidences* (Sage, In press, with Barbara Mitchels).

Ruth Nicole Brown is an assistant professor in Gender & Women's Studies and Educational Policy Studies at the University of Illinois, Urbana-Champaign. Her research interests include examining the ways in which girls of color, particularly African American girls, negotiate decision making, the rhetoric of self-esteem, and punitive social policies in the contexts of their everyday lives.

Phoenix de Carteret is a Research Fellow in the Faculty of Education at Monash University, Australia.

Julianne Cheek is a professor in the Division of Health Sciences and director of the Early Career Researcher Development program at the University of South Australia. She holds honorary professorships in South Africa and the United Kingdom and is currently a visiting professor at the Institutt for sykepleievitenskap og helsefag at the University of Oslo, Norway. She is the author of *Postmodern and Poststructural Approaches to Nursing Research* (Sage, 2000) and coauthor of *Finding Out: Information Literacy for the 21ˢᵗ Century* (Macmillan, 1995) and *Society and Health: Social Theory for Health Workers* (Longman Chesire, 1996), which won the prize for the best Tertiary Single Book (wholly Australian) in the prestigious Australian Awards for Excellence in Educational Publishing for 1996. She is also coeditor of the journal *Health: An Interdisciplinary Journal for the Social Study of Health, Illness and Medicine*, associate editor of *Qualitative Health Research*, and is on the editorial boards of six other journals.

Carolyn Ellis is professor of communication and co-director of the Institute for Human Interpretive Studies at the University of South Florida, Tampa. She is the author of numerous books, including *The Ethnographic I: A Methodological Novel about Autoethnography* (AltaMira, 2004), *Composing Ethnography: Alternative Forms of Qualitative Writing* (AltaMira, 1996, with Arthur P. Bochner), and *Final Negotiations: A Story of Love, Loss and Chronic Illness* (Temple University Press, 1995). Her current research projects investigate autoethnograpy, narrative writing, and issues of illness and loss.

H. L. (Bud) Goodall, Jr., is professor and director of the Hugh
Downs School of Human Communication at Arizona State University, Tempe. He is the author or coauthor of twenty books,
including *Writing the New Ethnography* (AltaMira, 2000) and *A
Need to Know: The Clandestine History of a CIA Family* (Left Coast
Press, 2006), and over 100 articles, chapters, and papers. *A Need to
Know* received the 2006 Best Book Award by the National Communication Association Ethnography Division. A pioneer in the
field of creative nonfiction, he has authored works on high technology organizations, rock 'n roll bands, and alternative religions.
With Eric Eisenberg and Angela Trethewey, he is the coauthor of
the award-winning textbook, *Organizational Communication: Balancing Creativity and Constraint*, now it its 5th edition (St. Martin's
Press). His latest book is *Writing Qualitative Inquiry: Self, Stories,
and Academic Life* (Left Coast Press, 2008).

Jackie Goode is a Research Fellow in the School of Education at
the University of Nottingham, UK. For the last fifteen years, she
has worked as a full-time academic researcher on a variety of sociological and social policy projects in the areas of welfare, health,
and higher education. Her work as appeared in such journals as
British Journal of Sociology of Education, Qualitative Inquiry, and
Disability and Society.

Kenneth R. Howe is professor in the Educational Foundations,
Policy, and Practice program area, and director of the Education and the Public Interest Center at the University of Colorado,
Boulder. He is a specialist in philosophy of education, philosophy
and educational research, and policy analysis. He has conducted
research and published articles on a variety of topics, ranging from
the quantitative/qualitative debate to a philosophical examination
of constructivism to a defense of multicultural education. His
recent research has focused on education policy analysis, particularly school choice, and the controversies surrounding the nature
of scientific research in education. His books include the *Ethics
of Special Education* (Teacher's College Press, 1992, with Ofelia
Miramontes), *Understanding Equal Educational Opportunity: Social
Justice, Democracy and Schooling,* (Teachers College Press, 1997,
with Ernest R. House), *Values in Evaluation and Social Research*

(Sage, 1999, with Ernest R. House), and *Closing Methodological Divides: Toward Democratic Educational Research* (Springer, 2003). Professor Howe teaches courses in the social foundations of education, the philosophy of education, education policy, and philosophical issues in educational research.

Patti Lather is professor of education at The Ohio State University, Columbus. She is the author of *Getting Lost: Feminist Practices toward a Double(d) Science* (SUNY Press, 2007) and *Getting Smart: Feminist Research and Pedagogy with/in the Postmodern* (Routledge, 1991), which received the Critics Choice award from the American Educational Studies Association. She is also the editor (with Chris Smithies) of *Troubling the Angels: Women Living with HIV/AIDS* (Routledge, 1997), which was named a CHOICE Outstanding Academic Book.

D. Soyini Madison is a full professor in the Department of Performance Studies at Northwestern University, Evanston, Illinois. Professor Madison also holds appointments in the Department of African American Studies and the Department of Anthropology. She is the author of *Critical Ethnography: Methods, Ethics, and Performance* (Sage, 2005); coeditor of *The Sage Handbook of Performance Studies* (2006); and editor of *The Woman that I Am: The Literature and Culture of Contemporary Women of Color* (PalgraveMacmillan, 1993). Professor Madison lived and worked in Ghana, West Africa, as a Senior Fulbright Scholar conducting field research on the interconnections between traditional religion, political economy, and indigenous performance tactics. She received a Rockefeller Foundation Fellowship in Bellagio, Italy (2003) for her current book project, *Acts of Activism: Human Rights and Radical Performance* (in progress), based on fieldwork in Ghana. Madison also adapts and directs her ethnographic work for the public stage in such performances as: *I Have My Story to Tell*, a performance reflecting the oral histories of University of North Carolina laborers and service workers; *Mandela, the Land, and the People*, a performance based on the life and work of Nelson Mandela; *Is It a Human Being or A Girl?*, a performance ethnography on traditional religion, modernity, and political economy in Ghana; and *Water Rites*, a multimedia performance on the struggle for clean and accessible water as a human right. Professor Madison has won numerous teaching awards, including the Tanner University Award at the University of North Carolina-Chapel Hill for Outstanding and Inspirational Teaching.

Joseph Maxwell is professor in the Graduate School of Education, College of Education and Human Development, at George Mason University, Fairfax, Virginia. His most recent book is *Qualitative Research Design: An Interactive Approach*, 2nd edition (Sage, 2005). He has published widely on qualitative research and evaluation methods, combining qualitative and quantitative methods, medical education, Native American society and culture, and cultural and social theory. His present research interests focus primarily on the philosophy and logic of research methodology. Professor Maxwell also pursues investigations in cultural theory, diversity in educational settings, and how people learn to do qualitative research.

Michele McIntosh is a lecturer in the School of Nursing, Faculty of Health, at York University, Canada. Her research focuses on ethical issues in qualitative research and on participants' perspectives.

Lois Melina is a doctoral candidate at Gonzaga University in Spokane, Washington. She is exploring how women who entered their adult lives in the 1970s negotiated and performed gender at a time of rapid change in roles and expectations for women. She is representing her findings as ethnodrama, and is particularly interested in the intersections of narrative, identity, and performance.

Janice M. Morse is professor of nursing at the University of Utah, Salt Lake City. She is the author or editor of thirteen books, including *Nursing Research: The Application of Qualitative Approaches* (Stanley Thorne, 2003), *The Nature of Qualitative Evidence* (Sage, 2001), and *Preventing Patient Falls* (Sage, 2001). She is also the editor of the journal *Qualitative Health Research* and the Qual Institute Press.

Linda Niehaus is professor of nursing at the University of Alberta, Edmonton, Canada.

Ronald J. Pelias is professor and director of Graduate Studies in the Department of Speech Communications at Southern Illinois University, Carbondale. He is the author of many books on performance studies and performance methodologies, including most recently *Performance Studies: The Interpretation of Aesthetic Texts* (St. Martin's Press, 1992), *Writing Performance: Poeticizing the Researcher's Body* (Southern Illinois University Press, 1999), and *A Methodology of the Heart: Evoking Academic and Daily Life* (AltaMira, 2004). In 2000, he received the Lilla A. Heston Award for Outstanding Scholarship in Interpretation and Performance Studies and the Distinguished Service Award, both from the National Communication Association.

Laurel Richardson is Professor Emeritus of Sociology at The Ohio State University, Columbus. She is an international leader in qualitative research, gender, and the sociology of knowledge. She has written numerous groundbreaking books, including the landmark *Fields of Play: Constructing an Academic Life* (Rutgers University Press, 1997), which received the 1998 Charles Cooley award from the Society for the Study Symbolic Interaction. Other books include *Last Writes: A Daybook for a Dying Friend* (Left Coast Press, 2007), *Travels with Ernest: Crossing the Literary/Sociology Divide* (AltaMira, 2004, with Ernest Lockridge), *Writing Strategies: Reaching Diverse Audiences* (Sage, 1990), *Feminist Frontiers*, 1st–7th editions (McGraw-Hill, 2003, with Verta Taylor and Nancy Whittier), and *The New Other Woman: Contemporary Single Women in Affairs with Married Men* (Macmillan, 1985).

Lois Ann Scheidt is a doctoral student specializing in computer-mediated communication at the School of Library and Information Science at Indiana University, Bloomington. Her research focuses include adolescents in online social venues, human-computer interaction, and human subjects issues and policies relating to online research. She is a founding member of the Blog Research on Genre (BROG) Project at IU.

Clarence Shelley is currently a special assistant to the chancellor at the University of Illinois at Urbana Champaign. He has served the campus as dean of students and associate vice-chancellor. Shelley's assignments have included having primary responsibility for monitoring and managing the campus initiatives toward racial and cultural diversity.

Christopher Darius Stonebanks is an associate professor in the School of Education at Bishop's University, Quebec, Canada. He is also a founding scholars advisory board member for the Paulo and Nita Freire International Project for Critical Pedagogy at McGill University, Canada.

Ian Stronach is Research Professor of Education at the Education and Social Science Research Institute, Manchester Metropolitan University, UK. His research spans a range of qualitative approaches to educational research—teacher research, action research, illuminative evaluation, deconstruction of illuminative evaluation, research methodology, and theory from a poststructuralist/postmodernist point of view. He is an editor of the *British Educational Research Journal* and a member of the British Educational Research Association Council.

Harry Torrance is professor of education and director of the Education and Social Research Institute, Manchester Metropolitan University, UK. His substantive research interests are in the interrelation of assessment with learning, program evaluation, and the role of assessment in education reform. He has undertaken many applied, qualitative, and mixed-method investigations of these topics funded by a wide range of sponsors. He is an elected member of the UK Academy of Learned Societies for the Social Sciences.

Nick Trujillo is professor of communication studies at California State University, Sacramento, where he teaches and conducts research in the areas of organizational communication, media and sports, and narrative ethnography. A recognized pioneer in the study of the performance of organizational cultures from a critical perspective, he is the author of *In Search of Naunny's Grave:*

Age, Class, Gender, and Ethnicity in an American Family (AltaMira, 2006), *The Meaning of Nolan Ryan* (Texas A&M University Press, 1994), and *Organizational Life on Television* (Ablex, 1994, with Leah Vande Berg). His forthcoming book is about cancer and death written from the perspective of a cancer victim and her husband. Coauthored with his late wife and fellow communication scholar, Leah Vande Berg, *Uv Ou: Loving Through Cancer, Living Through Grief*, is expected to be published in Spring 2008.

Leah Vande Berg was professor of communication studies at California State University, Sacramento, from 1990 until her death in 2004. An expert on mass media, she taught classes on women in the media and television criticism. She wrote four books and published more than forty academic articles.

Stanley Varnhagen is academic director and evaluation researcher, University Extension Centre, at the University of Alberta, Canada.

Mary E. Weems is a poet, playwright, and imagination-intellect theorist. She has been widely published in journals, anthologies, and several books including *Public Education and the Imagination-Intellect: I Speak from the Wound in My Mouth* (Lang, 2003), which argues for imagination-intellectual development as the primary goal of public education. Her most recent book, *Tampon Class* (Pavement Saw Press, 2005), is in its second printing. Weems is currently a visiting assistant professor in the Department of Education and Allied Studies at John Carroll University, Cleveland, Ohio, and works as a language-artist-scholar in K-12 classrooms, university settings and other venues through her business Bringing Words to Life.

Carolyne J. White is professor and chair of the Department of Urban Education at Rutgers University-Newark, New Jersey.

Jonathan Wyatt works in staff development and training at the University of Oxford, England, and as a counselor in the UK's National Health Service. He is working toward an Ed.D. at the University of Bristol in narrative and life story research.